The Implacable Urge to Defame

Judaic Traditions in Literature, Music, and Art
Harold Bloom and Ken Frieden, *Series Editors*

SELECT TITLES IN JUDAIC TRADITIONS IN LITERATURE, MUSIC, AND ART

American Artists, Jewish Images
Matthew Baigell

Bridging the Divide: The Selected Poems of Hava Pinhas-Cohen
Sharon Hart-Green, ed. and trans.

The Image of the Shtetl and Other Studies of Modern Jewish Literary Imagination
Dan Miron

Intimations of Difference: Dvora Baron in the Modern Hebrew Renaissance
Sheila E. Jelen

Neither with Them, nor without Them: The Russian Writer and the Jew in the Age of Realism
Elena M. Katz

Rhetoric and Nation: The Formation of Hebrew National Culture, 1880–1990
Shai P. Ginsburg

Social Concern and Left Politics in Jewish American Art: 1880–1940
Matthew Baigell

With Rake in Hand: Memoirs of a Yiddish Poet
Joseph Rolnik; Gerald Marcus, trans.

The Implacable URGE to Defame

CARTOON JEWS IN THE AMERICAN PRESS, 1877–1935

Matthew Baigell

SYRACUSE UNIVERSITY PRESS

For a listing of books published and distributed by Syracuse University Press,
visit www.SyracuseUniversityPress.syr.edu.

ISBN: 978-0-8156-3496-6 (hardcover)
      978-0-8156-3510-9 (paperback)
      978-0-8156-5396-7 (e-book)

Library of Congress Cataloging-in-Publication Data

Names: Baigell, Matthew, author.
Title: The implacable urge to defame : cartoon Jews in the American press,
    1877–1935 / Matthew Baigell.
Description: First edition. | Syracuse, New York : Syracuse University Press,
    2017. | Series: Judaic Traditions in Literature, Music, and Art | Includes
    bibliographical references and index.
Identifiers: LCCN 2017000963 (print) | LCCN 2017001271 (ebook) |
    ISBN 9780815634966 (hardcover : alk. paper) | ISBN 9780815635109
    (pbk. : alk. paper) | ISBN 9780815653967 (e-book)
Subjects: LCSH: Jews—Caricatures and cartoons—History. | Jews—Press coverage—
    United States. | American wit and humor, Pictorial—History—19th century. |
    American wit and humor, Pictorial—History—20th century. | Antisemitism in art. |
    Antisemitism in the press.
Classification: LCC NC1763.J4 B35 2017 (print) | LCC NC1763.J4 (ebook) |
    DDC 741.5/3529924073—dc23
LC record available at https://lccn.loc.gov/2017000963

For Tali, my favorite (and only) granddaughter

Contents

Illustrations

Preface

IN THE COURSE of researching and writing this book, I constantly discussed my findings and thoughts with Renee Baigell and, as always, took her advice and observations to heart, for which I am ever thankful. I also want to express my thanks to Donald Kuspit, whose support, council, and suggestions over several decades have been very important to me, especially while I gathered material for this book. I take full responsibility, however, for its contents, all inadvertent errors of fact, opinions expressed, and the tone I assumed in its text.

I also thank Anne-Marie Belinfante and Amanda (Miryem-Khaye) Seigel, librarians in the Dorot Jewish Room of the New York Public Library, for their patience, good cheer, and professional expertise in making available books, articles, and many rolls of microfilm. I owe debts of gratitude to Robert DeLap of the New-York Historical Society, Thomas Lisanti of the New York Public Library, Bradley Olson of the New Britain Museum of American Art, Lauren Robinson of the Museum of the City of New York, and Erin Schreiner of the New York Library Society for providing illustrations in their institutions' collections.

I also want to express my appreciation to Shlomo Edelstein for alerting me to the shockingly vast number of contemporary anti-Semitic cartoons one can find on the Internet and to Murray Zimiles for calling my attention to Sara Lipton's books on medieval anti-Semitic cartoons.

I also offer a profound thanks to Deborah Manion of Syracuse University Press for seeing the manuscript through from its early drafts to its publication. We all should be blessed with such supportive and patient editors. And I cannot thank Annie Barva enough for her incredible copyediting skills both in catching inadvertent and overlooked errors and in suggesting ways to improve awkward passages in the text. I also owe a debt of gratitude to the anonymous readers whose suggestions of what to leave in, what to add, and what to abandon were extremely helpful.

I read some works as Kindle transfers to my tablet, so I added "Kindle ed." to the citations to them in the text because pagination is not always identical with that in printed books.

A few words about the illustrations reproduced here. I photographed most of the cartoons from *Puck*, *Life*, *Judge*, *Judge's Library*, and *New Masses*. Other images were taken from *Frank Leslie's Illustrated Newspaper*, from the occasional book and contemporary journal, or from digitized images available on the Internet, all indicated in the captions. Quality varied, especially of those images taken from the Internet. Depending on how the page was reproduced, some images were so blackened as to be unusable. Others were too pale to be read clearly. In some, edges and lines had grown fuzzy. Those illustrations I found in actual magazines, some dating from the 1870s, had been bound into volumes that had grown quite fragile with age. As a result, librarians, rightly so, would not allow flash and did not want volumes opened completely for fear the bindings would break. And weighing down a page so that it would lie flat was not always possible, either. Therefore, some illustrations appear wavy as a result of paper warping. Rectangular illustrations might appear slightly trapezoidal. When possible, some institutions provided acceptable copies of illustrations, for which I am very grateful.

The names of several illustrators were often illegible in the cartoons. Rather than try to guess their names, I listed them as "unknown artist" in the captions. For those whose names were known, tracking down their original drawings for the cartoons became an impossible task.

I provide the publication information (magazine, date, and page number) for all cited and described cartoons directly in the text.

Some articles or short items were published in magazines as untitled fillers or under the general heading "NO ARTICLE." Rather
than clutter my works cited list with a raft of entries titled "NO
ARTICLE," I listed these items under the magazine titles.

A note about figure 62, *Capital Embraces Religion* by William
Gropper. Its caption in the essay in which it appeared states that it
was reproduced from an issue of *Der Apikeures* published in 1934. I
was unable to find any further references to that magazine. For other
works whose estate representatives or owners I could not locate, I
offer my apologies and hope to add the proper acknowledgments to
them at the earliest opportunity.

The Implacable Urge to Defame

Introduction

A PERSONAL NOTE at the start. I was born in 1933 in Brooklyn and remember playing on the street and going to public school in the late 1930s with children of refugee families who had escaped Hitler's Germany. In the mid-1940s, I went to a Jewish summer camp run by refugees from eastern Europe. Photographs of famous individuals killed in the murder and concentration camps were prominently displayed, and we all took part in playlets of ghetto round-ups and other similar events taking place in Europe. I also remember, among other things, being interviewed in 1945, a time of heightened anti-Semitism in America, by a reporter from *PM*, a liberal New York newspaper, who wanted to know if an attack on my person had anti-Semitic overtones. As an adult, I married into a Holocaust survivor family and over the years have heard many stories of brutality and murder committed by those who participated in the destruction of East European Jewry.

My point in mentioning all of this at the start of this book is to say I have known since childhood about the plight of Jews in Europe and have experienced Jew hatred in America, and it has influenced the tone of this book, which is about cartoons and caricatures of Jews in American magazines published in the late nineteenth and early twentieth centuries. I have also included some works that counter those caricatures.

After completing *Social Concern and Left Politics in Jewish American Art, 1880–1940* (Baigell 2015), a book that was clearly written from a Jewish point of view and that contains several cartoons by Jewish artists, I wanted to explore the ways in which Jews were presented in cartoons in the mainstream American press during that same period. Were Jews seen as individuals or as stereotypical examples of a particular group? Were they shown in sympathetic or hostile ways?

After spending seemingly endless days looking at digitized pages on the Internet and turning actual pages of humor magazines such as *Puck*, *Life*, *Judge*, and *Judge's Library*, I stopped counting anti-Jewish cartoons when the number went higher than one hundred. (For information about these magazines, see Mott 1938, 268, 520–32, 552–56.) The sheer quantity was shocking, and the images and captions equally so—the negative myths and stereotypes portrayed were repugnant and required in my mind's eye constant confrontation. As one commentator noted in 1940, "No other people precipitates such a reversion to primitive terror and folkloristic mental helplessness among civilized nations. Regarding no other people could such 'inaccuracies' and 'exaggerations' be given currency" (Samuel [1940] 1988, 10–11). As another observer noted in 2007, the decades covered here were the years of the most "virulently bigoted illustrations" (Dewey 2007, 25; see also Dobkowski 1979; Weingarten 1979; Kraut 1982; Higham 1984; Gerber 1987; Dinnerstein 1994).

To be sure, Jews were not the only religious, national, ethnic, or racial group to be savaged in America's periodicals. I came upon several hundred, perhaps thousands, more cartoons that denigrated and demeaned Native Americans and African Americans as well as Irish, German, and East Asian immigrants. If we agree with Clifford Geertz that "works of art are elaborate mechanisms for defining social relationships, sustaining social rules, and strengthening social values," that "they materialize a way of exploring, bringing a particular cast of mind out into the world of objects, where men can look at it" (1976, 1478), then clearly these turn-of-the-century cartoonists were not interested in understanding the nature and condition of individual members of these groups or in helping them navigate their way in modern America.

Immigrants were ridiculed rather than welcomed to their new country, and certainly no effort was made to accelerate the process of welding together into a single cohesive nation the people from so many disparate groups. Cartoonists seemed rather to exhibit a xenophobic, Anglo-Saxon-based aversion to all minority groups. Whether it was their intention or not, they participated in keeping different religious, racial, and ethnic groups apart and perhaps hindered their entry into mainstream culture for the simple reason that the cartoons they drew told those who rarely interacted directly with minority persons what they might expect, how such strangers might respond, and how immoral or just plain stupid they might be. In fact, cartoons became the major visual medium to dehumanize and discredit American minorities, to caricature stereotypical behavior patterns, and to reduce all those in the line of attack to creatures considered not fully qualified to become decent, responsible citizens of the country.

Native Americans often appeared helpless before the steady encroachment of "peaceful" white settlers, or they were presented as barbaric predators hindering the arrival of "civilization" on their lands. African Americans were presented as childlike, lazy, and not above resorting to theft when the opportunity presented itself. The Irish, often portrayed with simian-like faces, were ignorant. *Puck* especially attacked Catholicism and the papacy through its cartoons and articles (Thomas 2004). Germans drank a lot of beer. But Jews, among all immigrant groups, were shown in more and as many negative ways as possible: they were money-hungry Shylocks and thieving Fagins, social climbers, arsonists ready to claim insurance for property loss, and disagreeable, scheming parvenus who would take advantage of any situation in which they found themselves. And by some inscrutable, delusional process, Jews, despite their relatively small numbers, were also thought to be organized to take over global commercial and financial markets. To be sure, there were actual Jewish gangsters and Jews who cut moral and legal corners a bit too sharply, as there certainly were among other minority and mainstream groups, but "among the derogated ethnic groups, late-century cartoonists seemed to labor most over the Jews" (Dewey 2007, 30). This ill will toward Jews continues to this day (Stephens-Davidowitz 2014, 4).

In the very limited literature about the humor magazines and their cartoonists, there is occasional mention of anti-Semitic cartoons, but it is as if such acknowledgment has been carefully monitored, even consciously repressed. For example, the only instance of acknowledgment I could find in *Wikipedia* entries for *Puck*, *Life*, *Judge*, and *Judge's Library* is a brief passage in the entry for *Life* acknowledging the magazine's bias against Jews. This factoid can be borne out by thumbing through the pages of the different magazines, an observation corroborated by Martha Banta, who wrote the following about *Life*: "It was not easy for *Life* to accept that Jews possessed an unbroken existence in time that far exceeded the paltry centuries claimed by Anglo-Saxons of London or the Anglo-Americans of New York, or that their spiritual leaders attended to strict codes of conduct that reached back thousands of years before Europeans stumbled upon America" (2003, 149).

It should be noted that these periodicals were not primarily hate magazines. Most articles were concerned with politics and included items and issues of general interest (Press 1981, 254–62; Fisher 1996, 70). However, by my count, very few articles and not one single cartoon praised Jews in anyway, and the author of the one nineteenth-century article I found expressly about cartoons did not mention negative images of minority figures (Mitchell 1889, 728–45). But, as I point out, a few favorable images were published in nonhumorous publications during the years in question.

In retrospect, it is arguable that Jews were considered the quintessential Other, the most unalike and unlikeable among the Others, whose values and goals differed from those of the majority culture. It was most frighteningly believed that their presence, aggressiveness, and intelligence could challenge, change, and overwhelm local cultural patterns as well as alter worldviews. They were basically seen, certainly in cartoons, as the Nefarious Other, capable of breaking traditions of conduct and time-honored laws, a willful people and a disturbing presence in normal society.

In articles about Jews, certain descriptive words and phrases appeared consistently: *greedy, merciless, tricky, vengeful, lacking in humanity, crafty, clannish, parasitic dealers in money exchanges, unscrupulous middlemen.* They are cunning schemers after control of the world's money supply and various commercial enterprises. They refuse to integrate, assimilate, and mix with Christians, and they will remain separate. They will remain strangers who seek the best bargains, destroyers of Christian civilization, owners of the best land, unpatriotic, not nationalistic, and known for refusing to do manual labor. They are Christ killers, illiterates, members of a racially inferior race, people who represent foreign-dominated eastern American cities; they have bad hygiene and challenge Anglo-Saxon cultural hegemony. They are adept at criminal behavior, such as arson and unscrupulous business tactics. Their mercenary aggressiveness is instinctive, and they are socially vulgar and pushy people, destroyers of the American work ethic, political radicals, and members of a community unable to understand democratic principles.

The many fewer positive words and phrases included *sober, industrious, law abiding, willing to take care of their own kind, peaceable, not brutal or violent,* and *family involved.* Because I found so few favorable opinions, I was inevitably reminded of that old joke in which a person states to a friend that Jews and bicycle riders are responsible for all the ills in the world, and the friend then asks: "Why also the bicycle riders?" One is left to conclude that anti-Jewish rhetoric, stereotyping, and caricaturing became a familiar, not to say prominent, part of the age and functioned in word and image as respectable forms of discourse.

But all of this was nothing new. Since the Middle Ages, images hostile to Jews have appeared in paintings, prints, cartoons, and sculpture in Europe and, in more recent times, in the United States and the Middle East (see Fuchs 1921; Glassman 1979; Gilman 1991, 169–93; Lipton 1999, 2014; Stav 1999; Kotek 2009; Nirenberg 2013; Forman 2014). In his book *The Jew in Early American Wit and Graphic Humor* (1973), Rudolf Glanz writes, "In his own way over the millennia, the Jew was both a target on his own and used as an expression of the general criticism of social conditions. He was, in addition, the subject of an unbridled folk imagination in the folklore of nations as well as in their literary and graphic humorous creations" (11).

When writing this book, I narrowed Glanz's observations to one nation alone, the United States, because, first, the number of cartoons in American periodicals was so great and the level of vilification of Jews was so aggressive, debasing, and varied and, second, cartoonists in different countries emphasized different aspects of their "Jewish problem." In 1908, roughly the midpoint of the years covered in *Social Concern and Left Politics in Jewish American Art, 1880–1940* (Baigell 2015), a writer for the *Chicago American* (1908) scolded the editors of *Life* for an anti-Semitic article by pointing out the differences between Jews as individuals and Jews as embodiments of the larger community: "If you have a fight with any particular Jew, FIGHT HIM. Don't fight his mother, or his religion, or his race. That is out of date, and, what is more serious, IT DOESN'T WORK ANYHOW" (untitled filler, qtd. in "Anti-Semitic Life" 1908, 3).

This was a nice idea and gesture at the time, but the anti-Semitism this writer referred to was not out of date in 1908 and, alas, is still not out of date today, nor has it been since the days of ancient Egypt (Nirenberg 2013, chap. 1). I chose the title for this book, therefore, because it describes the conscious or unconscious assumptions of anti-Semitism as part of or integral to the belief systems of many people over the centuries and certainly in America.

When exploring the literature, I came upon similar assessments by several scholars, which I have taken as my point of departure. For example, Sir Harold Evans (b. 1928), the British-born journalist and historian, writes,

> Antisemitism is a very peculiar pathology that recognizes no national borders. It is a mental condition conducive to paranoia and impervious to truth. Its lexicon has no word for individuality. It is fixated on group identity. It is necessarily dehumanizing when people become abstractions. Once an emotional stereotype has been created—of Jews, of blacks, of Catholics, or Muslims—it is readily absorbed into the bones like strontium 90, an enduring

poison that distorts the perceptions of the victims. All minority groups have suffered but none have [sic] been stereotyped more heinously and more durably than Jews. (2012, ix)

A brief comparison of three cartoons about possession of territory makes this point clear. In the May 19, 1880, issue of Puck (p. 183), a Native American watches helplessly as the borders of his reservation are eaten away by adventurers, trespassing miners, and renegades (fig. 1). The federal government is clearly not interested in protecting his interests. For the November 24, 1880, issue of Puck (p. 189), the same cartoonist, Frederick Burr Opper, drew a map of Manhattan Island seemingly inundated by Irish immigrants (fig. 2). The main thoroughfares are named "Kelly Boulevard," "Dublin Street," and "Tammany Avenue," the last for the Irish political machine. Central Park has been renamed "Shamrock Park"; Long Island Sound is now called "Long Irish Sound"; and so on. This cartoon seems to be an exercise in clever renaming of sites rather than in showing fear of an Irish takeover of Manhattan. By comparison, fear and hostility would seem to be the subtexts of the cartoon titled New York in the Future, published in the December 19, 1901, issue of Life (p. 535) in that it suggests what Manhattan as a Jewish city

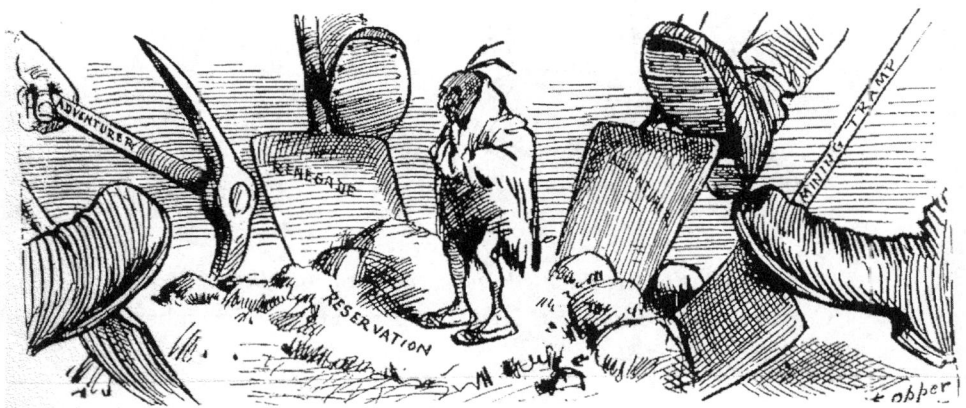

1. Frederick Opper, Untitled, from Puck, May 19, 1880, 183.

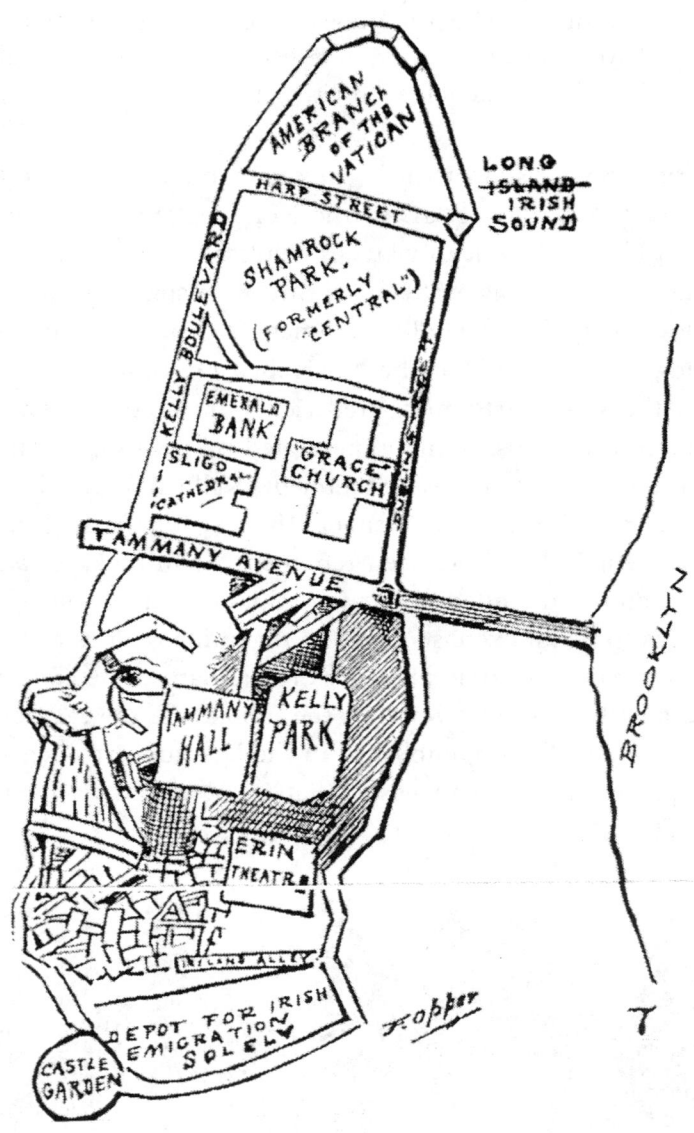

2. Frederick Opper, *Puck's Revised Map of the City of New Cork, Formerly Known as New York*, from *Puck*, November 24, 1880, 189.

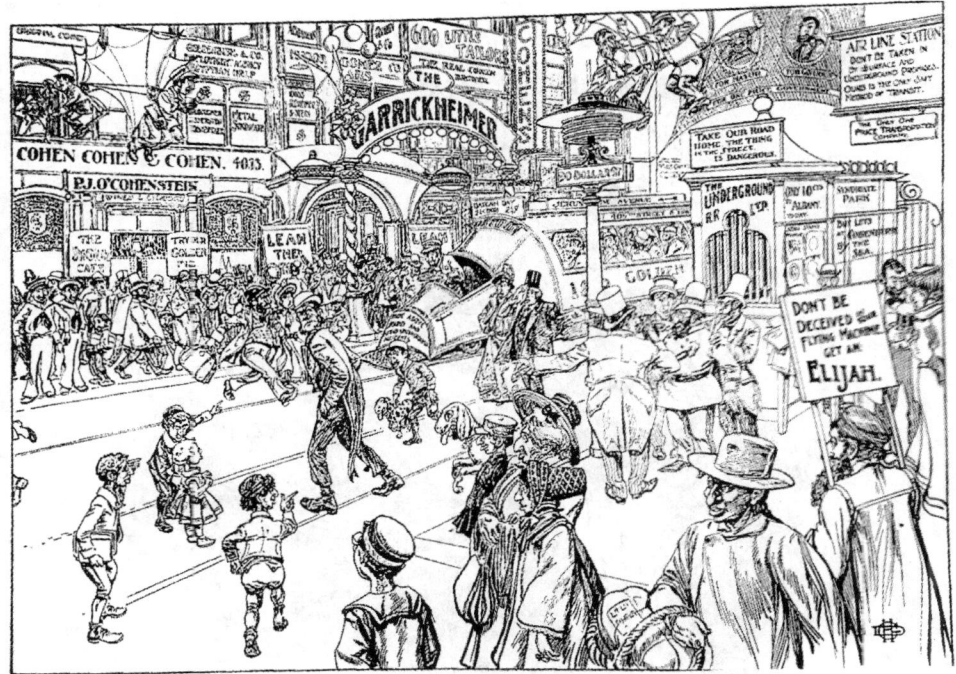

NEW YORK IN THE FUTURE. ONLY A QUESTION OF TIME.

3. Harrison Cady, *New York in the Future. Only a Question of Time*, from *Life*, December 19, 1901, 535.

would look like (fig. 3). All the stores are owned by Jews; the police are Jews; all the seemingly self-satisfied people on the street are Jews except for the tall man surrounded by jeering young boys, whose actions the police watch but do not stop.

If we were to choose the one cartoon around the turn of the twentieth century that symbolizes the fear and hatred as well as the ambivalent and grudging respect for commercial success generated by the Jewish presence at the time, it might very well be the one titled *Dominant Races* published in the issue of *Puck* for July 27, 1898 (p. 11) (fig. 4). The cartoonist, Louis Dalrymple, summed up in two short lines of text Christians' distress about what they perceived to be Jewish aggressive self-confidence, business acumen, and increasingly

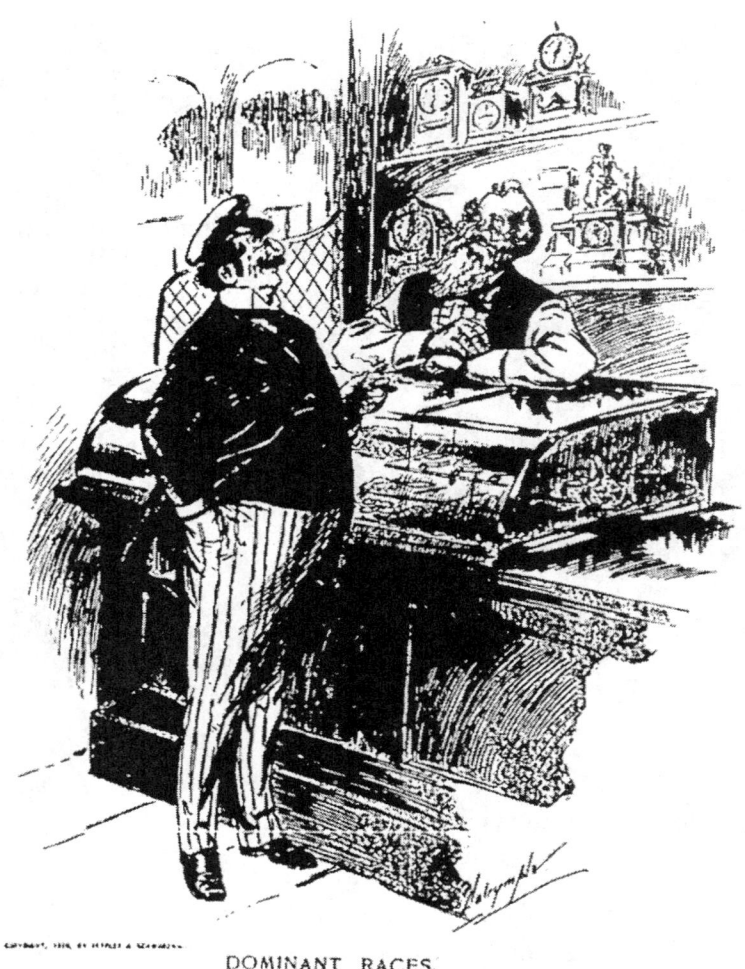

DOMINANT RACES.

4. Louis Dalrymple, *Dominant Races*, from *Puck*, July 27, 1898, 11.

unavoidable presence. Two large-nosed (the inevitable defining facial characteristic of cartoon Jews), middle-class businessmen are reflecting on the place of Jews in America vis-à-vis the dominant culture givers. Isaacs asks in the cartoon world's ever-present Jewish English dialect, "You t'ink der Anglo-Zaxons vos going to rule der eart'?" Cohenstein responds: "Vell, may be dey mighd, but dot von't brevent der Hebrews from owning id!"

On the one hand, the cartoon can be read, at least by Jews, as affirming the financial success many had already achieved in America as opposed to the limited chances for advancement in the Old Country. But the infuriating self-satisfied smiles on the men's faces, reflecting their belief that someday Jews will replace Anglo-Saxon Christians as the dominant cultural and economic force in the country, bluntly announces the approaching American nightmare—becoming subservient and beholden to uncontrollable, uncultured, unethical Jewish landlords and businessmen. Obviously, not all Christians subscribed to the cartoon's negative implications, but it is illustrated here to make the point that it reflected the covert and overt anti-Semitism exhibited in so many cartoons.

Many of the illustrations and passages of text visualize or discuss Jews as a stereotype. Such a stereotype, "first and foremost, . . . means losing the ability to define yourself. It means being defined by those who believe they know you before you've even met" (R. Cohen 2015, 1)—a point central to my underlying premise. That is, a Jew becomes his or her stereotype. Or, to say it another way, the stereotype shows Jews "as being something other than what they actually are" (Marcus 2015, 130, Kindle ed.).

For cartoons about Jews in the late nineteenth and early twentieth centuries, it was not always necessary to read the captions that were usually written in what passed for Yiddish-inflected (or infected) English to identify the subjects as Jews because they were easily identified by the size of their noses (figs. 5–7).

In fact, I cannot recall a single cartoon in which a Jewish person is not given a bulbous nose. In figure 5, the nose is part of an object. In figure 6, it is part of a human interaction. In figure 7, it is a part of a recognizable person, the esteemed editor Joseph Pulitzer (1847–1911), who appeared in at least four cartoons, twice in profile alone and twice with other editors in cartoons concerned with elections. In this cartoon in the issue of *Life* for March 9, 1899 (p. 200), he appears in an advertisement describing the magazine's excellent qualities. (See also "NO TITLE" in *Puck* 1884, 248; 30; Keppler 1891, not paginated; "NO TITLE" in *Life* 1897; and

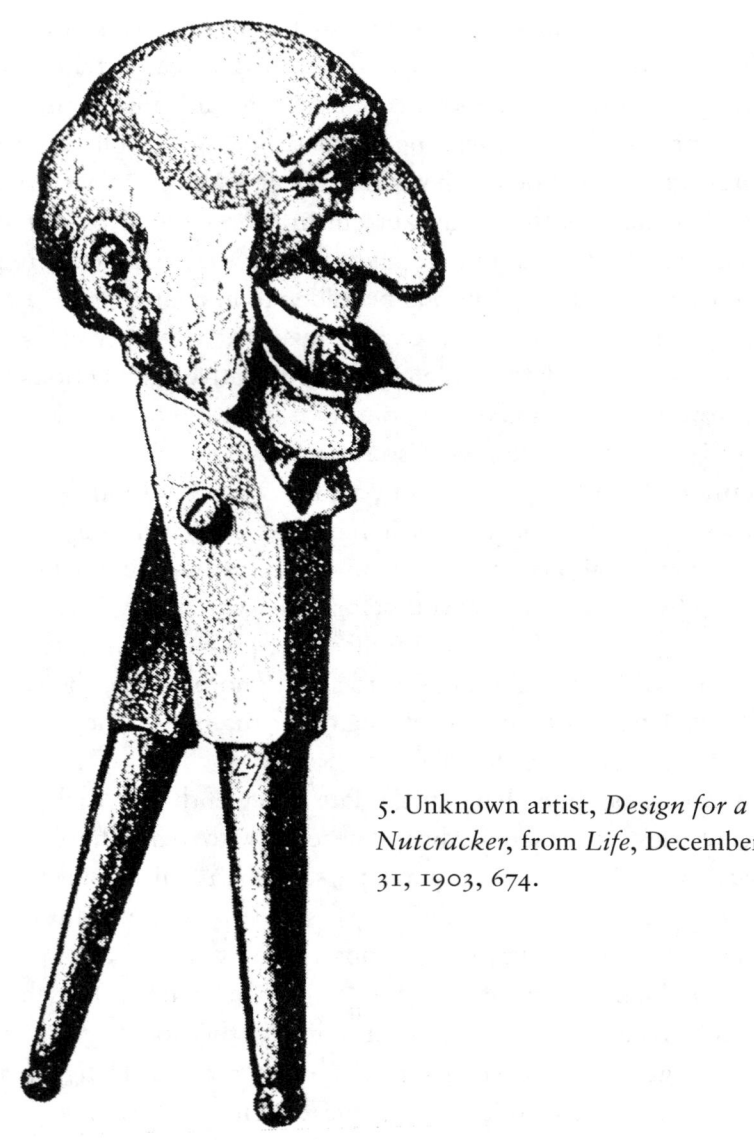

DESIGN FOR A NUTCRACKER.

5. Unknown artist, *Design for a Nutcracker*, from *Life*, December 31, 1903, 674.

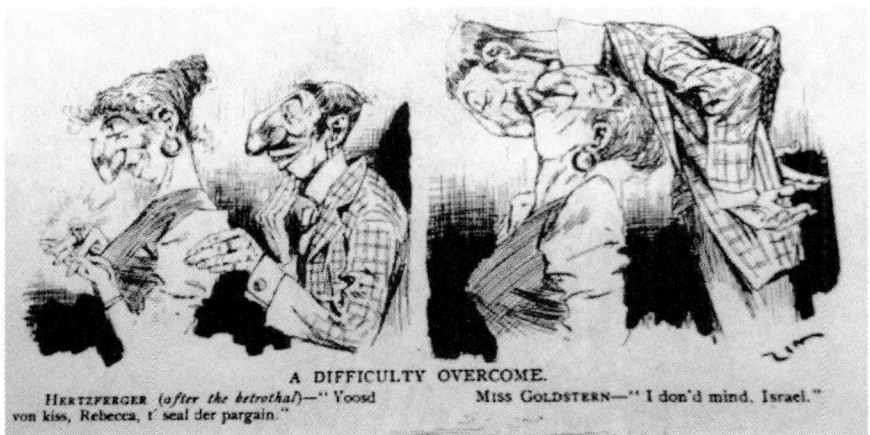

A DIFFICULTY OVERCOME.

HERTZFERGER *(after the betrothal)*—" Yoosd von kiss, Rebecca, t' seal der pargain."　　　MISS GOLDSTERN—" I don'd mind, Israel."

6. Eugene Zimmerman, *A Difficulty Overcome*, from *Judge's Library*, January 1892, not paginated.

Glanz 1973, 137–43. For a normal portrait of Pulitzer, see Hills 1977, 39.)

Pulitzer, with an unbelievably large nose, is shown wearing gaudy clothes and sporting an immense diamond stud, an outfit often worn by cartoon Jewish subjects, especially Jewish women flashing their wealth and nouveau riche bad taste. The caption reads: "Our Worst Editor. Joseph Pulitzer, and his opinion of *Life.*" Probably in response to a dispute with Pulitzer, the editors of *Life* assert that he "is known wherever bad English is read and depraved minds everywhere hail him as a source of inspiration. He has probably done more harm to morals, and has fostered with more real persistency the rapid undergrowth of American degeneracy than any other living man."

The editors then imagine Pulitzer's response in cartoon language meant to typify the broken, heavily accented English spoken by recent immigrants, even though Pulitzer had emigrated from his native Hungary in 1864 when he was a seventeen-year-old youth, some thirty-five years before the advertisement was published—certainly time enough to lose such an accent. Besides, a Hungarian accent was quite different from the Polish and Russian accents that were more common in New York's Lower East Side. What this means very simply is

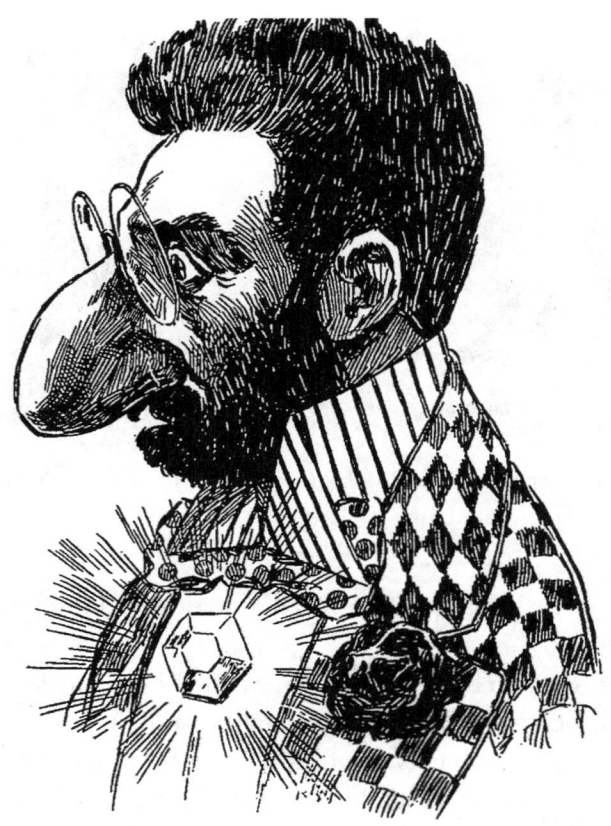

7. Unknown artist, *Joseph Pulitzer, Our Worst Editor,*
from *Life*, March 9, 1899, 200.

that the visual image and the printed word enhanced and reinforced
each other so that through physiognomy and language Jews could be
easily identified and their unsavory characteristics emphasized by the
circumstances in which the cartoonists placed them. As a result, the
appearance, the accent, and the dialogue invariably reinforced each
other, thus placing Jews in a triple lose-lose-lose situation.

On occasion, language and facial features alone were not necessary to set Jews apart. In a cartoon titled *Why Not Let the Apparel
Proclaim the Man?* in the February 23, 1898, issue of *Puck* (p. 2),
the Jewish man is distinguished by his short height, wide girth, and

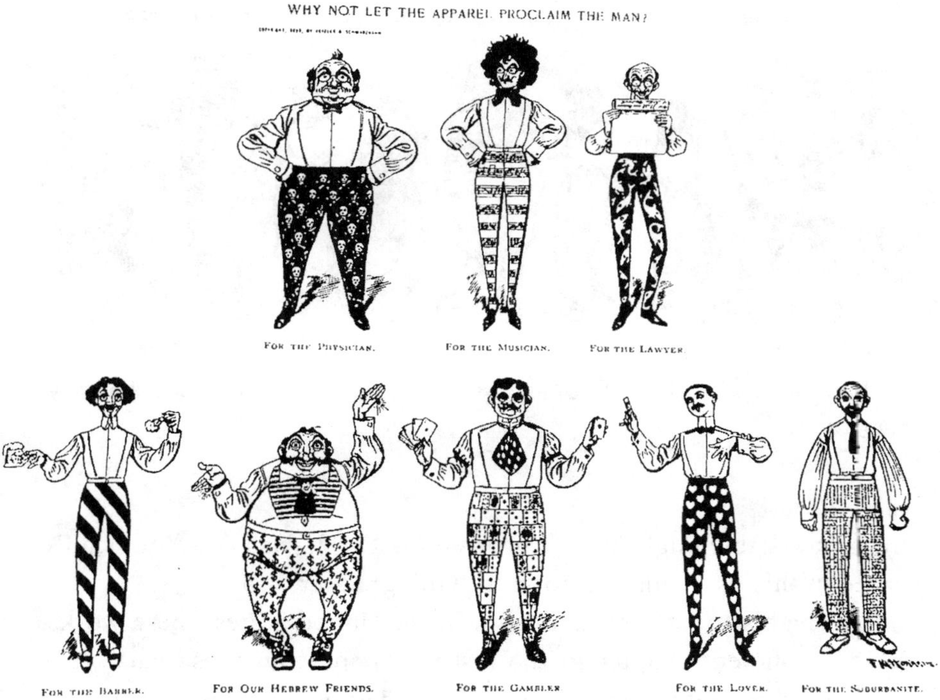
WHY NOT LET THE APPAREL PROCLAIM THE MAN?
FOR THE PHYSICIAN.
FOR THE MUSICIAN.
FOR THE LAWYER.
FOR THE BARBER.
FOR OUR HEBREW FRIENDS.
FOR THE GAMBLER.
FOR THE LOVER.
FOR THE SUBURBANITE.

8. T. M. Honning, *Why Not Let the Apparel Proclaim the Man?* from *Puck*, February 23, 1898, 2.

bowed legs (fig. 8). In addition, he is the only man identified by his religion, not by his profession, residence, or social preferences. And in a fantasy All-American football team selected by *Puck*'s nameless expert and composed of men whose last names indicate their country of origin, which appeared in the January 7, 1914, issue (p. 3), it is easy to pick out the Jewish man: he is the only one identified by his religion insofar as he is nationless; he is also knock-kneed and stoop-shouldered and does not have an aggressive look (fig. 9, *fourth from the left*).

His name also gives away his identity. For cartoon Jews, the last syllable of their names is usually *stein* or *berg*, and the first syllable is often *Cohen* or *Isaac*. Or, to associate Jews with monetary obsession,

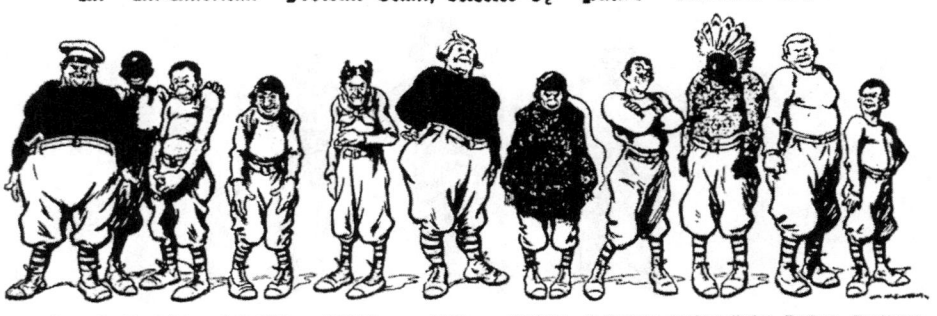

9. Unknown artist, *An "All American" Football Team*, from *Puck*, January 7, 1914, 3.

the first syllable might be *Silver* or *Gold*. The Jewish All-American's name in this particular cartoon is "Goldgrabber."

In the history of anti-Semitism in the United States, these works form a coherent chapter in the history of the country's visual culture, but this chapter has not been studied as assiduously as it might. Because continued stereotyping serves a dehumanizing function, the same cultural, political, and religious attitudes evident in the late nineteenth and early twentieth centuries that permitted anti-Semitic acts ranging from casually stated nasty asides to restrictions on employment, residence, and college entrance continued through the 1930s and 1940s.

Although this book is about cartoons created in the past, it can be argued that both these older cartoons and cartoons published abroad today have played a role in encouraging distrust, misunderstanding, and therefore hatred of minorities. Such hatred has encouraged hostile actions particularly against Jews. I have personally experienced anti-Semitic incidents directed at me as an individual and apparently as a representative of the entire Jewish community, as in "You Jews . . . ," meaning that I am defined as a person through a stereotype. Certain of my experiences have been startlingly like those described by Nina Morais in 1881: "In the popular mind, the

Jew is never judged as an individual, but as a specimen of a whole race whose members are identically of the same kind" (269).

Given the rise of anti-Semitism in our own time, as witnessed in public actions and publications both here and abroad, including physical attacks, murders, swastikas painted on buildings, Jewish tombstones overturned, as well as threats to destroy Israel and the intent, once again, to murder Jews, I saw no reason to remain polite or neutral in my presentation here, and so I express on occasion feelings similar to those voiced by friends and colleagues outraged when they viewed the cartoons I had collected. This book, then, is scholarly in intent but personal in delivery.

1 The Cartoons

SCHOLARS OF JEWISH AMERICAN HISTORY have noted that periods of anti-Semitism waxed and waned between the Civil War and the Second World War, but animosity toward Jews, as revealed in cartoons, remained constant and was especially virulent in the 1880s and 1890s, the years of heavy immigration from eastern Europe. A cartoon might occasionally have had a topical reference, but there seems to have been little correlation between a cartoon and a specific public event or to periods of greater or lesser anti-Semitic activity. As historian Roger A. Fischer observes, cartoons did not necessarily relate to editorial purposes or political events (1996, 71, 90).

The general mindset, evidently, was to caricature, caricature, and keep caricaturing. At least, this is what I found in *Judge* (1881–1932), *Judge's Library* (1887–1910), *Puck* (1871–1918), and *Life* (1883–1936), from which I drew most of the illustrations discussed and included in this book. Circulation numbers vary, but estimates put *Judge's* readership at about 85,000 in the 1890s and 100,000 by 1912. *Life* readers numbered around 250,000 in 1920. And *Puck* had between 80,000 and 100,000 readers around 1900. The intended audience had to be middle-class Protestants because any other religious, racial, or ethnic group would have been constantly offended by the images and captions (Thomas 2004, 214; see also the *Wikipedia* entries for these magazines).

Grotesque and demeaning caricatures in overwhelming numbers appeared in issue after issue, and editors seem to have taken pleasure in adding offensive covers to the insulting cartoons inside those covers, especially in those issues devoted to a single subject. For example, written in large letters across the cover of the April 1890 issue of *Judge's Library*, a monthly compilation of material taken from the weekly *Judge*, were the words "OUR FRIEND THE HEBREW." And the cover of the June 1892 issue reads, "ALL ABOUT OUR COLORED BRETHREN. COONS." *Judge's Library* insulted all groups equally: the November 1900 issue was titled "FUNNY GRAFS," probably short for "graphics," and just below the title the following list appeared: "10 cents, Irish Jokes, Dutch Jokes, Jew Jokes, Nigger Jokes, etc."

If the cartoons and their captions are an index of feeling, it would appear that hatred and fear of immigrants and native minorities remained intense, steady, and publicly expressed. Stereotypes endured. By 1900, however, as circulation of these magazines began to decline, cartoons began to grow repetitive and predictable. By the second decade of the twentieth century, fewer grotesque caricatures appeared in print, with the exception of the Communist press. But, as if in compensation, the number of books and articles that demeaned minorities increased exponentially in the mainstream press, as discussed in chapter 3.

Several contemporary scholars have recorded many examples of disparaging remarks about Jews printed in eighteenth- and early-nineteenth-century American books, magazines, and various public documents. But all agree that anti-Semitism grew dramatically after the Civil War (Morgan 1899; "The Escape of Daniel Emanuel" 1917; Harap 1974, 19–46; N. Cohen 1979, 191; Sarna 1981; Dinnerstein 1994, 3–34). During the Civil War, the most notorious anti-Semitic act was General Order No. 11 issued by General Ulysses S. Grant on December 17, 1862, expelling all Jews from the territory under his command, which extended from northern Mississippi to Cairo, Illinois, and on December 28 removing all Jews from Paducah, Kentucky. The charge was that Jews as a group had violated "every regulation of trade established by the Treasury Department as well as department orders." The order was revoked on January 17, 1863, at the behest of President Abraham Lincoln (Ash 1982; Sarna 2012, 7).

(For Brigadier General Thomas Ewing's different General Order No. 11 of August 25, 1863, recorded in George Caleb Bingham's famous painting *Order Number 11*, which exists in two versions, see Grose-close 1978 and Rush 1991, 184–215.)

Over the next fifty-odd years, an avalanche of anti-Jewish cartoons appeared in the humor magazines. Altogether, they reveal an abiding animosity to Jews and all aspects of Jewish life in America, whether real or imagined. With the arrival of increasing numbers of immigrants after the Civil War, levels of hostility rose, and Jews began to be categorized in cartoons by their assigned stereotypical rather than actual appearance and behavior patterns and to be demeaned by their accents and mangling of the English language (Handlin 1951b; N. Cohen 1979, 187). Given our contemporary sensitivities to and support of minority rights, it is shocking to realize that cartoonists and editors of the time seemed to have no qualms about and no control mechanisms with respect to contributing to and reinforcing the negative stereotypes that proliferated through the mainstream press. It is equally shocking to read articles and books written during these decades, especially in the early twentieth century, in which authors revealed so openly and sometimes at great length why they disliked Jews and found them untrustworthy. They basically wrote prejudice porn.

Among the representative cartoons illustrated and discussed here, subject matter hostile to Jews can be divided broadly into two overlapping groups: those ridiculing Jewish social behavior patterns and those essentially condemning Jewish business practices. Many cartoons show two people engaged in a conversation recorded in the caption. Objects placed in the background indicate the context—for example, clothing store or family living room. Multifigure cartoons, although fewer in number, became more common toward the turn of the century. Double-page spreads appeared from time to time and could be especially scurrilous because they might include as part of a narrative sequence individuals engaged in different but related activities that mock the cartoon's principle subject and show Jews to be morally corrupt or, at best, unsavory.

A few cartoons that express objections to Jewish social behavior dating from the late 1870s represented two events worth considering in some detail because of the then growing hostile attitudes toward Jews. Both events involved the denial of admission to hotels—in Saratoga Springs, New York, and in Manhattan Beach in Brooklyn, then a city separate from New York (Higham 1984, 127–29; Mayo 1988, 95). Although not the first time Jews had been turned away from hotels, these particular instances caught the attention of cartoonists and the press, meaning that they became viable public issues and risible events to entertain magazine readers. (Scholars of anti-Semitism in America subsequently highlighted these events as harbingers of worse things to come.)

In 1877, Judge Henry Hilton, owner of the Grand Union Hotel in Saratoga Springs, New York, denied admittance to Joseph Seligman, a German Jewish banker who had previously vacationed there. Two years later Austin Corbin, president of the Manhattan Beach Corporation, denied admission of Jews to his hotel at the eastern end of Coney Island in Brooklyn (Moore 1981, 36–39; Dinnerstein 1994, 39–40; "Joseph Seligman" n.d.). Both Hilton and Corbin held that Christian vacationers did not want to socialize with Jews and would avoid hotels where the latter rented rooms. Corbin especially found Jews to be pretentious, vulgar people who expected more for their money than other paying guests. Not surprisingly, both Corbin and Hilton were active in a short-lived organization called the American Society for the Suppression of the Jews.

Cartoonists found much humor in these rejections and lampooned Jews who were looking for summer resorts and trying to gain access to places where they were not welcome. In the June 17, 1877, issue of *Puck* (pp. 8–9), a montage of images sprawled across two pages (fig. 10). On the left, a pigeon-toed Seligman scratches his head as he says, "Where, oh, where is my summer home?" Immediately below him, pigs grace the hotel flag, the porch roof, and the columnar supports for the roof. Insofar as pork is one of the forbidden foods mentioned in the Hebrew Bible, the caption explains the choice of that decorative motif: "A sure device to keep them out."

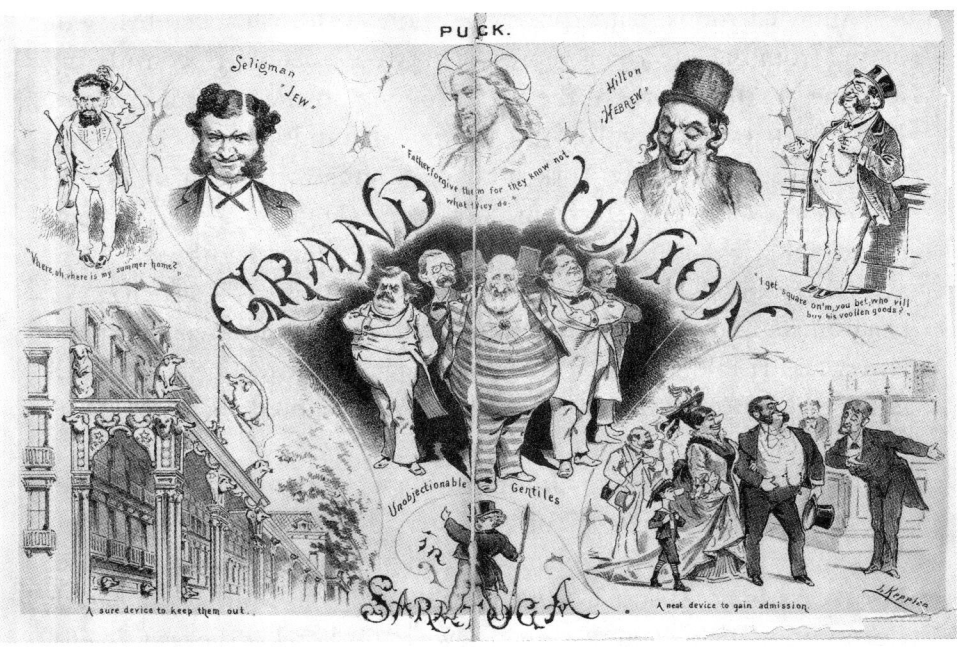

10. Joseph Keppler, *Grand Union: Unobjectionable Gentiles in Saratoga*, from *Puck*, June 17, 1877, 8–9. Image 91905d. Photography © New-York Historical Society.

The center of the cartoon portrays a bevy of "unobjectionable gentiles." Above them, an image of Jesus surmounts his words during the Crucifixion: "Father, forgive them, for they know not what they do." These words were meant either for Jews who wanted to stay at the hotel or for the gentiles, as if excusing their behavior. On the top right, there are two stereotypical images of big-nosed Jews. Beneath them, Jews with prosthetic, upturned noses are seen passing as Christians to gain admission to the hotel.

Puck evidently could not abandon the matter. In a cartoon for the May 11, 1881, issue (p. 178), the cartoonist captured a Coney Island–like scene, including hotels, boardwalk promenaders, a sandy beach, bathers, sun bathers, and banners (fig. 11). This hotel clearly catered to Jewish guests. All of the figures on the boardwalk have huge noses, and some have pot bellies. The women are ostentatiously overdressed for a

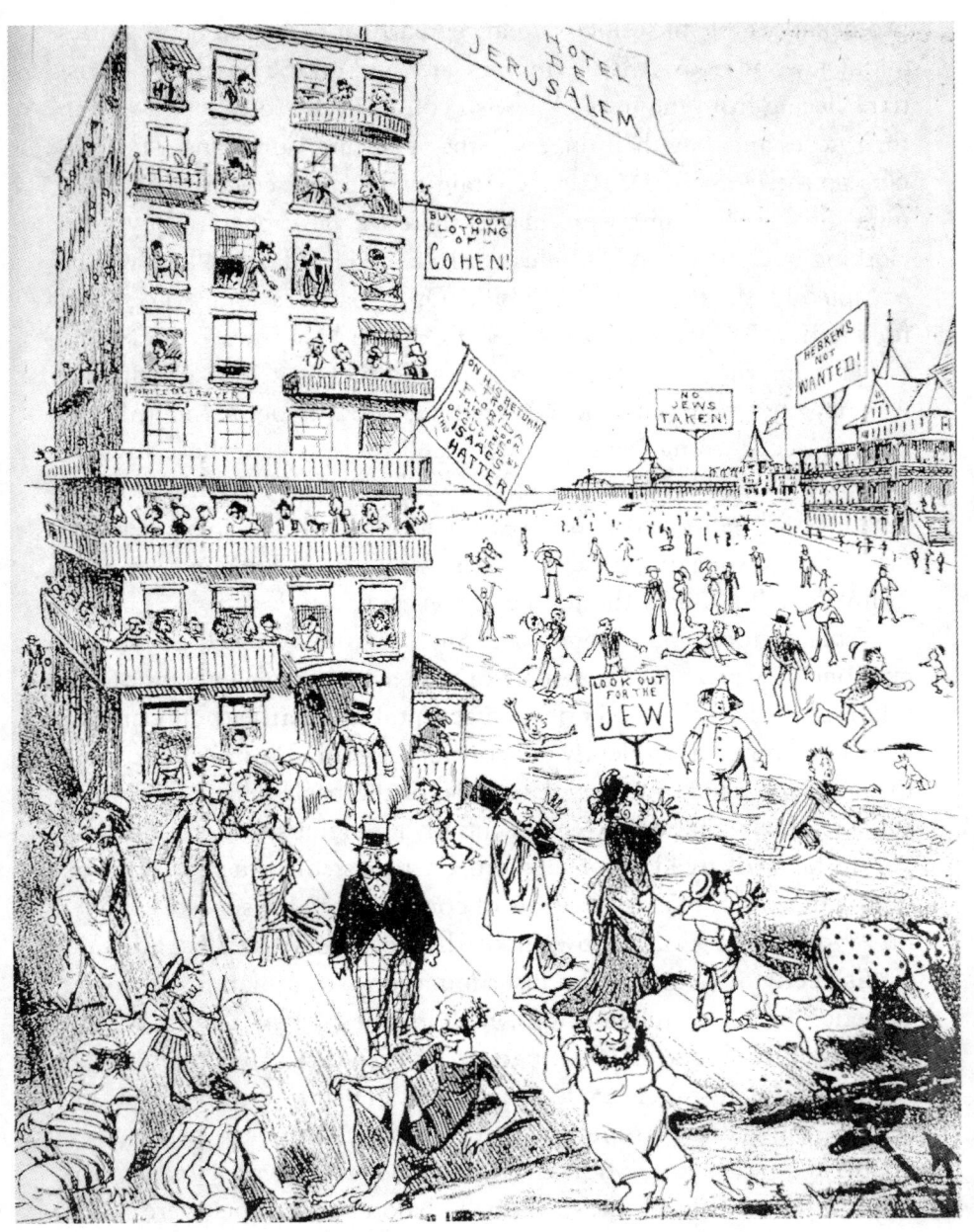

11. Unknown artist, *Untitled*, from *Puck*, May 11, 1881, 178.

promenade, a hostile criticism that regularly appeared in news stories about Jews at resorts. Those in the water and on the beach are Christians fleeing from the Jews. A Jewish couple in the foreground thumb their noses and wag their fingers at the departing Christians. The banners on the Hotel de Jerusalem contain two advertisements that in the mind of the cartoonist were placed there by vacationers: "Buy your clothing of Cohen," and "On his return from Florida, this floor will be occupied by the ISAACS HATTER." Other banners state: "Look out for the JEW," "Hebrews not WANTED," and "No Jews TAKEN."

Perhaps the ultimate in arrogant and haughty Jewish behavior was depicted years later in the April 10, 1902, issue of *Life* (p. 301) (fig. 12), concerning Jews who managed to register in hotels where they were not wanted. Lounging in front of a hotel on Mt. Olympus, where Greek gods and goddesses vacationed, Minerva, on seeing a fat-bellied Jew leaving the entrance, says to Juno: "Extrawdn'ry, isn't it, my dear Juno, how the Jews get in everywhere."

This cartoon dates from 1902. Such cartoons as well as the discussions they provoked were part of increasingly open expressions of religious disdain that had not been acceptable in earlier publications. Such contempt was evidently not considered printable or in good taste in the 1870s insofar as it violated one of the basic beliefs of Americans—namely, that they were essentially a religiously tolerant people and in favor of freedom of religion. Cartoons consequently acted as surrogates for public expressions of contempt for Jews. For example, in 1879, Austin Corbin, owner of the hotel in Coney Island, said as discreetly as possible that discrimination was a matter of "social esthetics" and not religion (qtd. in N. Cohen 1979, 209). Corbin's response also fit the classical pattern of prejudice. First, the deed is done—in this instance, exclusion of Jews. Then the rationalizations begin (Young-Bruehl 1996, 3, Marcus 2015, 14).

To maintain the notion that social behavior was a major reason for refusing Jewish reservations at hotels, attempts were made to explain differences between Jewish behavior patterns and acceptable Christian manners. For example, in an article in the *Jewish Messenger* in 1881, the author explained that Jews speak with great

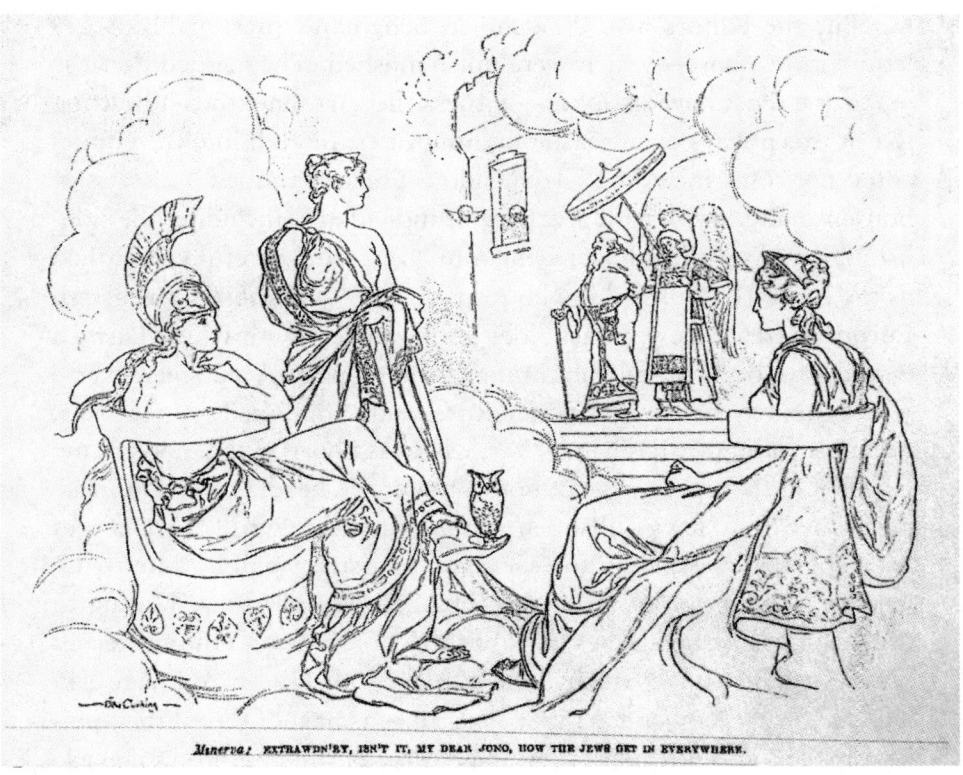

12. Otto Cushing, *Untitled*, from *Life*, April 10, 1902, 301.

vivacity and arm movements, like all inhabitants of southern Europe, and then he offered this interesting observation: "Some of our stolid Anglo-Saxon would-be actors might with advantage study the natural eloquence of these people" (Kounstamm 1881, 1). But such explanations only exacerbated the situation by calling attention to the very differences to which Christians objected and found repulsive. (It is perhaps not for nothing that in Irish tap dancing the dancers' arms remain vertical, unmovable, and close to the body.)

Despite the press's reticence to discuss anti-Semitic attitudes openly, the *Puck* editors made light of Seligman's predicament in the same issue in which the cartoon about his aborted vacation appeared (June 27, 1877). Under the headline "Hilton and the Jews," the editors noted that "right-thinking men will only condemn [Hilton's action]"

(2). But the editors also condemned Seligman's presumably angry letters in response—which were not published. They added that the magazine must have its jokes—witness the cartoon—thus admitting that it was always open season on minorities. In addition, the editors could not resist including "Tremendous Stir in Saratoga," a series of nonsense interviews with a variety of individuals, including the Englishman and prime minister Benjamin "d'Israeli," carefully identified as the earl of Beaconsfield, who responded to questions in an eastern European (read: Lower East Side) Jewish dialect with which Disraeli would have been entirely unfamiliar. And on page 4, a doggerel verse written under the name "Sydney Rosenfeld" contained four stanzas, each one ending with the line "Yet, why was I born with a hook in my nose?" On that same page, a notice under the heading "Puckerings" mentioned that Jews will open a hotel of their own. "No Gentiles need apply, at least no Hilton-Gentiles. Christians will be admitted."

Puck could not let go of the Seligman–Hilton story. Willing to dredge up yesterday's news, it published an article on Hilton's recent business failure under the headline "Alas! Poor Hilton" on page 2 in its issue for December 25, 1878. This time, as part of the editors' policy of working both sides of an issue, they outlined Hilton's debacle with little mercy. Then, noting that everybody in America "stands equal before the law and before society with all his fellow-citizens of whatever creed or nationality," they concluded that "it is the verdict of all thinking men that in everything he [Hilton] has done . . . , he has been a magnificent failure—and the Jews have won a grand success"—as if Jews were responsible for Hilton's failure or as if only they were concerned with Hilton's business ventures.

Jews understood that whatever other reasons might be given, the religion itself provided the core of Jew hatred. Of the various reflections on this matter written over the years, an article in the *Jewish Messenger* for August 31, 1888, was among the most succinct and to the point:

> Why is the word Jew a term of reproach? Simply because the Jew is made a kind of theological bogey to infantile Christian minds. . . .

The most fruitful of all factors it must be frankly stated, has been
the religious training of Christians. . . . That sentiment is at the
root of popular prejudice; it is taught to children in Sunday-School;
it is inculcated in sermon and text. . . . The man of sorrows and
acquainted with grief is the Jew in every Christian age. ("Christian
and Hebrew" 1888, 4)

The Hilton–Corbin connection was also used to implicate Jews
in unscrupulous business practices, as *Puck* demonstrated in a cartoon in the December 8, 1880, issue (pp. 226–27) (fig. 13). From the
left, Hilton and his janitor, a German named Bismarck—an insulting
reference to Otto von Bismarck (1815–98), chancellor of the German
Empire from 1871 to 1890—and then from the right Corbin kick out
of their hotels an itinerant Jewish salesman who sells all manner of
good Christian values as objects from his basket—sobriety, industry,
patriotism, poetry, literature, and prosperity, among other things. In
the background on the left, the viewer is reminded that no Jews are
allowed in the Grand Union Hotel in Saratoga, and on the right on a
porch at Corbin's hotel the words "Manhattan Beach" are written on
a banner. The caption at the bottom (not shown in the figure) reads:
"The Chosen People, I have thriven on this sort of thing for Eighteen
Centuries. Go on, gentleman, Persecution helps de Pizness."

Of the cartoons describing Jewish unprincipled business practices, subjects included purposefully committing arson to obtain
fire insurance; exhibiting miserliness; buying and showing off one's
jewelry; selling clothing; hustling unsuspecting individuals; teaching
children the value of making and keeping money; and a continuing
and open-ended sense of Jewish rapaciousness, acquisitiveness, and
money-grubbing materialism.

For example, Jewish businessmen were considered so untrustworthy because of the many workplace fires set in the 1860s—about
twenty years before the great migration from southern and eastern
Europe began—that seven major fire insurance companies agreed
not to insure Jewish-owned businesses in the future. But because no
arson cases were ever proven in court, companies began to insure

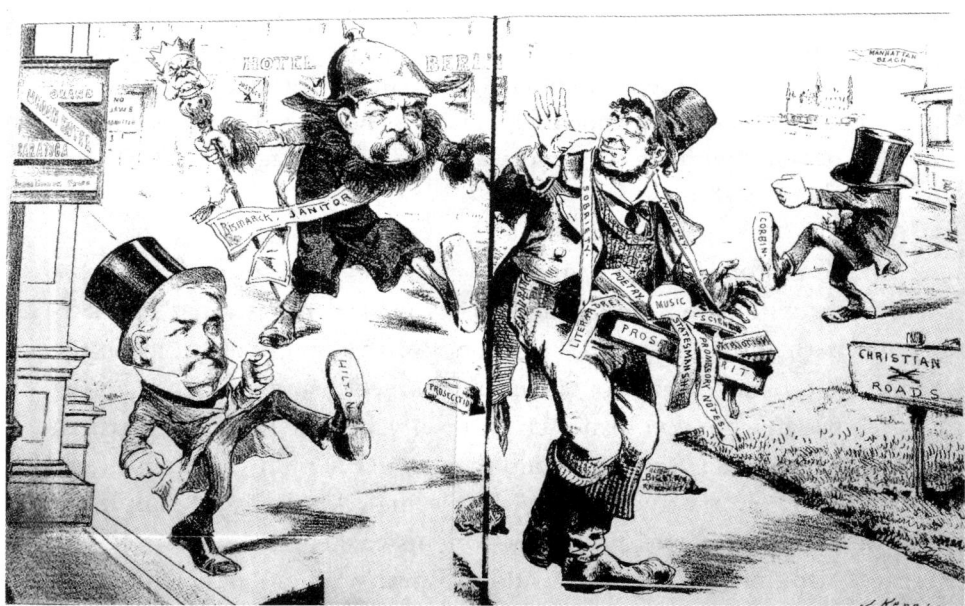

13. Joseph Keppler, *The Chosen People*, from *Puck*, December 8, 1880, 226–27.

them again (Gribayedoff 1897, 102, cited in Dobkowski 1979, 60–61; Dinnerstein 1984, 36–37; Mayo 1988, 92–94).

Nevertheless, several cartoons about "successful" or planned fires appeared even as late as 1900. In these cartoons, an exchange often takes place between two people in a store, in a home, or on a street. For the May 1900 issue of *Judge's Library* (not paginated), the caption tells the story pictured in the cartoon. In *For and Against*, two men— one the proprietor of a second-hand clothing store and the other his friend—speak to each other (fig. 14). The most important items are the bottles in a rack on the right and the sign beneath them: "Hand Granades to Be Used in Case of Fire," the misspelling as purposeful as the dialogue. The friend, Cohn, says: "I vas surbrised to see you take such brecautions against fire." Silvergold, the proprietor, with a Cheshire cat grin on his face, answers, "Don'd say a void! Dot's a brecaution against de fire goin' oudt; dey're filled mit kerosene."

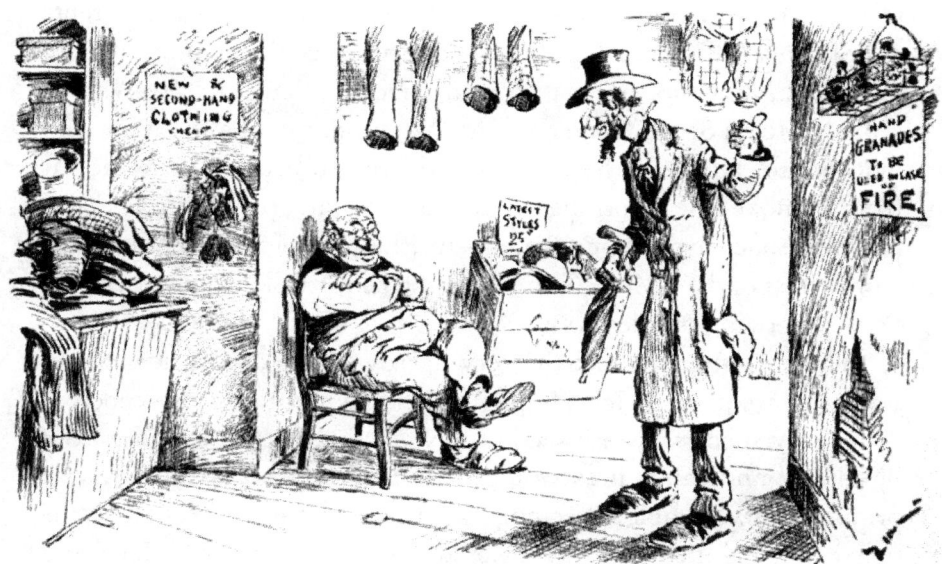

FOR AND AGAINST.

COHN—" I vas surbrised to see you take such brecautions against fire."
SILVERGOLD—" Don'd say a vord ! Dot's a brecaution against de fire goin' oudt ; dey're filled mit kerosene."

14. Eugene Zimmerman, *For and Against*, from *Judge's Library*, May 1900, not paginated.

Of the many variations on the theme of arson, here are four telling examples. *The Hebrew Clothing District*, published in the February 3, 1894, issue of *Judge* (p. 68), shows a newspaper reporter standing before his editor, who sits at a desk overloaded with papers. The editor says: "You neglect to say in your story who were the losers by the fire." The reporter responds: "I said it was in Chatham Street [in the Jewish section of the Lower East Side], didn't I? There were no losers; all winners." The untitled second cartoon for the May 17, 1900, issue of *Life* (p. 424) takes place in an office building lobby. It shows a Jewish man asking the Irish doorman, "Is Ibenstein and Rosenbaum in this building?" The doorman responds: "Go on wid yez. No—this is a foire-proof building." The third cartoon, titled *Not Smart*, in the February 1894 issue of *Judge's Library* (p. 13), shows two men talking to each other. Cohen tells his friend that he thinks his son, Isadore, is a fool. "I gives him ten thousand dollars to start in the clothing business and he goes to Omaha and rents a store in a fire-proof building." For the December 1900 issue of *Judge's Library* (not paginated), the cartoon titled *Why He Wept* is set on "Motza Street," where a very overweight man and a very thin man speak, while in the background firemen are removing goods from a smoke-filled clothing store as the weeping proprietor looks to heaven. Isaac says: "Vot's Rosenbein [the proprietor] veeping for?" Cohen responds: "Mein Gott, he can't help it! Shust see does fool firemen moving out der goods."

These cartoons reflect the very narrow range of attitudes about Jews and arson: first, Jews hoped for and helped along an expectant or already successful fire; second, Jews avoided renting in fireproof buildings; and third, fires would be even more successful if Jewish proprietors were able to remove goods for future sales before the date of the planned fire. The unspoken presumption is that Jews and planned arson go together. If someone of this era saw several cartoons of Jews associated with arson, then that person would begin to believe that this was a scheme that Jews used to make money.

Jewish chicanery based on one sort of "pizness" or another became a staple of cartoonists. In response to an item in a newspaper mentioning that the Catskill Mountains are filled with Jews ("Levy's Out!" 1881, 367), a cartoonist presents a Jewish man, the owner of a family hotel, who tells his son in doggerel verse written in dialect and entitled "Levy's Out" that he is closing the hotel to become a stock broker, that they will be able to wear the diamond rings, chains, and watches left by and unreturned to their boarders, and that his son will someday become a broker just like his parent. The underlying intention of the poem, dated "Jewly, 1881," seems to be to point out that for Jews honesty and a sense of morality are irrelevant in business enterprises. The poem also touches on another sensitive Christian issue—the rapidity with which Jews could switch from one business to another quickly and aggressively, leaving their American competition far behind.

Once these points were made—over and over again—it became easy to blame Jews for their actions, whether they were perpetrators or victims, because they were not sensitive to the feelings of their clients or of the public in general. Further, they certainly lacked moral values and had little or no self-respect. About the last quality, take, for example, an exchange in the June 1, 1876, issue of the *New York Tribune* between a Jew who disliked an advertisement for a resort banning Jews even before Joseph Seligman tried to reserve rooms at the Grand Union Hotel in Saratoga Springs. The editors replied to the complaint: "It is hardly wise for Hebrews to be so extremely sensitive. They certainly do not wish to go to a hotel which does not desire their presence, or, if they do, they have odd notions of self-respect" (qtd. in Mayo 1988, 95). At worst, the newspaper told Jews what their reactions should be to the ban but did not consider their sensibilities, histories, customs, or constitutional rights. At best, which is not saying much, the article reminded Jews not to be so sensitive to rejection or to other slights. The editors revealed neither sympathy nor interest in understanding Jews as newcomers to America. Jews were simply the Other, inferior persons who must be told how to behave in order to be tolerated, if not entirely accepted.

The response to the cartoon *Modern Moses* in the November 30, 1881, issue of *Puck* (pp. 200–201) (fig. 15) and the resulting fallout from the subsequent exchange only underline the mainstream position, indicated by an article in the *New York Tribune*, that victims are largely responsible for their victimhood. From left to right in the cartoon, Jews from varying social classes pass through the separated waters of the Red Sea under the watchful eye of the ghosts of Russian soldiers. People with monstrous noses walk safely between waves marked with the words *intolerance* and *oppression*. They are being welcomed by a very Jewish Uncle Sam wearing ill-fitting clothing and holding a baton labeled "Liberty." Most of the people seem pleased to be delivered into the Promised Land, one or two already appearing shifty-eyed, as if planning ways to accumulate their fortune in America. (For the December 16, 1912, issue of *Der Groyser Kundes* [The Big Stick], artist and cartoonist Saul Raskin substituted Marx for Uncle Sam as well as the words in Yiddish: "Karl Marx the Liberator Giver.")

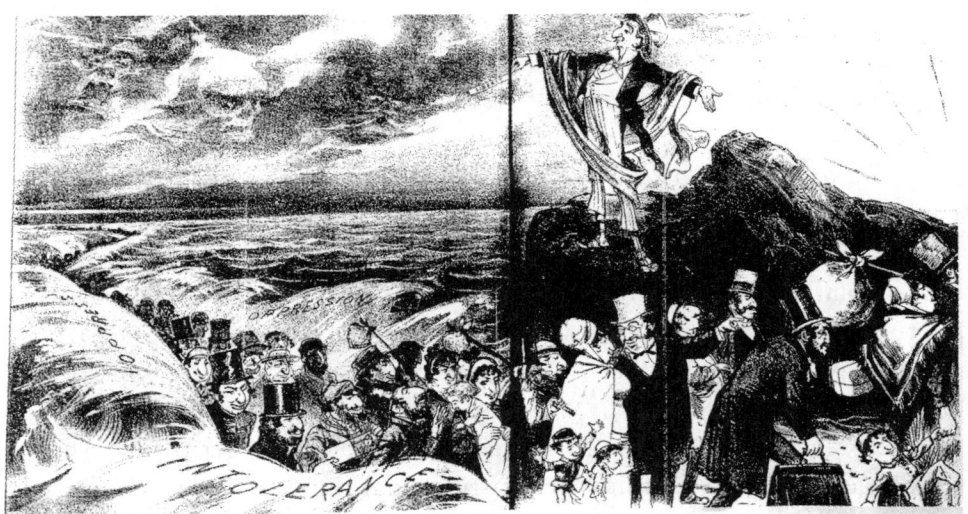

15. Unknown artist, *Modern Moses*, from *Puck*, November 30, 1881, 200–201.

The editors of the *Jewish Messenger*, offended by the cartoon, responded in an editorial article in the December 9, 1881, issue by condemning *Puck*, calling it a German comic weekly whose editors did not understand that Jews emigrated from Russia to escape persistent official and street-level hostility and that in 1881 alone the roughly 250 pogroms had already occurred. The editors explained their displeasure:

> In such a case, decency and humanity demand that so tragic an incident [*sic*] should at least be treated sympathetically. The caricaturist, however, sees in the journey of the unhappy emigrants only an opportunity for a vulgar ridicule. Evidently, *Puck* is not yet Americanized. In this country, decent people regard with painful interest the story of Jewish suffering, and the welcome of emigrants is hearty and generous. The only exception seems to be the cartoonist and this is not the first time that he has raised a laugh "making the judicious grieve." (*Jewish Messenger* 1881, 4)

In their double-speak way, the editors of *Puck* responded to this criticism by both praising and insulting Jews. They termed the *Jewish*

Messenger a denominational weekly that was, like all such publications, established as a means to make money by trading on its faith. After assigning negative motives to the magazine, *Puck's* editors then insisted, not for the first time, that they were not prejudiced and that their "Hebrew friends" should not be so sensitive and must learn to take a joke. "If they do not wish to be made fun of, they should not intensify the traditional peculiarities that so often make them subject of ridicule." These peculiarities included being clannish and clinging "to their antiquated puerile Oriental customs and mummeries. . . . They should become Americans . . . , mix and marry and associate . . . with non-Jews or Gentiles, and get rid of the silly idea that their race and religion are immeasurably above all others" ("Israel on the Crank" 1881, 227).

The *Puck* editors' statements call for two different kinds of observations. First, the editors implied that they really did not dislike Jews but rather that they were victims of Jewish oversensitivity and that their views were being questioned by those who objected to their statements. In this way, the editors hoped to control any discourse on anti-Semitism rather than allow the Jews to do so. Jews were not to decide who did and did not dislike them (B. Cohen 2012). I have inserted the word *anti-Semitism* here to point out that the editors denuded the word of any serious meaning. As one author wrote in 1945, "Anti-Semitism has no specific meaning. It is a weasel idiom, loose, and complaisant, capable of being emptied almost at will of one content and filled with another. . . . [It is] a prejudice in search of a pretext" (M. Steinberg 1945, 11, 54). What applied in 1945 also applied in 1881.

The second observation is that according to the editors Jews should give up their Jewish culture, memory, and probably their religion immediately on immigrating and become just like other Americans (Kaufman 1949, 239). In both the first and second instances, then, the editors put Jews in an untenable position—damned if they responded to anti-Semitic articles and depictions of them, damned if they didn't because it was their own fault for being disliked.

In any event, presumably those who could not make the Red Sea crossing seen in figure 15 could take, as another cartoon states, "the

'New Trans-Atlantic Hebrew Line'" (fig. 16), depicted in the issue of *Puck* for January 19, 1881 (p. 339). Even if illiterates could not read the sarcastic caption, "For the Exclusive Use of 'The Persecuted,'" they would know who the persecuted were: the people on the ship, the sailors, the ship itself, the fish in the water, and the bird in the sky—all have hooked noses.

Chicanery of one sort or another, social aggressiveness, and manipulation of another person remained popular subjects for cartoonists in connection with Jews. For example, in 1881, Frederick

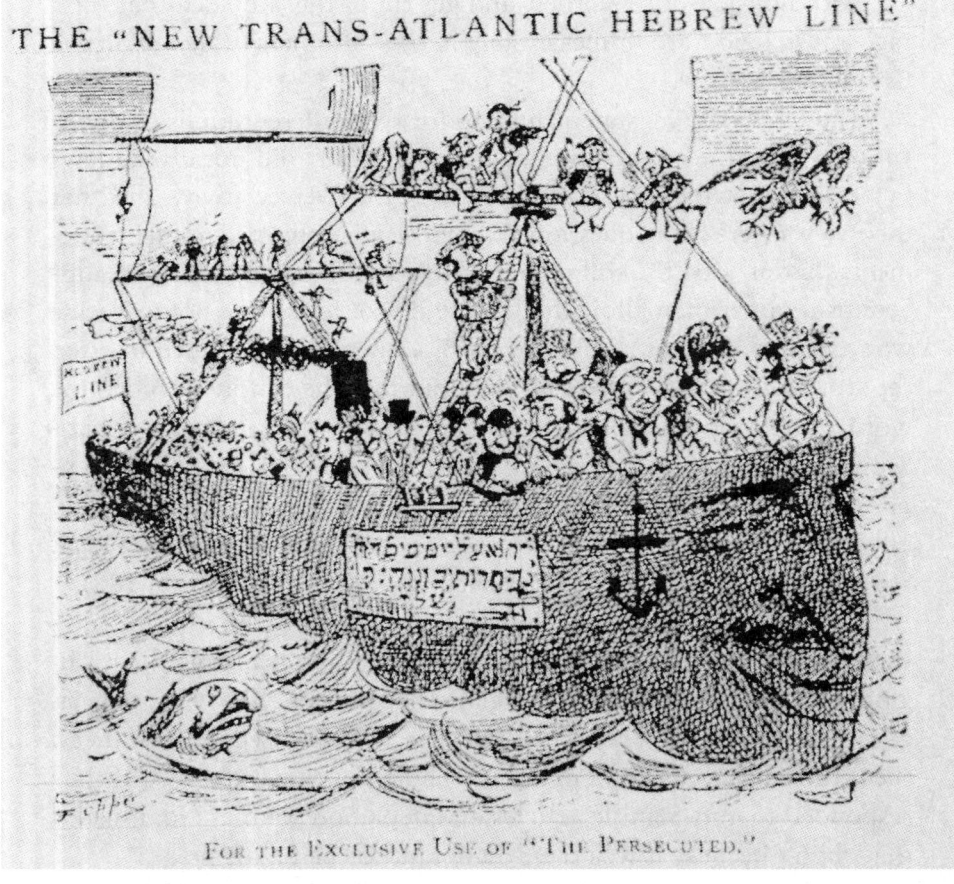

16. Frederick Opper, *The "New Trans-Atlantic Hebrew Line,"* from *Puck*, January 19, 1881, 339.

Opper drew for the May 18, 1881, issue of *Puck* (p. 196) a multi-figure cartoon showing different ways a salesman makes his sale. The cartoon, titled *The Salesman's Snares for His Annual Victims*, shows the salesman's various techniques, including literally fish-hooking an unsophisticated small-town person and getting a potential client drunk. Another cartoon in the December 7, 1881, issue (p. 216) shows an obviously Jewish claims agent along with other agents bothering Civil War pensioners. But it is the Jewish agent especially who is seen closing in on a wounded and therefore vulnerable veteran. In another cartoon that year in the March 9 issue of *Puck* (p. 60), a Jewish art dealer is altering a canvas in order to sell it as an old-master painting.

From the 1880s through the 1910s, cartoonists showed different and sometimes ingenious ways Jews supposedly took advantage of people. In the April 14, 1886, issue (p. 102), *Puck*, in one of its ongoing *The Streets of New York* cartoons, an old man creates and then takes advantage of a situation. In the first of a two-cartoon sequence, the "Benevolent Old Hebrew Gentleman" gives baseballs to small boys. We learn in the second cartoon that the Gentleman is a glazer who replaces the windows broken by the boys (fig. 17). As late as 1910, a cartoon in the January issue of *Judge's Library* (not paginated) shows a Jewish itinerant peddler confronted by the resident of a rural household, who says: "Clear out! You cheated me like the mischief last time you were here." Jacob, the peddler, responds: "Vell, dem's der gusdomers I don'd like to lose, so I calls again." The two lessons to learn from this cartoon are, first, that you should try to repeat a successful even if immoral sale; second, you should do so only if you are certain that you can outsmart your former customer again. The Jew in this cartoon, now made a laughingstock for the cartoon's viewers, does not learn the second lesson.

Cartoons of Jewish tailors, an especially popular subject, showed them to be experts at duping their customers. In the March 24, 1898, issue of *Life* (p. 226), the tailor says to a client who has complained about the tightness of a pair of trousers that rise up to just under his armpits: "Does pants fids you jusd beaudiful, mine frent, now

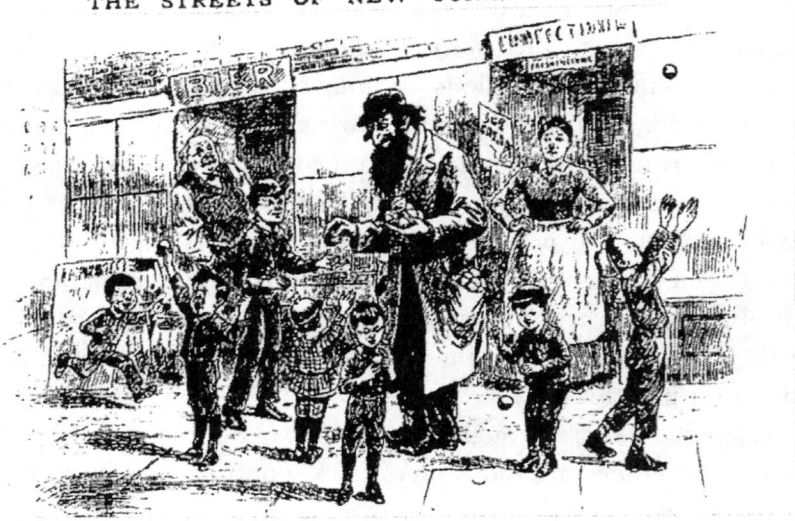

There was a Dear, Nice, Benevolent Old Hebrew Gentleman who Attracted Considerable Attention on the East Side of Town Lately by Giving Away Base-Balls to the Small Boys——

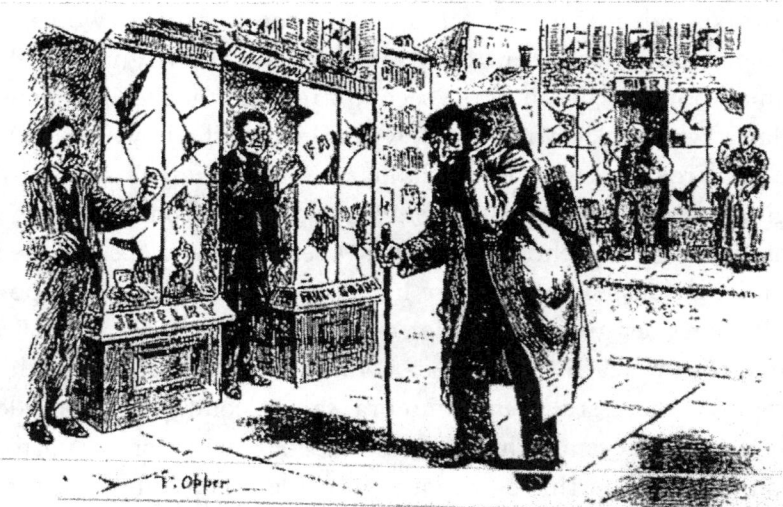

But it was Noticed that the Dear, Nice, Benevolent Old Hebrew Gentleman Always Appeared the Next Day with a "Glass-put-in" Outfit, and did a Rushing Business.

17. Frederick Opper, *The Streets of New York*, from *Puck*, April 14, 1886, 102.

ain'd id." In the March 1892 issue of *Judge* (p. 5), an overweight man complains to Cohen, the tailor, that his trousers are too short. Cohen replies: "My friend, dot vas my new spring sthyle, warrented nefer to get trodden down at der heels." And in the July 1892 issue of *Judge's Library* (p. 19), a farmer complains to Levy, the tailor, about the enormous size of the cuffs on his coat. Levy replies: "Vell, dot is vot is called de English coat of arms, mine friend."

Sometimes the scene is not in a tailor shop. For example, in a cartoon in the issue of *Judge's Library* for August 1892 (p. 91), Miss Hockheimer, who has fallen out of a rowboat or was pushed out by Loenstein, says: "Vat vill mommer say? Mein dress is spoilt." Loenstein, in water up to his waist and holding a small poster extolling Lowenstein dye mousse, says: "Here vas some readin'-matter vhile I pushes you on to der beach." Or in the issue of *Puck* for February 18, 1881 (p. 432), in a sequence of four images titled *How Rosenthal Avoided a Suit for Damages*, we see a man on the street reading a book; he falls into an open manhole in front of Rosenthal's clothing store and emerges covered with dirt. In the last scene, Rosenthal has put a signboard near the manhole that reads: "Look Out for Our Fall Opening." Despite the infantile humor, these cartoons might have been collected in a cartoon book titled *Duping and Conning: The Ways of the Jewish Tailor* insofar as all reinforce the notion that Jewish tailors are duplicitous to the core of their beings.

Cartoonists often showed one possible reason for Jews' duplicity and success: early training within the family. Grandparents and parents taught their children to be aware of and to take advantage of a situation. Cartoons on this subject usually included a father or grandfather sitting in a chair advising the younger person or making an observation based on years of experience. In the issue of *Puck* for December 14, 1898 (p. 26), a grown-up son elegantly dressed for horseback riding tells his grandfather: "Ven I vos oudt horseback riding dis morning, Gandfader, I dradet dot horse undt made feefty tollars." The grandfather replies: "Goot for you, Chakey! Dot vos der vay to enchoy horsepack riding!" (fig. 18). A subtext might be that even though the grandson has reinvented himself as a young American, he cannot

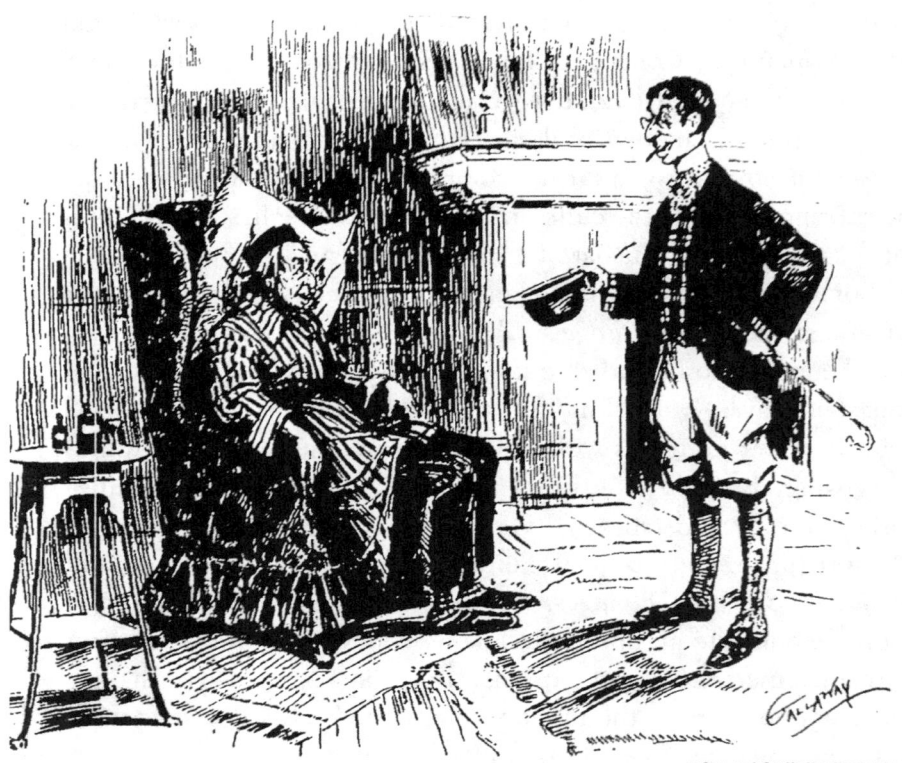

BUSINESS AND PLEASURE.

"Ven I vos oudt horseback riding dis morning. Grandfader, I dradet dot horse
undt made feefty tollars."

"Goot for you, Chakey! Dot vos der vay to enchoy horsepack riding!"

18. Walter H. Gallaway, *Business and Pleasure*, from *Puck*, December 14,
1898, 26.

escape his Jewish training, mangled English, or biological makeup.
Another subtext is that Jews, always alert to possible financial profit,
take advantage of every situation as it presents itself.

In a cartoon for the August 31, 1898, issue of *Puck* (p. 12), titled
True Happiness, the son asks: "Fader, dis book say as moneysh does
not print happiness." The father replies: "No, mein sohn, it's der
inderest vot you gets on der moneysh vot makes you happy." In other
words, the son is taught the important lessons that money creates

money and that making money is its own reward. In the December 7, 1898, issue of *Puck* (not paginated), Grabbenstein Jr. quotes from a schoolbook: "In 1776, Washington, Adams, Hancock, and Jefferson were among those who were making history." Grabbenstein Sr. interrupts: "Is dere a list of der men who vere making moneysh [in] dose times?" And in the April 18, 1894, issue of *Judge* (p. 261), Samy asks his father, "Good deeds speak for themselves, don't they, fader?" Mr. Isaacstein responds: "Yes, Samy, if dey vos on real estate." Even though the father still speaks with a heavy accent, the accent does not overrule his cleverness and his knowledge of the English language in teaching his son the difference between doing a good deed and owning a good deed. A few pages later in the same issue of *Judge* (p. 297), the son in a different family has already learned an important lesson. His father asks him if he has bought flowers for his sister's wedding. The son, holding the bouquet, answers that he purchased paper flowers so that they can be used again when his grandfather dies.

Such cartoons reinforced viewers' perceptions of Jews as a people who pass on to their offspring their money-hungry values. Such Jewish family values became accepted truths and inevitably triggered automatic responses toward Jews and even by Jews, for which I can personally vouch. Even I was momentarily surprised when I came on a cartoon in the Jewish press that presented a totally different point of view of a Jewish parent–child conversation. The then famous Jewish cartoonist Samuel Zagat (1890–1964) created a sympathetic cartoon in 1919 about the relationship between a father and son (fig. 19) (Zagat 1972, 19). Instead of the elder person sitting in a living-room chair dispensing wisdom, the two men sit together on a bench after a walk and obviously have spoken to each other about things not exclusively related to business practices. The old man is dressed in a way that suggests old-fashioned European styles, and the son is clearly an acculturated American. The caption reveals that they speak perfect, unaccented English. The son, looking at his father, says, "Terrible news again." The father, staring off into space as if responding to something remembered, says, "Don't take it too hard, son, we have been through them before." Given the date, their conversation could

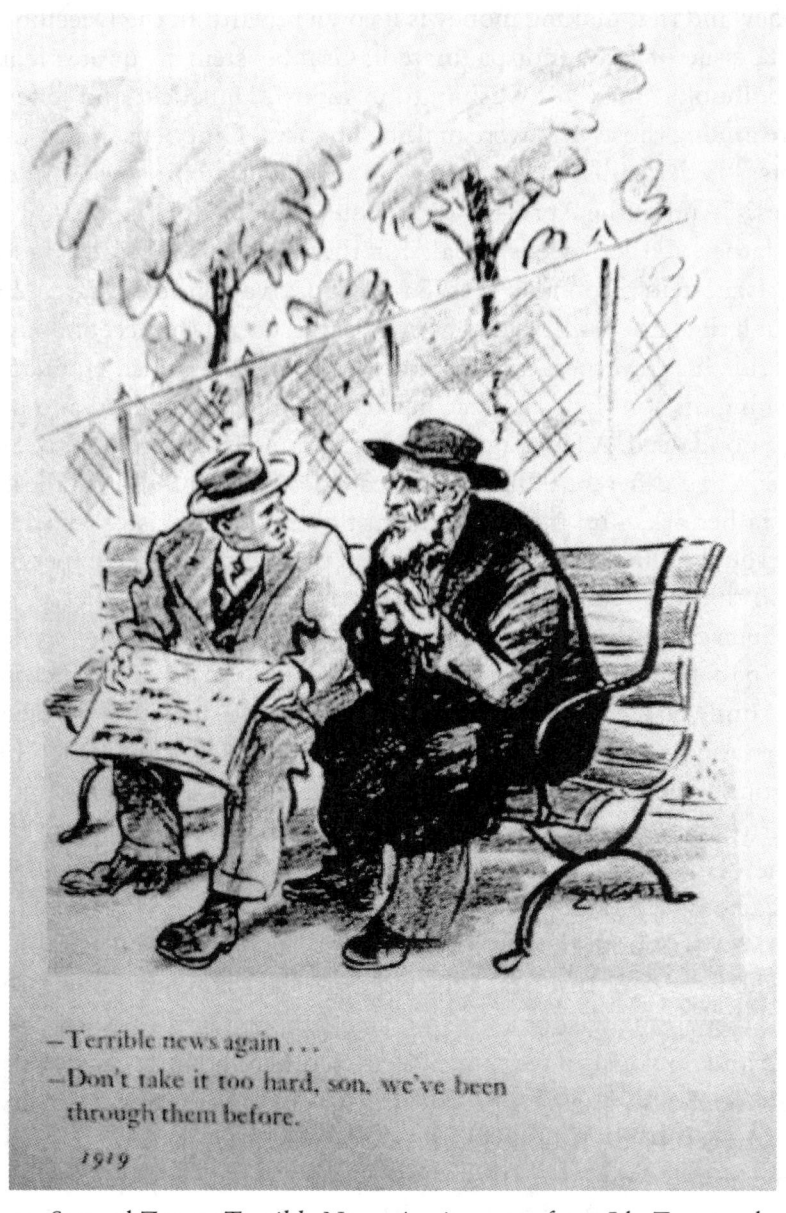

—Terrible news again . . .
—Don't take it too hard, son, we've been
through them before.

1919

19. Samuel Zagat, *Terrible News Again*, 1919, from Ida Zagat, ed.,
*Drawings and Paintings: Jewish Life on New York's Lower East
Side, 1912–1962* (New York: Rogers Book Service, 1972), 18.

be about a report of an anti-Semitic incident or yet another pogrom in eastern Europe.

This cartoon makes some important and corrective points in comparison to the usual negative stereotypes. Conversations between Jewish children and their elders were not limited to lessons in how to connive, make money, or dupe innocent persons. Sympathetic responses are instead both expected and given. Traits and habits of mind such as patience, resignation, and mutual understanding between generations as well as acceptance of the outcomes of specific situations can also be instilled in children and grandchildren. To say it bluntly, Zagat shows that Jews do have and reveal human feelings.

But more usually in the cartoons of this period, Jews inevitably sought out, bargained for, or stumbled upon good deals. For example, Jews apparently considered doctors' fees negotiable. Slick talking helped. In one such face-off in the issue of *Life* for February 20, 1896 (p. 133), the doctor tells Mr. Stein that he has complications from six different diseases, to which Mr. Stein replies, "How much discount you gif me on halef a dozen, doctor?" In another cartoon in *Life* on September 23, 1897 (p. 252), a husband explains to his wife, who has found a prescription on the ground and is not certain of its worth, "Vat a question! Do you think dot nobody vill never be sick?"

And a cartoon in the May 24, 1890, issue of *Judge* (not paginated) shows a patient in bed attended by his physician and a friend. The friend, realizing the patient is dying, asks the patient to make him a creditor before it is too late.

Looking for and taking advantage of bargains also suggests an underlying propensity toward cheapness despite presumed Jewish financial successes in business practices. In the January 1894 issue of *Judge's Library* (not paginated), Bergmann comments on recovering from a serious illness and looking so healthy after returning from Florida: "Bud I good haf had a funeral for halluf of vot der drip gost." Another cartoon in *Judge's Library*, this one as late as September 1910 (not paginated), shows the Isaacsteins on a ferry boat. Mrs. Isaacstein tells her husband that she is going to be seasick. His response: "Vhy couldn't you find dot oud pefore you eat dot feefty-cend dinner?" A cartoon in the December 8, 1897, issue of *Life* (p. 529) features the man who, after finding out that it will cost him fifteen dollars to buy a ticket to the Thousand Islands in the St. Lawrence River in Canada, asks the agent: "How much fer five hundred?" Another version of the "cheapskate joke," this one in the April 1890 issue of *Judge's Library* (not paginated), shows Mr. Rheinstein asking Mrs. Goldburg to marry him. She refuses him because she has just ordered, with no discount, expensive cards engraved with her maiden name. He will have to wait until she uses up all of the cards. In yet another version, this one published in the July 3, 1913, issue of *Life* (p. 11), three old and very bald Jewish men enter a barber shop and, showing the proprietor their bald heads, ask him if he can give them one portion of shampoo for three. And then in the March 6, 1895, issue of *Puck* (p. 36), in the most merciless, hard-hearted cheapskate joke of all, Mr. Grabheimer tells a penniless tramp who asks for a handout, "I don't see how I can make any money oud of you!"

As cheap as Jews were thought to be, they were also paradoxically seen as extravagant spenders, especially on jewelry and fine clothing, as we saw earlier in the hotel cartoons. A cartoon that overwhelms in this regard and at the same time makes a point of commenting on Jewish masculinity is *History as It Might Have Been: The Return of the Prodigal Son*, published in the October 10, 1912, issue of *Life* (p. 1956) (fig. 20). Not humbly seeking forgiveness, as in the legend, but ostentatiously traveling in an automobile driven by a uniformed driver, the prodigal son returns to visit his parents, who are dressed in what appears to be Middle Eastern—that is, not American—garb. This choice of clothing style is probably a comment on the notion that Jews originated in central Asia (see chapter 3). Their son seems to have adopted both Western clothing styles (his hat) and Western customs, such as traveling with golf clubs, tennis rackets, and a copy of *Sporting News*, in addition to displaying the affectations of a rich, spoiled child.

The parents' home, Cohenhurst Manor, reflects their obvious wealth. Their son, accompanied by his bulldog, extends a limp hand to

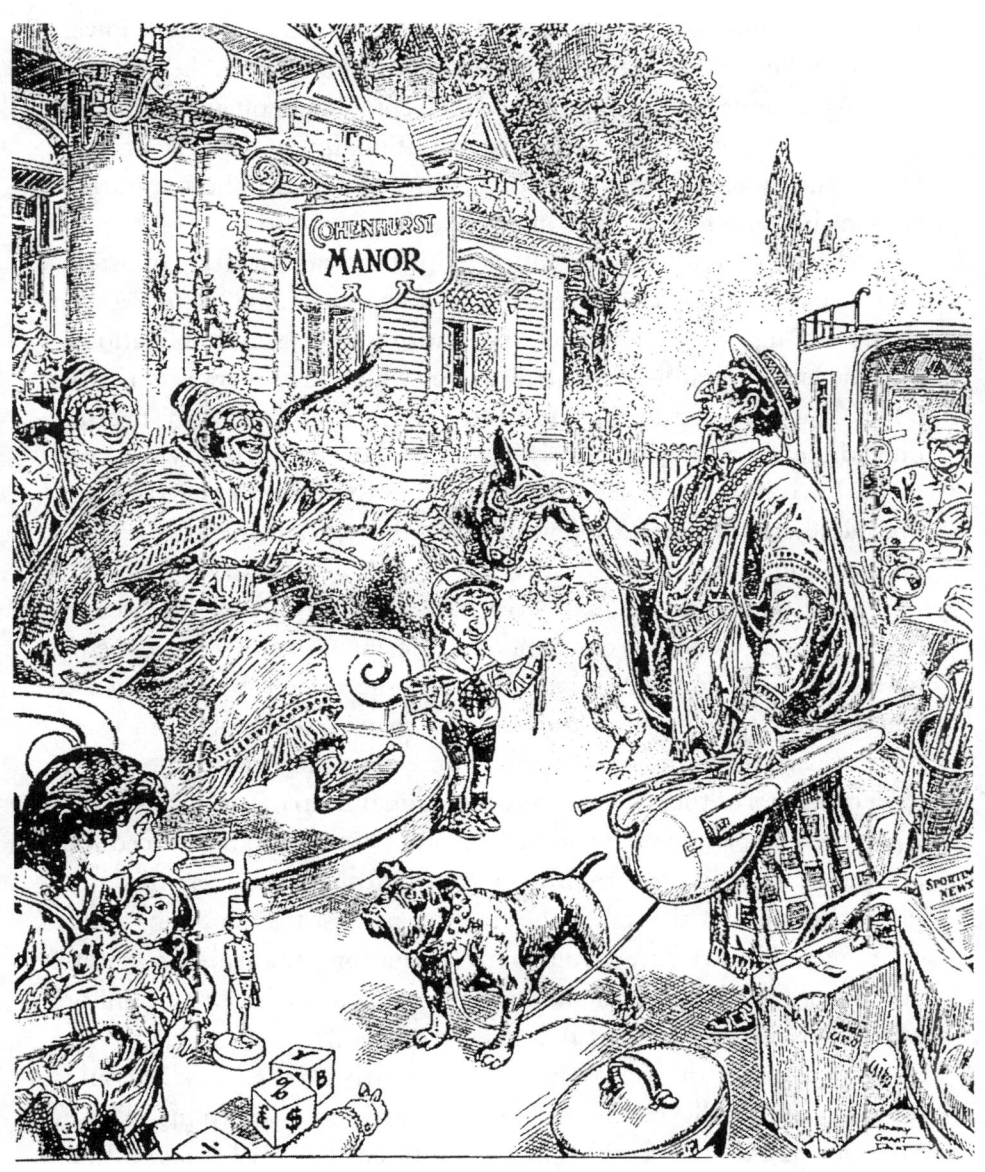

HISTORY AS IT MIGHT HAVE BEEN
THE RETURN OF THE PRODIGAL SON

20. Harry Grant Dart, *History as It Might Have Been: The Return of the Prodigal Son*, from *Life*, October 10, 1912, 1956.

his parents, who rush to greet him. The woman and child on the lower left might be the family the son had abandoned insofar as the bulldog, wearing an apparently diamond-studded color, faces off against them, suggesting, whether the cartoonist intentionally intended it or not, that in the choice between a life of pleasure and a life of humanitarian responsibility to family, the son has selected the good life.

Whatever its other ramifications, this cartoon is a study in ostentation, emphasizing the parents' overblown emotional exuberance, the collecting of gaudy objects, the ignoring of personal obligations, and the lack of manliness—qualities for which Jews were often criticized. It also suggests that however the parents previously overindulged their son, they obviously accept and forgive his behavior as an adult. He is less the Prodigal Son than a brother of the spoiled-rotten mythic Jewish Princess (on Jewish masculinity, see Boyarin 1997 and Gilman 1998, 68).

In cartoons of individuals from other minority groups, we rarely, if ever, see individuals so determined to appear a certain way, so seemingly in control of their situation, and at the same time so unaware of the effect they have on the viewer—that is, so involved in their own lives as to be oblivious to the impression they make on others, even members of their own family. Once again, cartoons of this type, when seen by people who had little contact with Jews, reinforced the point that all Jews were rich, wore gaudy clothes, and were disdainful of those about them. (At the start of my first teaching job, when my wife and I were barely able to make rent for a semirundown half-double in a garden-apartment development, our next-door neighbor asked my wife how many fur coats she owned.)

Especially in the 1890s and the very early 1900s, jewelry could play a role literally in life-and-death situations in cartoons. These cartoons might be assembled in a book titled *Jews and Jewelry*. In a cartoon in the December 21, 1899, issue of *Life* (p. 536), Goldstein and a friend are floating in the ocean after a shipwreck (fig. 21). The friend, who is staying connected to Goldstein by holding on to his enormous diamond necklace, asks Goldstein: "If you don't come up again, Goldstein, can I keep the diamond?" In the July 1892 issue of *Judge's Library* (not paginated), a cartoon shows an older Jewish couple having dinner during a visit to Washington, DC. The husband says to his wife, who wears large diamond earrings, "Chew real hard, Kate. It makes them dimuns sparkle like new coppers," meaning that her earrings move and reflect the light when she eats. In the issue of *Judge's Library* for March 1892 (not paginated), a father holds his infant son out of the apartment window, reciting, "Twinkle, twinkle little star," and when he gets to the line "Like a diamond in der shky," the infant asks: "Vere is dot dimond, fader?" In a cartoon in the May 17, 1890, issue of *Judge* (p. 82), Mr. Hirschkind and his wife are sitting in a theater box behind a lady wearing a huge feathered hat. The man is looking though opera glasses directly at the diamond earrings the lady is wearing. When his wife notices that the lady's feathered hat blocks her husband's view of the stage, he answers that nevertheless he is satisfied with the view. In the June 7, 1890, issue of

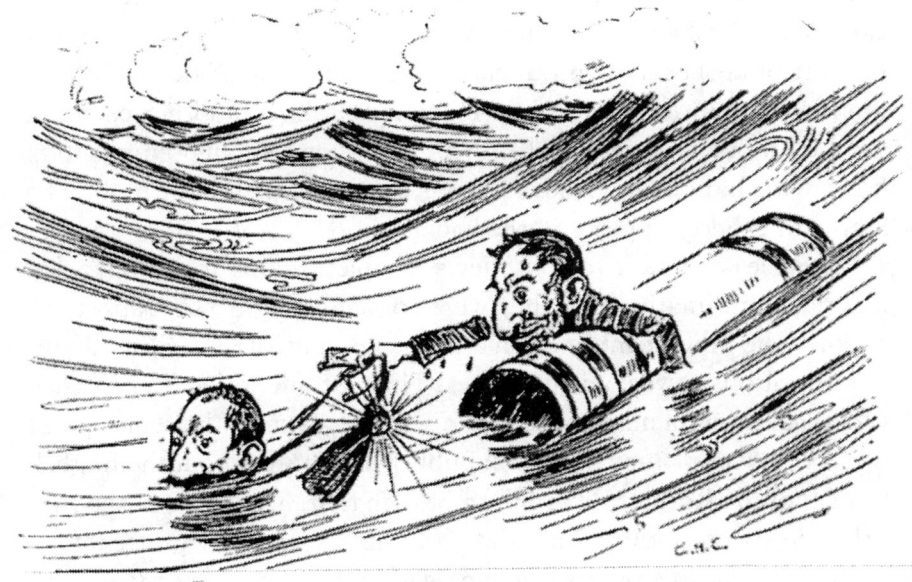

"IF YOU DON'T COME UP AGAIN, GOLDSTINE, CAN I KEEP THE DIAMOND?"

21. C. M. C., *If You Don't Come Up Again, Goldstein*, from *Life*, December 21, 1899, 536.

Judge (p. 134), Mr. Feelstein, kneeling before Miss Guggheim, says that her eyes are like diamonds. When she asks, "How many carats, Abe?" the only kind of comparison he can offer is to say that the carats are the biggest ever, that they were in the pawn shop for thirteen months. And, finally, a really insulting cartoon in the April 11, 1907, issue of *Life* (p. 515) shows a Jewish parrot named Polly Goldstein warning a duck, who is staring at a fake diamond, "I vouldn't eat dat. I tink it vor an imitation!"

Although the last cartoon is about birds searching for something edible, it is among the very few with food as the subject, despite the fact that overweight Jews appeared in many cartoons. In one cartoon published in the January 30, 1902, issue of *Life* (p. 99), Mrs. Jacobs, in a panic, tells her husband that their son, Ikey, just swallowed the giraffe from his toy Noah's ark kit. Mr. Jacobs, not upset by the news, says that at least it was not the pig, an animal whose meat is forbidden to Jews (fig. 22). One wonders if Mr. Jacobs would have been upset even if it were the pig rather than the giraffe. (This cartoon, published in the January issue, is not a commentary on the boycott of kosher meat products on the Lower East Side that began months later in May 1902 [see Hyman 1980].) In another cartoon, for the July 11, 1907, issue of *Life* (p. 58), a young man holding a box filled with ham sandwiches is being chased by a Jewish mob. The Statue of Liberty appears in the background.

In at least three cartoons, Jews are pictured as many-tentacled octopuses, intimating that they were voracious, not to say rapacious, people who sought international financial control as well as dominant positions in various industries. The first one, titled *The English Octopus*, shows a map of the world with England as the center point (fig. 23). It was printed in a book published in 1894 about the English branch of the Rothschild family, a branch that, according to the subtitle, "feeds on nothing but gold" and has spread its eight tentacles around the world from its London headquarters (Harvey 1894, 141).

This illustration reverberates in different ways, none to the benefit of Jews. First, as recorded in a long article in *Harper's New Monthly Magazine* in 1874, the Rothschild "monomania has been

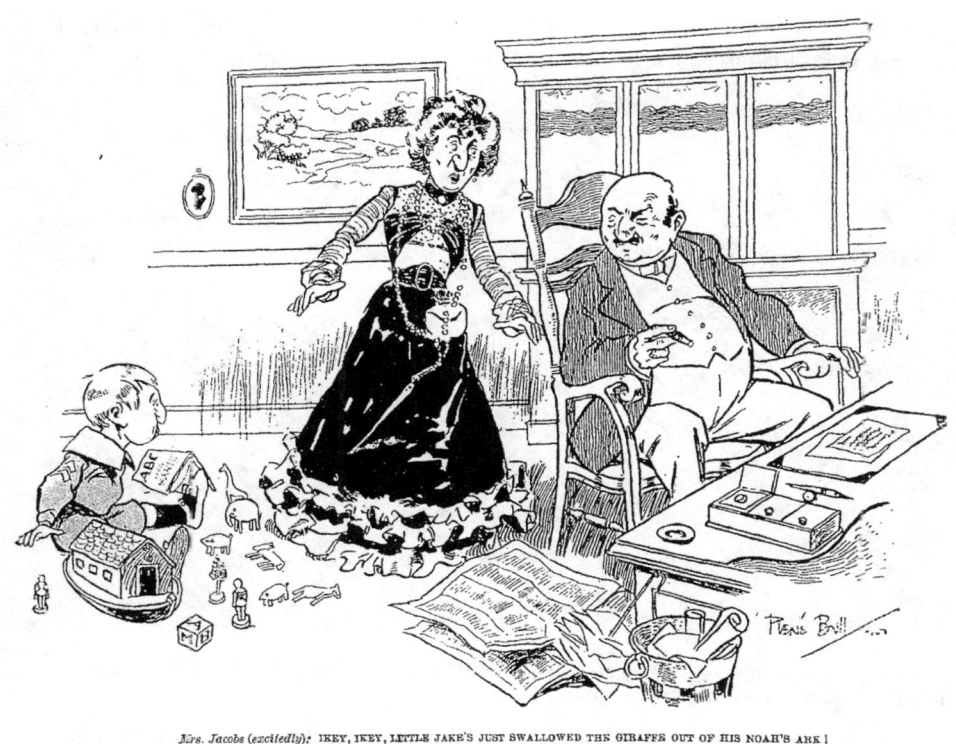

Mrs. Jacobs (excitedly): IKEY, IKEY, LITTLE JAKE'S JUST SWALLOWED THE GIRAFFE OUT OF HIS NOAH'S ARK !
Mr. Jacobs (philosophically): VELL, VELL, THANK GOODNESS IT WASN'T THE PIG !   —Moonshine.

22. René Brill, *Untitled*, from *Life*, January 30, 1902, 99.

money mania" (Browne 1874, 221; see also Dobkowski 1976, 20). Second, Jews were parasites who produced nothing but schemes to control industries. And the third way devolved from the second. As one scholar notes in trying to explain anti-Semitism in terms of the rise of capitalism and the control of international finance, "The Jew symbolized the hostile world of capitalist domination while the true community was based on so-called productive labor" (Mosse 1993, 45). However one parses the place of the Rothschild family in international finance, fault will be found, and Jews will be blamed.

The second octopus cartoon of concern here, titled *The Jewfish and the Octopus Start a Pawn-shop*, appeared in the January 16, 1902, issue of *Life* (p. 54) (fig. 24). This cartoon makes a double

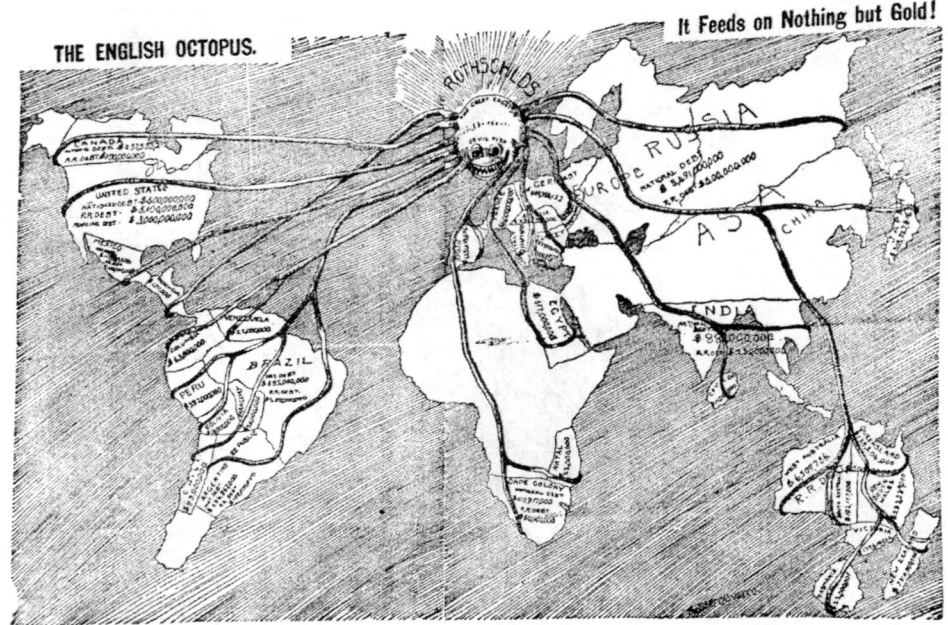

"The Rothschilds own 1,600,000,000 in gold."—*Chicago Daily News*. This is nearly one-half the gold in the Chicago wheat pit.

23. Albert[?] Cassotto, *The English Octopus, It Feeds on Nothing but Gold*, 1894, from William Harvey, *Corn's Financial School* (Chicago: Corn, 1899), 141.

reference—first, to the close association of Jews with pawn shops (the "Jewfish," of course, has a huge nose) and, second, to Jews' desire to squeeze out competitors.

The third cartoon, *Our Old Friend to the Octopus. In His Great Character, the Theatrical Trust* (fig. 25), appeared in the December 9, 1897, issue of *Life* (p. 520). Its subject is the Theatrical Trust, also known as the Theatrical Syndicate, formed in 1896 as a theater-booking monopoly by six Jewish speculative theater managers who dominated the nationwide "theatrical business of America." Their actions were considered "morally iniquitous," especially by those who could not function independently of the syndicate's power ("NO TITLE" in *Life* 1905b, 488; Hendrick 1913, 144–47; Winter 1918,

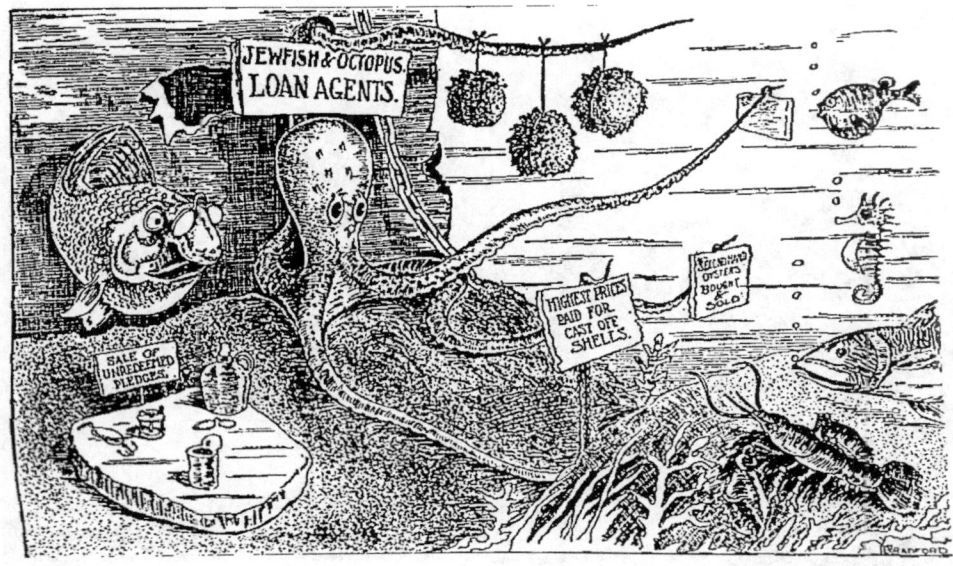

THE JEWFISH AND THE OCTOPUS START A PAWN-SHOP.

24. L. Crawford, *The Jewfish and the Octopus Start a Pawn Shop*, from *Life*, January 16, 1902, 54.

2:156, 19, 155). To ensure that the viewer knows the theater managers' religion, the word *Jerusalem* appears at the left margin.

The octopus image used in *The Theatrical Trust* cartoon is perhaps the ugliest of all images published during these decades. Not surprisingly, in an article in *Life*'s issue for April 23, 1903 (p. 372), titled *"Life's* Confidential Guide to the Theatres," the editors called New York Jews vulgar and stated that they have made money faster than they have acquired good manners or education, are ostentatious in demeanor, are an "undigested" element in New York, and sit through the wretched theater productions they deserve. However, the hope was that in a generation or two the typical Jew will become a splendid person "of refined taste, broad education, and chivalrous manners." Until then, they are at the mercy of "persons who have regarded it [the theater] only as a money-maker, that these persons happened to be vulgar, ignorant, and grasping, and that they also

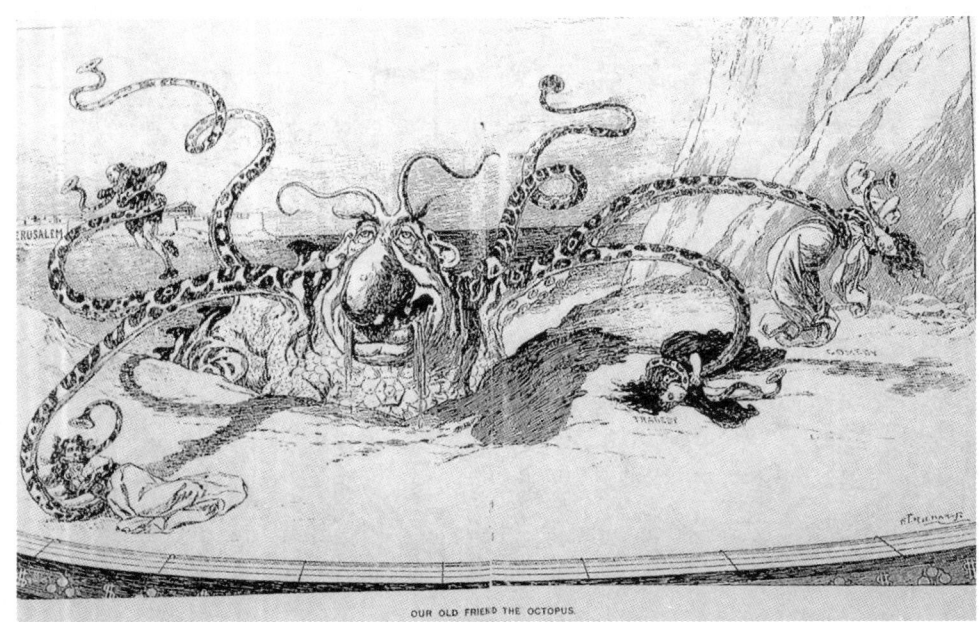

OUR OLD FRIEND THE OCTOPUS.

25. F. T. Richards, *Our Old Friend to the Octopus. In His Great Character, the Theatrical Trust,* from *Life,* December 9, 1897, 520.

happened to be Jews. Their chief supporters and best patrons have
been Jews of the same kind" (372).

OK, so the reptilian octopus image was reserved for Jewish theatrical and financial interests. A simple question then follows. How
come even a handsome, WASP-looking octopus was never used to
illustrate the political and economic reach of Big Oil, Big Steel, and
other trusts whose activities included taking over companies, breaking strikes, and even murdering strikers? The answer, the only logical
answer, is that those in control of these industries were not Jewish.

It is worthwhile to note here that some forty-odd years after
these three cartoons were printed, in 1942, the connection of Jewish
business interests with octopuses still held firm. The famous sociologist Talcott Parsons noted that "the House of Morgan which has
often been held to be the octopus of American finance cannot by any
stretch of the imagination be called a Jewish firm" (1942, 122).

One imagines, then, that Jews back in the day anticipated the worst kinds of comments and images about their particular situations or the shapes of their body parts. In the November 1892 issue of *Judge's Library* (p. 17), for example, a cartoon shows an Irish man and a Jewish man lost on a road between villages. They ask a local farmer for directions. He says that they should keep going and follow their noses. But because the Irishman's pug nose points up, and the Jewish man's parabolic-arched nose points down, the Jewish man responds: "But we wanted to stay together. Is dere no odder way"?

By 1910, the Jewish population of New York was estimated to be 542,000 (Rebak 2012, 49). As a result, New York itself, the hub of Jewish life in America, became the subject of cartoons. A curious and interesting cartoon in the February 6, 1913, issue of *Life* (p. 275) shows around two dozen well-dressed men in heaven looking down at a vision of "Little Old New York" (fig. 26). Their garments style them as Jews either from different parts of the world or from different centuries. The caption reads, "History as It Might Have Been (and in This Case Partly Was). The View of the Promised Land." What does this caption mean? It is true that many Jews looked upon America as the country in which they no longer felt they were in the Diaspora but finally in a homeland. The cartoonist must have been aware of this notion because he showed New York as an image of the New Jerusalem, the city to which Jews will be taken when the Messiah arrives and resurrects the dead. But—and here is the kicker in this cartoon—the men carry the accoutrements of their trade, presumably, as would have been said at the time, ready to do some serious business. To the cartoonist and the caption writer, then, New York had in part become the image of heaven and the kind of place where Jews could buy and sell to their hearts' content.

The fear of New York becoming "Jew York," if not the Promised Land, had evidently not been lost on the editors of *Life*, who in the December 19, 1901, issue (p. 535) published the cartoon titled *New York in the Future. Only a Question of Time* (see fig. 3, p. 9). The theater and the shops are Jewish owned. The only obviously

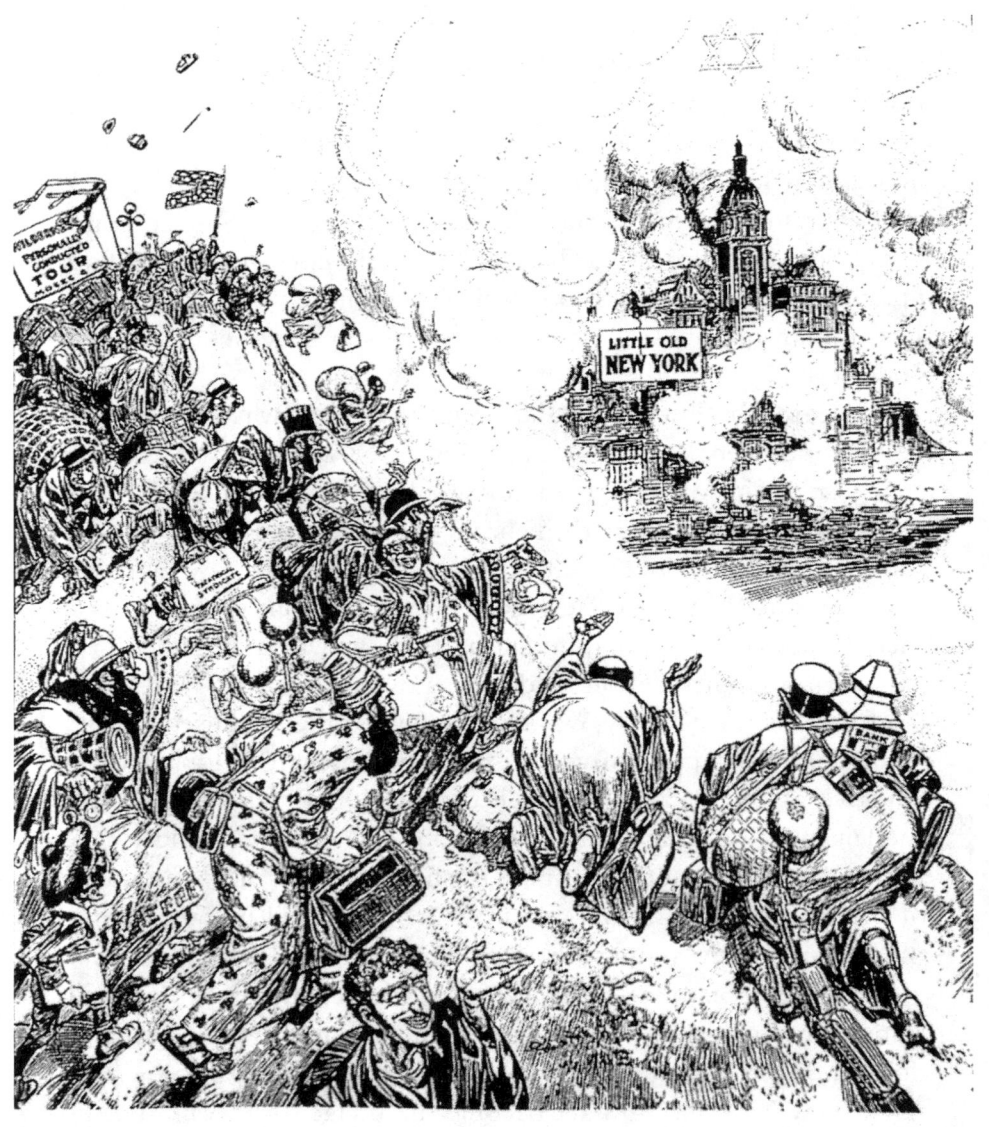

HISTORY AS IT MIGHT HAVE BEEN (AND IN THIS CASE PARTLY WAS)

26. Unknown artist, *History as It Might Have Been (and in This Case Partly Was)*, from *Life*, February 6, 1913, 275.

non-Jew, the tall man in the center left, is being mocked by a group of children as the police look on.

And what would happen on a Jewish holiday if all the inhabitants of Manhattan or all of its shops' owners were Jewish? As seen in the cartoon for the August 22, 1906, issue of *Puck* (p. 3), Broadway would be empty, businesses would be closed, the economy would suffer, non-Jews would not be able to shop or seek theatrical entertainment (fig. 27). The day after the holiday, Jews would presumably be back on the streets en masse. A cartoon published in the July 4, 1912, issue of *Life* (p. 1355) shows Fifth Avenue so packed with Jewish men that couples as well as a mother and her daughter are forced to walk in the gutter (fig. 28). A sign on the right reads: "Hungarian Kosher Restaurant," perhaps suggesting that Hungarian Jews were as ill-mannered as Polish Jews, the usual butt of jokes about bad behavior. But the point of the latter two cartoons was that Jews wielded economic power in New York, their city, but not in a nice way.

And should a Jewish mayor be elected? The cartoonist Harrison Cady drew *The Surrender of New York Town*, a fantasy double-page cartoon for the May 12, 1910, issue of *Life* (p. 882) imagining the extravagant, grandiose, over-the-top, ostentatious installation of said Jewish mayor (fig. 29). On the left side, the mayor approaches city hall accompanied by a huge honor guard that includes ballerinas wearing male masks and tutus (a long-standing negative comment on Jewish men's masculinity as well as Jewish women's overzealousness). Signs on buildings in the background proclaim "New Jerusalem Building, "Passover Towers," and "Synagogue Jerusalem."

On the right side, the mayor is given the key to the city along with donations from various industries in which Jews are prominent—diamonds, clothing, dry goods, and real estate. In the background, a group of men stand under a sign, "Ancient and Honorable Order of Pawn Brokers," an industry considered to be controlled by Jews. Because the cartoonist omitted references to donations from the gas, electric, street railway, and other special-interest corporations, the not-so-hidden message is that Jewish money alone bought the election.

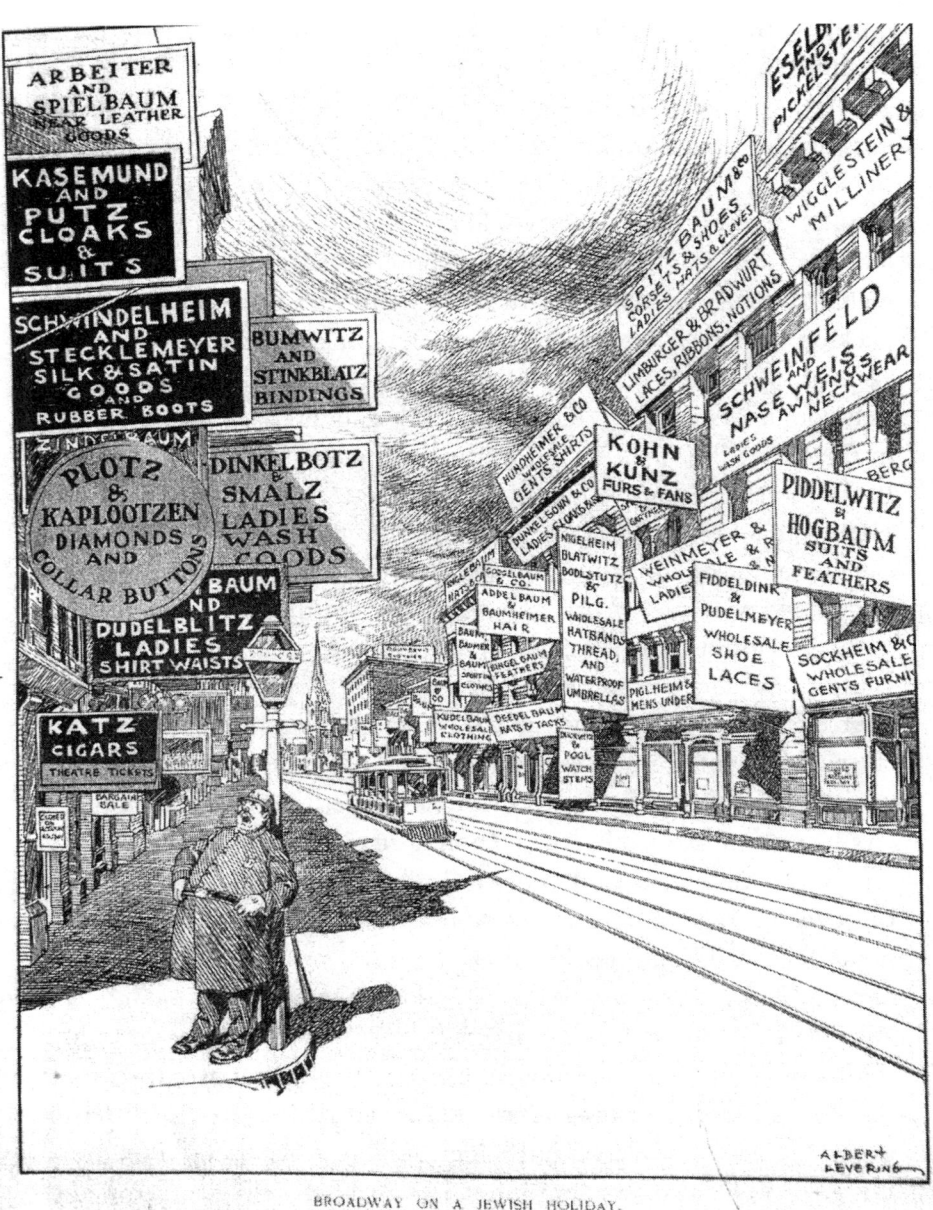

BROADWAY ON A JEWISH HOLIDAY.

27. Albert Levering, *Broadway on a Jewish Holiday*, from *Puck*, August 22, 1906, 3.

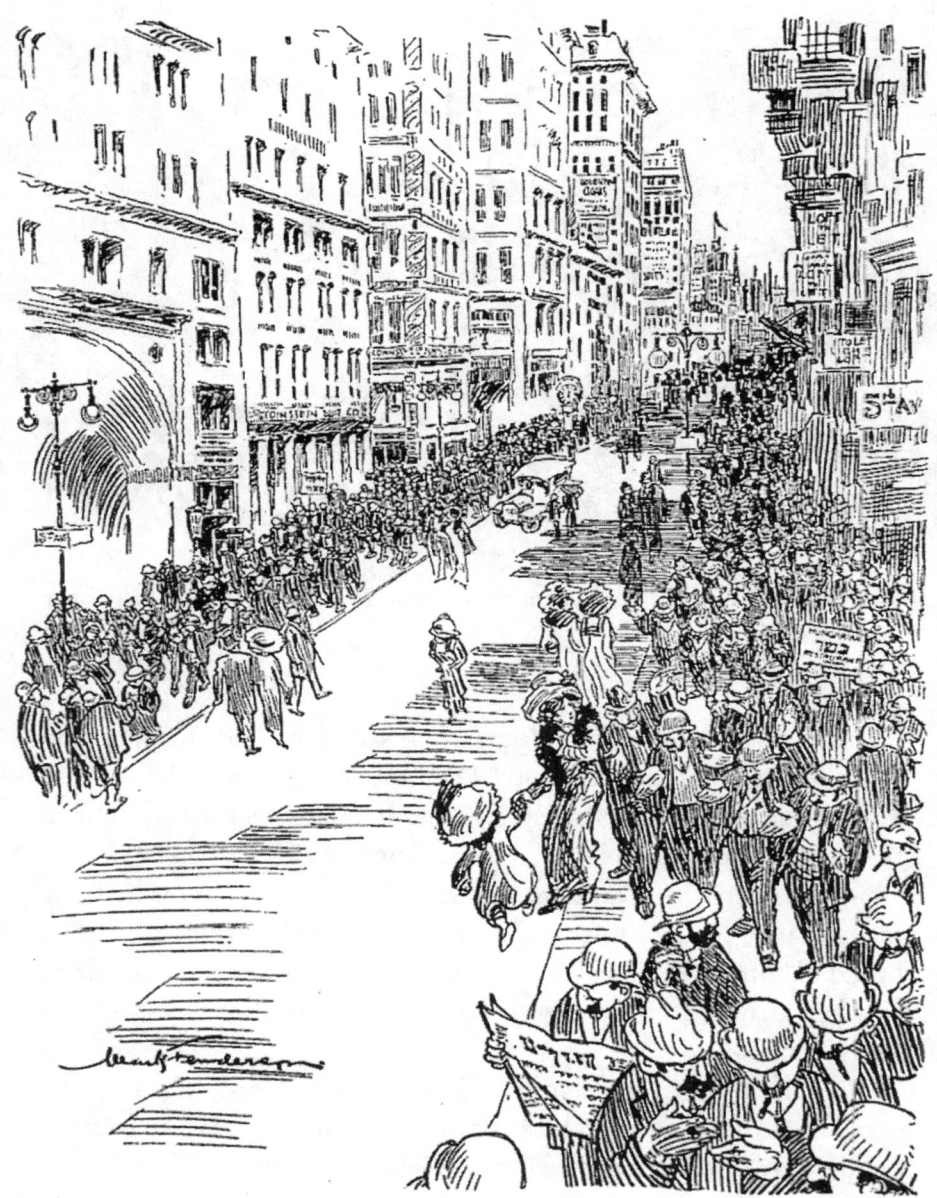

THE NOON HOUR ON FIFTH AVENUE

28. Mark Henderson, *The Noon Hour on Fifth Avenue*, from *Life*, July 4, 1912, 1355.

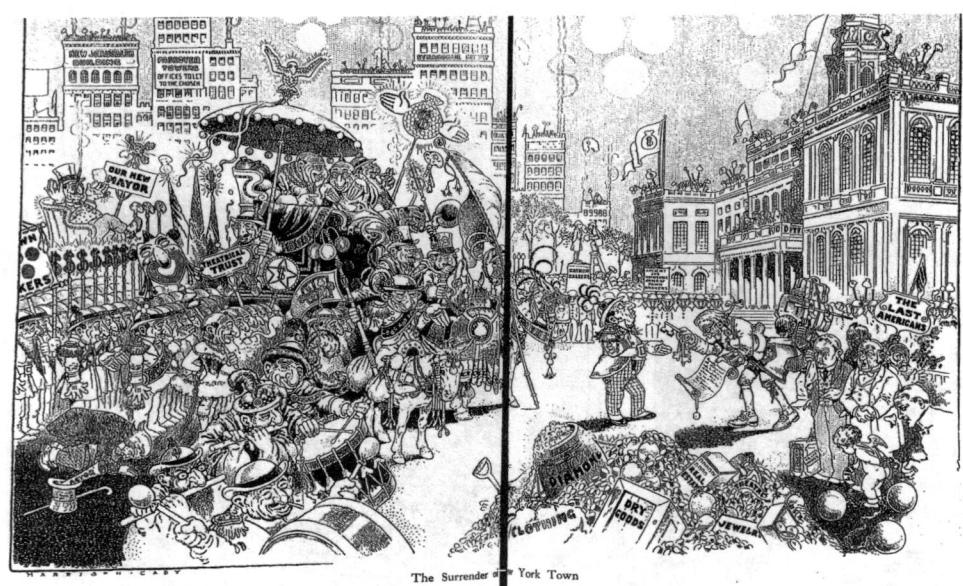

29. Harrison Cady, *The Surrender of New York Town*, from *Life*, May 12, 1910, 882.

Also on the right, another group of sad-faced and shocked men stand under a sign proclaiming "The Last Americans." The suitcase next to the man wiping his eyes with a handkerchief reads, "Off to the Mines." Beneath the men, a naked angel, its hands tied behind its back, is tethered to a large round ball. The sash falling off its body reads "Life," perhaps referring to the demise of the magazine and its brand of humor. We have, then, pomp, graft, and fear—an American city being turned into a Jewish-dominated New Rome, not a New Jerusalem.

Despite fears to the contrary, Jews did not secretly plan to take over New York, rename all of the stores, claim the most important public offices, turn the city into a New Jerusalem or New Rome, and be rude to non-Jews. But the influx of immigrants was evidently so massive that compromise, cooperation, and hospitality between them and long-established populations were not considered possible because in cartoonists' imaginations Jews were intent on maximizing their strength. Articles assessing the effects of such a massive influx appeared regularly. Some were balanced appraisals, some not. The editors of *Life* asserted that no other city in the world contained as many Jews and that the majority of its lawyers were Jewish ("NO TITLE" in *Life* 1905a, 480). On that same page in *Life*, the editors wrote similarly about Boston but agreed that the Irish in that city would not turn it into another Dublin because the Irish would become Yankees instead.

The editors also found that the large numbers of Russian Jews "accumulate in this town [New York] very much as mud accumulates at the mouth of a great river" ("NO TITLE" in *Life* 1905a, 480). The editors then asked a few questions rhetorically. What sort of Jewish delta will the Jews make of New York? Will New York make Knickerbockers of its Jews, or will Jews turn New York into another Jerusalem? The editors included a recommendation from former congressman Fitzgerald that the Irish should emulate Jews by going into business. So on the same page that Jews were compared to mud—as so many grains of dirt washed up on shore—they were also regarded as strong and multitudinous enough possibly to change the character of a city and as having enough commercial acumen that another minority group, the Irish, should emulate their business practices. Fear, loathing, and jealousy are revealed in these cartoons and editorials as well as an ambivalent sense of grudging respect that did not paper over the deep-seated hatred. (For similar editorials, see also "Objectionable Immigrants" 1891; Hendrick 1907, 1913; Reid 1908; Gibbons 1921).

If one chooses to read cartoons as indicative of public feelings, it is interesting to note that hostility to Irish immigrants, although profound, did not reach the level of hostility to Jews. For example, as just noted, Boston would probably remain a Yankee city, but New York might be turned into an Irish city. A generation earlier there appeared in the October 27, 1880, issue of *Puck* (p. 117) a cartoon in which the Irish had turned New York, or "New Cork," into another Dublin. It is titled *"Herald"—Hoax No. 2—"The Cath'lics Are Coming!" Bennett's Prophetic View of the City Hall, If W. R. Grace*

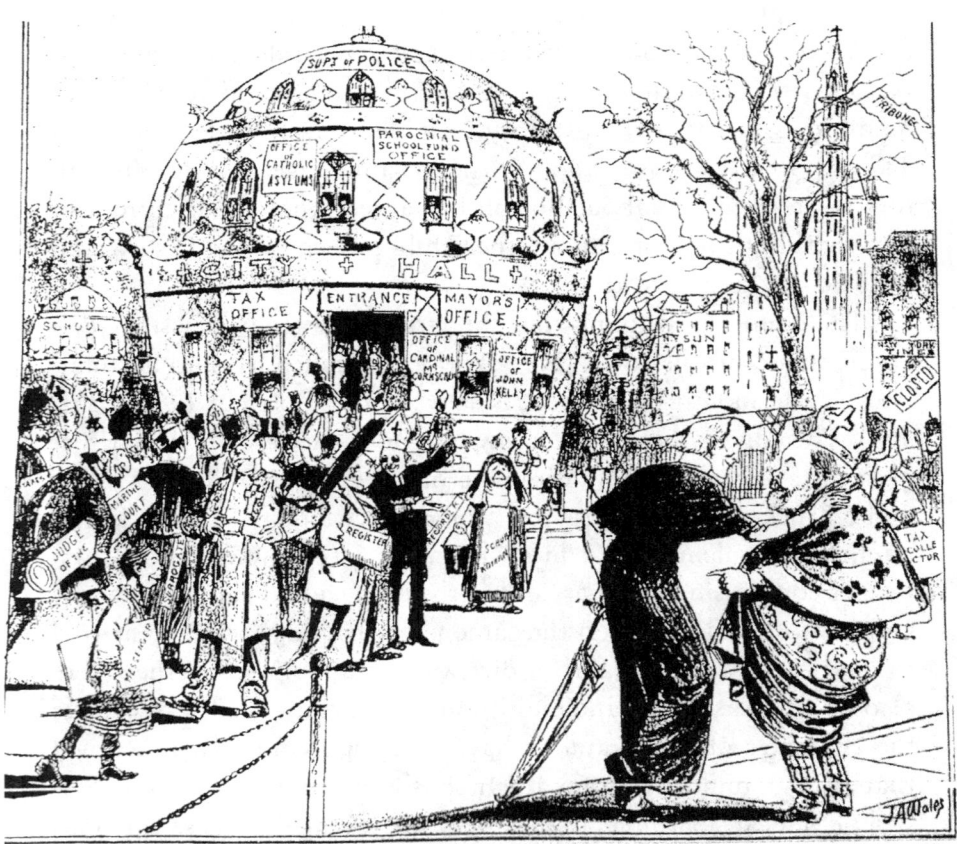

"HERALD"-HOAX No. 2.—"The Cath'lics are Coming!"
BENNETT'S PROPHETIC VIEW OF THE CITY HALL, IF W. R. GRACE IS ELECTED MAYOR.

30. James Albert Wales, "Herald"—Hoax No. 2—"The Cath'lics Are Coming!" Bennett's Prophetic View of the City Hall, If W. R. Grace Is Elected Mayor, from Puck, October 27, 1880, 117.

Is Elected Mayor (fig. 30). In fact, William Russell Grace (1832–1904), an Irish American, was elected mayor, the first Catholic to be so honored, and he served from 1880 to 1882 and again from 1884 to 1886. In the cartoon, all the officials are Catholic, and city hall had become, in effect, New York's Catholic headquarters. Even if the celebration at the election of an Irish mayor was much more muted and contained than the possible celebration at the installation of an imagined Jewish mayor, fear of an Irish takeover prompted the poem "No Yankee Need Apply" by "Slowcus," which was printed in the December 8, 1880, issue of *Puck*. The same line ends each stanza, and the fourth and last stanza goes,

> The Pope will send a Bishop or
> A Cardinal our King to stay,
> Or p'r'aps we'll crown him Emperor
> Of Irish Free Americay!
> (The crown shall wear the cross, you see.)
> And to his service all will fly—
> For favors bend the pregnant knee,
> But there—No Yankee need apply! (Slowcus 1880, 225, also given
>   in Thomas 2004, 219–20)

So much for New York remaining a Knickerbocker city. Despite the poem's hostile tone toward the Irish, Jews, according to historian Roger A. Fischer, invariably fared worse than the Irish and worse even than African Americans in any kind of cartoon comparison (1996, 78, 90) and quite likely in magazine articles.

Soon after the century's turn, there appeared one of the most paranoid articles in the anti-Jewish literature of the day. It was the second part of a two-article series by different authors published in the *Independent* in November 1908. The first article (Bernheimer 1908) asked why there was such anti-Jewish prejudice. Its author decided that this prejudice resulted mostly in social ostracism and rejection—for instance in trying to book hotel rooms, joining college fraternities, and getting children into private schools. But religion was also held against Jews. Gentiles simply did not like them. Why? The rationalization was that because some Jews' habits and manners were objectionable, therefore all Jews were objectionable.

In the second article (Reid 1908), the author promised anonymity to his interviewees if they spoke the truth, and, evidently, they jumped at the opportunity to unload years of pent-up anger, rage, and hatred toward Jews. Jealousy and an inability to meet Jews' level of competition seemed also to underlay the litany of dislikes, along with imagined Jewish dishonesty, persistent shrewdness, cunning, skimming, arson (starting fires in stores after stock is removed to gain insurance), fraudulent bankruptcies, pickpocketing, bad personal hygiene, and rank displays of their prosperity. Of Jews, it was said, "Where they contest they win" (Reid 1908, 1215). Gentile criminals were evidently not as well organized or as clever and unscrupulous. After mentioning the "Hebrew octopus" that now ran theater productions (see fig. 25), the article continued, "We see the Hebrew octopus seizing one enterprise and then another and we can't stop it. They are beating us. They beat us in the schools, in the colleges, in business everywhere, and we are not used to being beaten and don't like it" (1215). The "we" meant, of course, those of Aryan or northwestern European descent.

Two of the most pernicious cartoons in this regard, published in 1891 in *Puck*, provide visual confirmation of the hostile attitudes toward Jews held around the turn of the century. In the issue for January 21, 1891 (p. 372), we see a Jewish Uncle Sam–type figure but here a symbol of the most exploitative, uncaring, money-hungry American, a racist as well as a westward expansionist literally killing Native Americans and taking advantage of Africans and Asians by selling inferior and rotted goods to them (fig. 31). The boxes placed around him are labeled "Spoiled Meat," "Mouldy Bacon," and "Mouldy Bread." Too clever by far, the seller is identified as a Russian Jew by the can around his neck. The overall effect is to elevate the Jewish presence in immoral international commerce, which is personified in the figure of a Russian Jew, who stands as a surrogate for the most destructive, unscrupulous aspects of uncontrolled, predatory American capitalist behavior. But to viewers of this cartoon, it was not an American who behaved in such an immoral way, but a Jew. As suggested earlier, Jews came to symbolize the hostile world of capitalist domination (Mosse 1993, 45) but were perhaps never before presented in such brazen, heartless fashion as in this cartoon. The Rockefellers, Carnegies, and Morgans of the world, however, were evidence that Jews held no patent on producing rapacious businessmen.

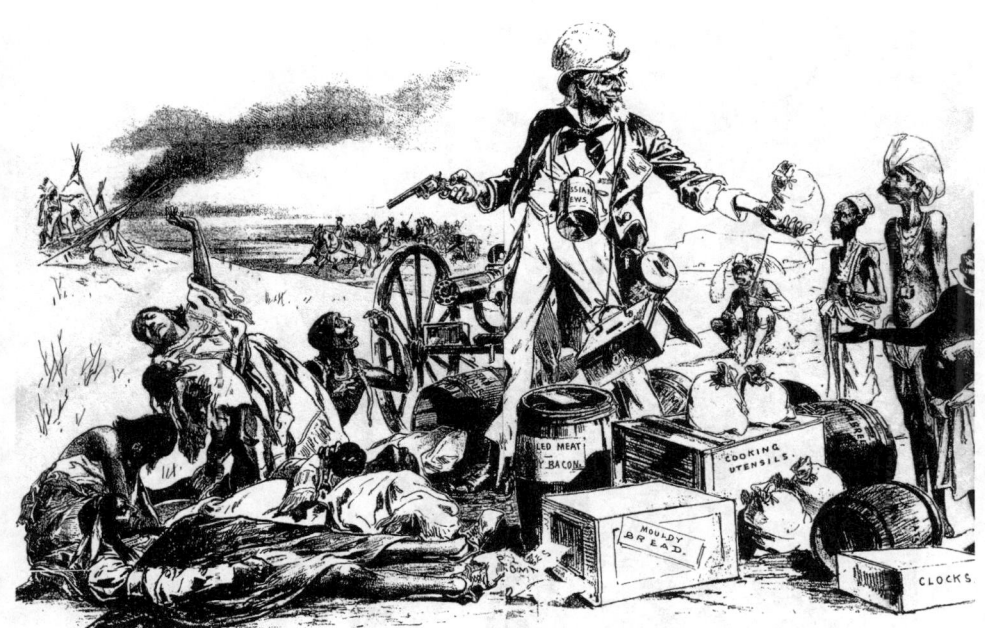

31. Joseph Keppler, *Consistency*, from *Puck*, January 21, 1891, 372.

For images that did not encourage mythic belief in the all-devour-
ing Jewish merchant, one has to look in the Jewish press to find out
how most Jews earned a living, many just barely. Sam Zagat, in a
series titled *East Side Professions*, noted in his caption that tinsmiths'
"short, short season lasts only 2–3 days when [they] solder and scour
pots and pans for Passover" (Zagat 1972, 33) (fig. 32). Their season
was short because for the eight days of that holiday many Jews used
alternate rather than everyday sets of dishes and kitchenware. In the
cartoon, we see the tinsmith on his knees scouring a pot as a man,
possibility its owner, looks on.

The second pernicious cartoon, a two-page spread published in
the July 29, 1891, issue of *Puck* (p. 368), shows a top-hatted, obese
man wearing what is probably a gold chain with two attached
watches and standing astride Broadway (fig. 33). He is surrounded by
memories of departures and evictions of Jews from various countries
dating back to ancient Egypt. The caption reads: "We Are the People.

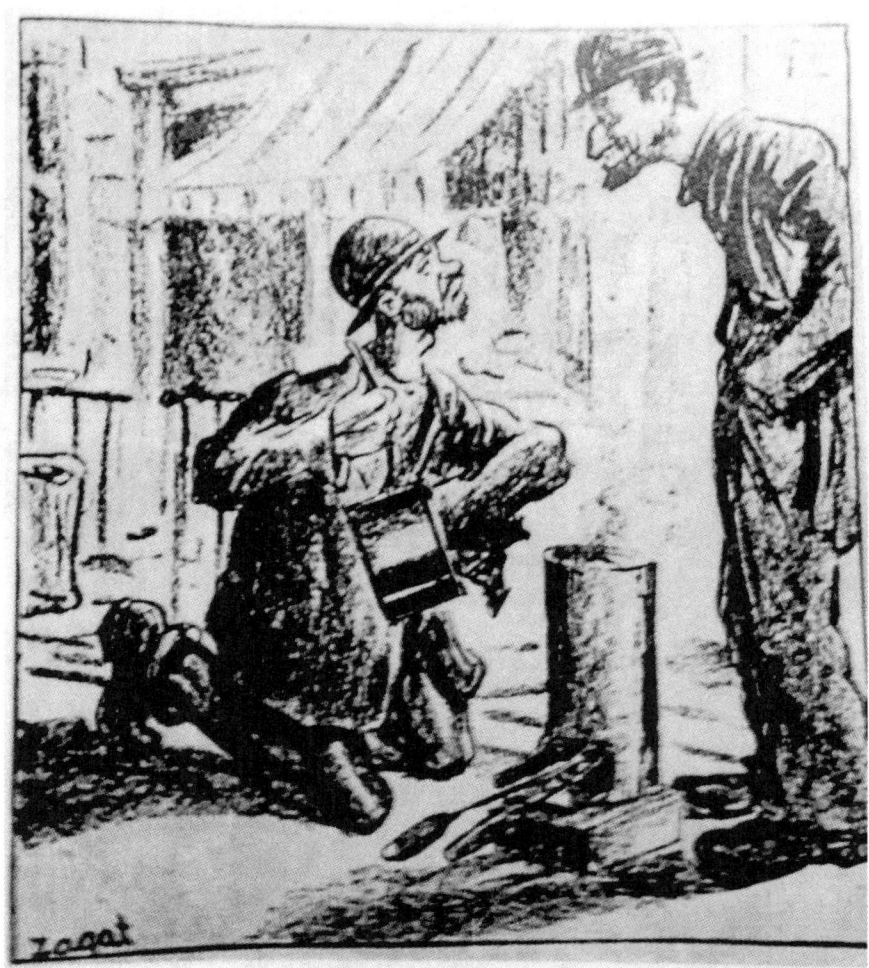

32. Samuel Zagat, *Tinsmith's Short Season,* 1920, from Ida Zagat, ed., *Drawings and Paintings: Jewish Life on New York's Lower East Side, 1912–1962* (New York: Rogers Book Service, 1972), 33.

The Downtrodden One.—They Have Always Persecuted Us, but We Get There All the Same!" One might read this cartoon as a celebration of Jewish strength and fortitude in face of continuous hatred and overwhelming odds, but the central figure, with his victory pose, ample girth, and face that suggests a sly and cunning swindler,

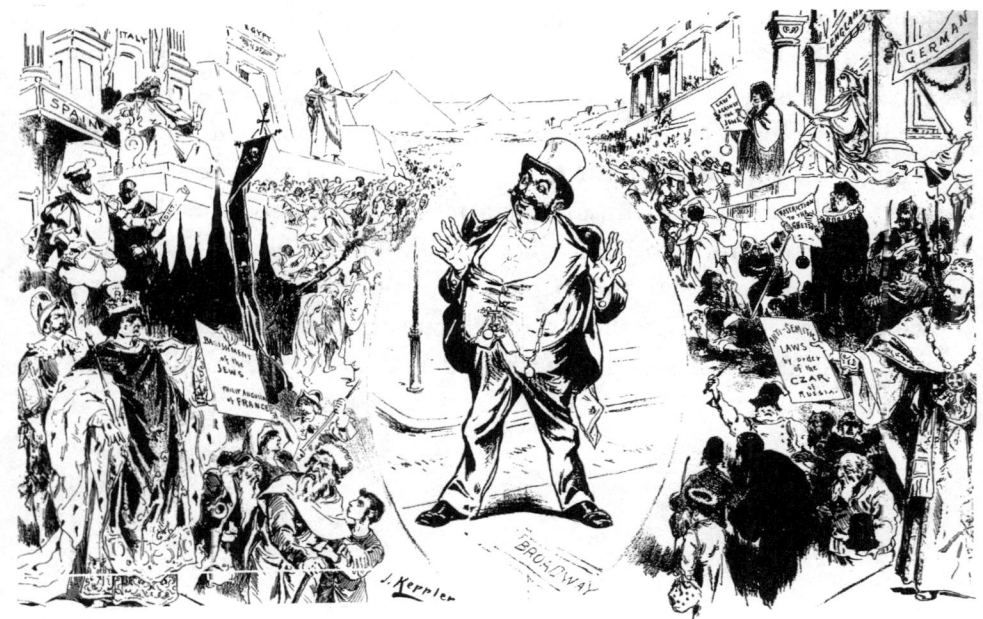

33. Joseph Keppler, *They Are the People*, from *Puck*, July 29, 1891, 368.

was *the* image of the Jew for many people of this era. Of the Jews depicted in cartoons, he is arguably the most loathsome-looking one of all. Who would want to socialize with him over a cup of coffee, let alone engage in a commercial transaction with him? Who would trust him? Both we and he can assume that he would not be welcome anywhere at any time—and, even worse, he seems not to care.

Was there any organized opposition to the publication of such images? In the early years of the twentieth century, Jewish organizations as well as Irish and African American groups regularly challenged the ugly, stereotypical presentations of minority figures in theatrical productions (Kibler 2015, 1–14, 117–24). For example, the Anti-Defamation League, founded in 1913 by B'nai B'rith, which had been formed in 1843 to ameliorate the conditions of Jews in America, complained that "whenever a producer wishes to depict a betrayer of public trust, a hard-boiled usurious money-lender, a crooked gambler, a grafter, a depraved fire-bug, a white slaver or other villains of one kind or another, the actor is directed to represent himself as a Jew" (qtd. in Roche 1963, 93). And so representations of repellant Jews on the stage lessened as a result of the league's efforts. But I could find no evidence of protests by individuals or organizations that advocated reduction of unpleasant cartoon images. As a consequence, magazines still published them, although fewer and fewer appeared over the years from 1900 to 1940. They persisted until the mid-1930s and then primarily through the encouragement of the Communist Party, which shamelessly used them through most of the interwar period in their political battles with Jewish leaders of non-Communist leftist groups (see chapter 4).

2 Explanations and Responses

IN HIS HISTORY of American graphic humor published in the early 1930s, William Murrell stated, "The cartoon in the modern sense is—with or without humor—a forceful presentation by means of exaggeration of a topical political or moral issue. It is intended for a wide audience and it makes use of popular symbols and slogans. The grotesque is often more in evidence than the comic because the political cartoon is designed to make something ridiculous, not merely laughable" (1933, 4).

The cartoons illustrated here raise political and moral issues, and their subjects are usually depicted as grotesque and ridiculous and are meant to be not merely laughable. But what of their creators, the cartoonists? Perhaps if we knew more about their mindsets, then we might be able to offer some explanations for their decades' long disparagement of Jews. Unfortunately, we do not, and in several instances we do not even know who they were. They quite often did not sign their work, or if they did, their names are unreadable. For the most part, they remain largely anonymous.

Only Vienna-born cartoonist Joseph Keppler (1818–94) has been the subject of a large-scale monograph (West 1968). His biographer avoided commentary about his attitudes toward minorities. We learn only that Keppler "was perhaps a bit more restrained than most of his cartoonist contemporaries" and that he had created "several notable cartoons that challenged his audience differently about race and ethnicity" (345), which is as diplomatically noncommittal as can be. Of the comments accompanying a virulently anti-Semitic cartoon by Keppler, *Consistency* (see fig. 31, p. 61), the text states only that Keppler was concerned about injustices done to Native Americans (36).

Of Keppler's fellow cartoonists, West states, "Information about Keppler's colleagues is scarce," as indicated by the inclusion of very short biographical summaries of their lives and works (1968, 438, 427–34). Keppler founded *Puck* as a German-language magazine in 1871. He worked for newspaper owner Frank Leslie in 1873 and then brought out *Puck* as an English-language magazine in 1876. It ceased publication in 1918. His cartoonist colleagues include Frederick Burr Opper (1857–1937), James Albert Wales (1852–86), Eugene Zimmerman (1862–1935), Edward Windsor Kemble (1861–1933), and Louis Dalrymple (1865–1905) (West 1968, 427–34; see also Dormon 1985, 490, "*Puck* Illustration Collection" n.d., and "*Judge* Magazine Illustration Collection" n.d.). But we know little of their temperaments, likes, dislikes, interests, or prejudices.

The historian Ernest Gellner suggests that people "have always been endowed with culture: a shared style of expression in words, facial expression, body language, style of clothing, preparation and consumption of food, and so forth. Culture is not identical among all [people]" (1997, 1, 3). A simple enough statement—culture is the basic social bond—but to try to explain why cartoonists tagged Jewish people with such a negative culture and as a people so preoccupied with financial matters and with criminal intentions in all business enterprises and why their cartoons remained popular for so many years, we would have to speculate almost endlessly. The effort would extend from religious and psychological hypotheses to first-person accounts of deep-seated prejudices and preferences. And within that range, one can invoke racist, nationalistic, economic, antimodern, and in-group versus out-group factors.

And to say that individual cartoons—or all of them collectively—can be examined on more than one level is to say that they are important artifacts that can contribute to discussions within American cultural history concerning the effects of immigration, especially from southern and eastern Europe; maintenance of nineteenth-century Anglo-Saxon cultural hegemony; religious and racial tolerance and intolerance; the replacement of a national agrarian culture by urban centers; and certainly the disparate elements that make up American visual culture. I touch on some of these subjects in this chapter, but each obviously requires more study than I can provide here.

One explanation that combines abstract speculation with religious and psychological factors is based on two observations Sigmund Freud made in *Moses and Monotheism* (1967, 116–17). In the first, he discussed the idea of the ur-jealousy between the younger brother religion, Christianity, and the older one, Judaism, as a variant of an Oedipal relationship, and in the second he noted the difficulties Christians had in living up to the ethical proscriptions found in the Hebrew Bible.

Although Freud's second observation was not published (in the original German) until 1939, the difficulties of living up to and honoring Jewish ethics and moral codes had been discussed in at least two articles in American magazines as early as 1887. The theses considered in these provocative articles were considered again in publications in the 1930s and 1940s.

In one of these articles, part of an ongoing series in the *North American Review* by individuals who maintained ties to their particular religious heritage, Pereira Mendes (1887) did not review and rebut attitudes of the moment toward Jews but instead ranged over the history of Judaism and its interactions with other religions and religious groups. Certainly a well-read and deeply knowledgeable person, Mendes included 108 footnotes in his article, which he titled "Why Am I a Jew?" His reasons for remaining a Jew were devoted to explaining why it was essential that humankind recognize the moral and ethical precepts of the Hebrew Bible, including treatment of women, patriotism, avoidance of trickery and abuse of the public trust, and the promotion of peace (601). He thought it ironic that he had been treated so poorly by Christians "when my only sin was that I was a more truthful follower of the teachings of him they adored [Jesus] and a worthier exponent of his views of peace and good will than they were themselves!" (601). He ended his essay by stating that the Jew is necessary to the world in order to achieve

"Universal Peace," "Universal Brotherhood," and "Universal Happiness" (607–8).

In similar fashion, the anonymous author of an article published in *Harper's* in 1893, "The Mission of the Jews," assigned Jews the role of bearers of spirituality as opposed to Greek sensuousness and related aspects of Christianity. The author stated: "It is this which may lie at the bottom of a certain antagonism which exists between the pronounced types of the Jews of Europe and the pronounced representatives of the Northern peoples, especially the Saxon race. . . . The Jew . . . stands as the representative of intellectual and emotional sensibility." The opposite of Jewishness, which the author termed "Germanism," "represents the more physical aspect of the soul, namely character" (264).

In a moment of parity between Jewishness and Germanism, the author described how intellectual and spiritual qualities without basis in character development could lead to "subtlety and trickiness and even cowardliness" and contrasted these qualities to that of sheer physicality, which, lacking in intellect and emotion, could produce "stubbornness and brutality." The author praised Jews for their presumed high level of morality but did caution them to retain a sense of balance in their approach to life. Otherwise, they as a people might come to grief ("Mission of the Jews" 1893, 264, 265). The proper behavior for Jews, then, was to be one of balance, a balance that blended their intellectual and spiritual attainments with physical activity. Probably with good intentions, the author thought of Jews as a people apart from the rest of the world who needed some help in becoming and remaining what he considered to be normal beings.

This author, clearly sympathetic but not quite seeing Jews as the equals of Christians, also provided an excuse for their interest in finance by acknowledging the humiliations and limitations forced upon them over the centuries. "Jews are in no way to be held accountable" ("Mission of the Jews" 1893, 265). And then in an astonishing statement that challenged assumptions of American nationalism, the author argued that Jews living in Diaspora would be the ideal facilitators for the increasingly interrelated, international economic system (the word *global* would be an anachronism in the context of 1893). In this respect, "the Jews are nearest to realizing the future ideal of man" (266), implying that the future lay in the hands of Jewish cosmopolitanism and internationalism, qualities for which Jews were usually condemned. The author, probably basing his analysis on the ethical values he found in the Hebrew Bible, decided that "it is the vocation of the Jews to facilitate international humanitarianism" (265), but without asking if that idea was acceptable to them. The idea is an interesting one, but in assigning Jews their place in the universe, it is an example of rank colonialism.

It is impossible to say if cartoonists and their readers agreed with this assignment, but one can imagine varying degrees of hostility to the idea that Jews represented higher moral ideals and were or should be leaders in a modern antinationalist, international movement at a time when hundreds of thousands were immigrating to America to the dismay of American nationalists, who felt that these immigrants would compromise the nation's heritage. One can see the headline: "Jews: Shock Troops of Advancing Internationalism!"

Notions of Jewish morality as a cause of anti-Semitism was considered again in the 1940s, especially by Maurice Samuel in his book *The Great Hatred*, originally published in 1940, several years after Hitler's Germany had denied Jews civil rights as German citizens. Samuel developed the thesis that the root cause of anti-Semitism was the ethical contents of the Hebrew Bible and the Jewish people it represented (see also Sarolea 1936; Sacher 1940; M. Steinberg 1945). Samuel's thesis was that Christians actually feared Christ—who as a Jew offered a message of loving others, helping others, respecting each person's individuality, and maintaining a personal sense of ethics—because his standards of conduct were simply too high. Therefore, Jews were hated for being both Christ killers and Christ givers (Samuel [1940] 1988, 127). In effect, Christians transferred their negative feelings about the ethical precepts of their own religion, which were based on the Hebrew Bible, to Jews (139). As a consequence, Jews were incapable of halting anti-Semitism because it was ultimately a Christian problem. Jews were, in effect, innocent bystanders and victims (173–74). As one observer succinctly put it in article published at the same time, "[Because] the Jews brought ethics, the whole concept of sin, into the Western World . . . , anti-Semitism is the European's revenge on the Prophets; it is his protest against the morality of the Bible" (Sacher 1940, 245).

Kenneth L. Marcus has noted more recently that "the excluded Jew is a distorted mirror image of the Gentile's self-conception" (2015, 82, Kindle ed.). In other words, the in-group accuses the out-group of the in-group's negative characteristics, intentions, or actions. "The in-group, despising these internal traits[,] . . . projects the disowned characteristics upon those positioned as outsiders. Thus, the Jewish political outsider is imagined as demon-beast" (82).

In the period discussed here, Jews, then, were assigned the role of surrogates for what Christians rejected in their own failed ideals and behavior. Rudolf Glanz proposes a similar kind of surrogacy, arguing that because Americans could not quite face the fact of their own intense and increasing concern for money in the newly urbanized, industrial, financially driven modern post–Civil War world, they blamed the Jews, who then became the symbol of rampant and uncontrollable American and world capitalism (1973, 13–28; see, e.g., fig. 31, p. 61).

Glanz's argument is based in part on the fact that biblical images or those derived from ancient or modern Jewish history rarely appeared in cartoons. In the few that did have such references, religious values of any sort were omitted.

For example, in the March 1, 1918, issue of *Puck* (p. 18), the caption reads: "King Solomon's Wives Find a Strange Blonde Hair on His Dinner Jacket" (fig. 34). What we learn from the cartoon is that Solomon had many, many wives and that the chief wife could not account for the strange blond hair. In two cartoons about Jonah, a submarine replaces the whale that in the biblical story swallows Jonah. In the issue of *Life* for June 6, 1907 (p. 749), a cartoon titled *The First Submarine Excursion* shows Jonah in a cutaway section of the whale's belly, steering the whale in a dive. The other cartoon, published in the February 19, 1916, issue of *Puck* (p. 9), is titled *If*

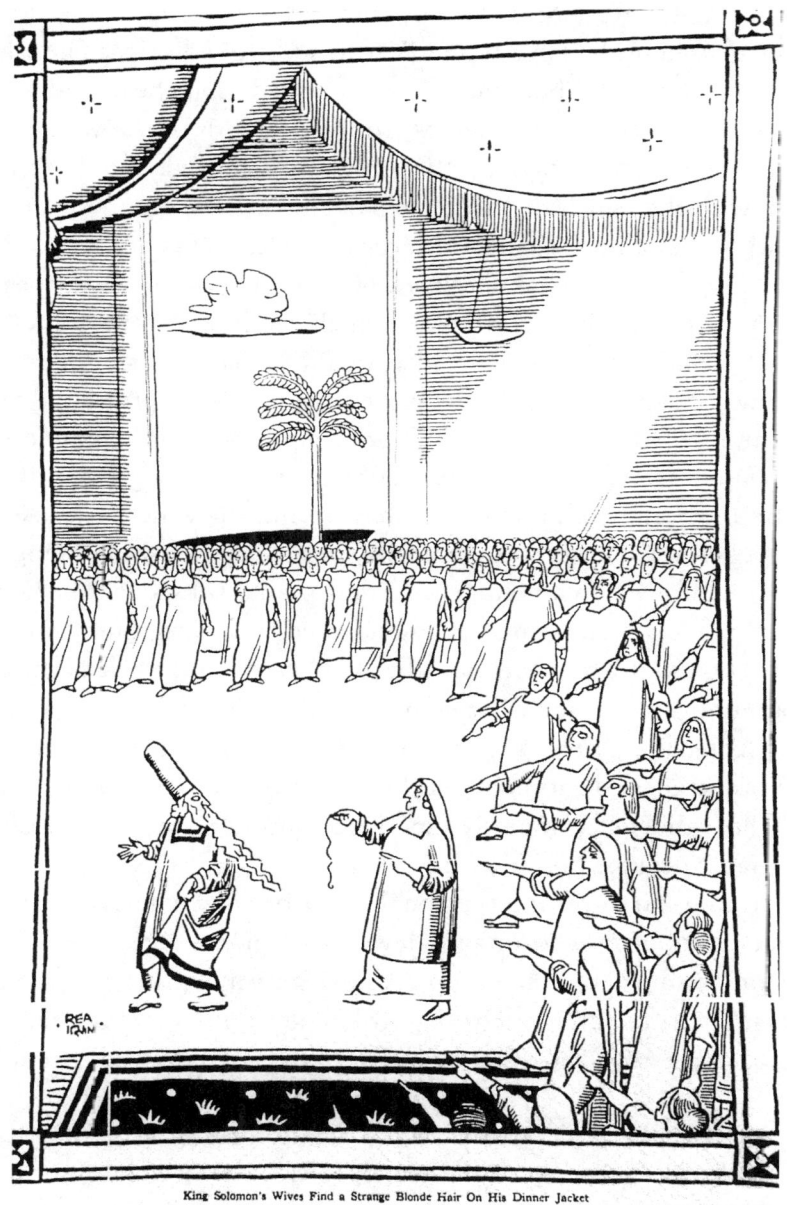

King Solomon's Wives Find a Strange Blonde Hair On His Dinner Jacket

34. Rea Irvin, *King Solomon's Wives*, from *Puck*, March 1, 1913, 18.

the Jonah Act Were Stated Now. It includes a reference to German U-boats used in the First World War to sink Allied ships. The whale has "U 2" (as in "U-boat number 2") marked on its head and is half out of the water. Jonah emerges from the mouth of the whale, and the caption has him saying, "If I only had a torpedo, couldn't I get hunk with the bunch that threw me overboard!"

Maurice Samuel, Kenneth Marcus, and Rudolf Glanz, each in his own way, describes characteristics of scapegoating or the scapegoat theory of prejudice, according to which the in-group projects onto an out-group, Jews in this instance, qualities that it abhors in its own behavior. Scapegoating is a form of self-protective, projective identification by which the individual or group chooses to remain essentially unaware of its actions by blaming the out-group for attitudes found unacceptable in its own behavior and for which it refuses to accept responsibility. But, ironically, by unconsciously blaming the out-group for its own inadmissible desires and subsequent behavior, the in-group is tied intimately to and needs the out-group for better or worse, usually for the worse. In plain street talk, it needs the out-group to disparage for what it chooses to ignore and to maintain its own sense of well-being. Art historian Ziva Amishai-Maisels notes as a broad generalization in her discussion of the Other in the visual arts that insiders feel morally superior to outsiders, the latter position invariably occupied by Jews (1999, 44).

From a narrower interpersonal point of view, what can be said about cartoonists who imaged Jews as despicable creatures? Some general comments about scorn and disparagement are in order. In *Leviathan*, first published in 1651, Thomas Hobbes laid out the general parameters of the discussion that have been followed ever since.

Sudden glory is the passion which makes those *grimaces* called LAUGHTER, and is caused either by some sudden act of their own that pleases them or by the apprehension of some deformed thing in another, by comparison whereof they suddenly applaud themselves. And it is incident most to them that are conscious of the fewest abilities in themselves, who are forced to keep themselves in their own favor by observing the imperfections of other men. And therefore much laughter at the defects of others is a sign of pusillanimity. For of great minds, one of the proper works is to help and free others from scorn and compare themselves only with the most able. ([1651] 1958, 57)

Beyond that assessment, both Freud and Henri Bergson offered insights into the minds of those "insiders" who consider themselves culturally superior, if not necessarily morally or intellectually superior, to "outsiders."

In *Wit and Its Relation to the Unconscious* (1938), Freud's insights into the personality of "insiders" might provide us with some comprehension, if not appreciation, of the character of the cartoonists and their editors. In the context of caricaturing Jews (and other immigrants), the person possessing a sense of wit, which is subjective, can create a situation that allows the observer of the cartoon to be the "Superior Subject," never the "Object" and never the "Voluntary Object" (633). The "Superior Subject" can observe the "Object" in a situation where the latter is comical because of social factors rather than personal qualities. The "Object" is defenseless in a comical situation established by the "Superior Subject" (776). A cartoonist, then, can set up a recognizable social situation in which the Object will look foolish, and because in the cartoon the Object engages in the stereotypical activities of his particular group, he or she will also reflect the generalized characteristics assigned to that group.

Freud also indicated that people tend to lose inhibitions about violence and verbal invective when dealing with foreigners and with those who are not clansmen or members of their nation. So the caricaturist enlists the "Observer," the third person—the viewer of the cartoon in our context—against the Object or enemy. "By belittling and humbling our enemy, by scorning and ridiculing him, we directly obtain the pleasure of his defeat by the laughter of the third person, the inactive spectator. . . . Wit allows us to surmount restrictions" and opens up otherwise inaccessible sources of pleasure to the inactive spectator (1938, 697–98). With the cartoons I describe in this book, therefore, pleasure came from both looking at the caricatured figures' exaggerated features and reading the captions written invariably in dialect or with mispronounced English words.

Freud could not fully explain the motivations of caricaturists, but he suggested that such individuals might possess a neurotic personality or a dissociated personality component that allows for "brutal mockery" of others (1938, 730). He was certain, however, that caricature provides a way to express indirect criticism or aggression rather than direct physical force. Regarding the distortion of a person's features, Freud held that degradation occurs "by rendering prominent one feature. . . . Only by isolating this feature can the comic effect be obtained which spreads in our memory over the whole picture" (777). Because the turn-of-the-century cartoonists typecast Jews as having big noses, fat lips, and enormous bellies, African Americans as possessing huge eyes and big lips, and the Irish as displaying simianlike faces, clearly more than one facial feature was and could be caricatured and comic effect achieved, but Freud's point is well taken.

Freud held that such comic effects pervaded one's memories of how figures are presented. As a result, seeing the same exaggerated features of minority figures in issue after issue of the humor magazines from 1877 to 1935 might have prompted viewers to forget the human qualities of individuals in minority groups and instead to remember only stereotypical features associated with these groups. Such individuals no longer possessed any sense of innate dignity, let alone personhood; they could have no bruised feelings or the ability to react in normal ways; and they no longer looked like normal human beings. They had truly become Objects.

Freud also held that "the effect of the caricature is not essentially impaired through [the] falsifying of reality" (1938, 777). In this sense, falsifying reality only magnified the Objects' stereotypical facial features and patterns of behavior. Seeing these stereotypes over and over again in cartoon form, year after year, decade after decade, ad nauseam, the viewer probably began to believe that the stereotyped images were what Jews and other minorities looked like and how they always acted, that the stereotyped patterns were the norm and therefore quite believable.

And, finally, Freud suggested that parody and travesty degrade through the use of lowly utterances (1938, 777). In the captions, the "lowly utterances," many of a truly perverse nature, were written in the voices of the Objects—Jews and others who mangle the English language as they brag about stealing, taking advantage of innocent white folk and other such activities, or just acting stupid. These captions were evidently within the bounds of decency back then but are totally unacceptable today, as suggested by the recent apology issued by the *Indianapolis Star* discussed in chapter 4.

In short, Freud profiled a typical caricaturist by describing a person with psychological issues based on fear of foreigners and the need to express superiority over them, a person who channeled his aggressive feelings by distorting bodily features and language as well as by assigning perverse intentions to those he chose to denigrate and belittle. Passive viewers who enjoyed looking at the images and reading the captions were apparently only too happy to be entertained by the cartoonists, who played to their own fears and prejudices about the immigrant Other or Object.

In *Laughter* (1956), a long and rambling collection of three essays, Henry Bergson echoed Freud's thoughts and added some further notions of his own. He suggested that the comic element in caricature can include a "favorite distortion toward which nature seems particularly inclined" but that "for exaggeration to be comic, it must not appear as an aim, but rather as a means" (77). What Bergson seemed to be implying here is that the observer already knows what the aim is, that he is in cahoots with the caricaturist and only has to be entertained by the means of delivery. As an example, Bergson noted, the caricaturist who alters the size of a nose by lengthening it is really making the nose indulge in a grin. Henceforth, the viewer will inevitably look upon the original as having determined to lengthen itself and then start grinning. The face we laugh at is, so to speak, its own caricature (78). An important by-product is that the resulting laughter is intended, as Bergson noted, "to intimidate by humiliating" (88).

Bergson went on to say that viewers laugh at somebody embarrassed by his own body (1956, 3), but this observation is not quite fair to those whose bodies are caricatured and who might not actually be embarrassed at all by their bodies. But in the context of the cartoons discussed in this book, it seems that the cartoonists wanted the individuals of certain groups to be embarrassed by their bodies. This sounds all the more ominous when juxtaposed to a question Bergson raised: "What bond of secret relationship can there be between the physical defect and the moral infirmity?" (96). In the same way, one can ask the cartoonists, Did you intend to make a connection between physical defect and moral infirmity? Do you arbitrarily alter a normal shape so that it will suggest a moral defect? Do you believe that a person with a physical defect can exist without a moral infirmity? Does a large nose or bowed legs imply moral defects?

Bergson described a situation that applies directly to our cartoonists when he suggested that comedy begins with a growing callousness to social life (1956, 147). Particularly in the context of one type of cartoon—in which Jews are shown trying to gain admission to summer resorts that reject them—an individual is comic by automatically going his or her own way without understanding that which troubles his fellow beings. The cartoonists in this instance seemingly responded to the wishes of resort proprietors and their Christian guests by portraying such scenes. As Bergson pointed out, cartoonists and their viewers "always find an unavowed intention to humiliate, and consequently to correct our neighbor, if not in his will, at least in his deed" (1956, 148). In this regard, the cartoonists not only revealed what should embarrass Jews but also suggested not so subtly that they should vacation among their own kind.

The cultural historian Wylie Sypher, who wrote an appendix, "The Meaning of Comedy," for the book in which Bergson's essays appeared, added three trenchant comments that serve to emphasize Freud's and Bergson's views:

[First,] [m]alice . . . is the only one of many obscure motives for laughing, which has been explained as a release from restraint, a response to what is incongruous or improper, or a sign of ambivalence—our hysteric [*sic*] effort to adjust our repulsion from, and our attraction to, a situation. . . .

[Second,] [o]ne of the strongest impulses comedy can discharge from the depths of the social self is our hatred of the "alien," especially when the stranger who is "different" stirs any unconscious doubt about our own beliefs. . . . In this role, the comic artist is a "conservative" or even a "reactionary" who protects our self-esteem. . . . To this extent the comic response is tribal. . . .

[Third,] [a]ny majority secretes venom against those who trouble it, then works off this venom in mocking some figure like Shylock the Jew, the Usurer, hated by right-thinking Christians precisely because he lives in the free and open market on a premise of ruthless competition. Shylock is the naked image of renaissance "initiative," whose thrift is called greed only because he is Hebrew. (Sypher 1956, 202, 242–43)

In an article discussing Jewish self-hatred, written in the midst of the Second World War, Kurt Lewin looked at the issue from a different point of view. He held that members of the majority group think of minorities as homogeneous groups. "This stereotype is created in the growing child by the asocial atmosphere in which he grows up, and that degree of prejudice is practically independent of the amount and kind of actual experience which the individual has had with members of the minority group" (1941, 226). A similar analysis appeared three decades later when folklore historian Alan Dundes stated that American stereotypes come not from personal knowledge or acquaintance with members of minority groups but "from proverbs, songs, jokes, and other forms of folklore we have heard all our lives" (1971, 187, qtd. in S. Cohen 1985, 209). And more ominously, a basic premise of historian David Nirenberg's book *Anti-Judaism: The Western Tradition* (2013) is that Christians' ideas about Judaism, their insistent belief in Jews' material, commercial, and financial interests as well as in Jews' culpability for the world's ills, might have a greater impact on the conditions of life for real Jews than anything those Jews might actually do or have done (see especially 423–60).

Nirenberg's observation points out something very basic regarding the cartoons at issue here and reinforces Lewin's suggestion—namely, that there was (and still is), whether purposeful or not, confusion between imagined Jews and real Jews. Following this line of reasoning, cartoonists with little or no contact with Jews or other minorities came to their cartooning with stereotypes already in mind. A case in point. Although not a cartoonist, the liberal columnist Randolph Bourne (1889–1918) famously argued for a "transnational America." He would never be accused of fomenting anti-Semitic thought, but he did use a barefaced anti-Semitic trope to argue a point he wanted to make in an article written in 1916: "It is not the Jew who sticks proudly to the faith of his fathers and boasts of that venerable culture of his who is dangerous to America, but the Jew who has lost the Jewish fire and become a mere elementary grasping animal" ([1916] 1992, 254). Of course, the question that needs to be asked, which Bourne does not ask or answer, is, Did immigrants who were not Jewish and who lost the faith of their fathers also become "elementary grasping animal[s]," or was this a singularly Jewish trait?

One can agree or disagree with author Herbert Gold's not quite tongue-in-cheek, over-the-shoulder notion that anti-Semites often claim they are not Jew baiters but rather that they despise villainy and aim only to point to the danger that Jews manifest. Gold suggests that this claim is meant to objectify the menace of the devil that lives in Jews. Perhaps the anti-Semite, he says, "is not a Jew baiter at all, but merely needs to destroy the Jew-host in order to kill the devil-tenant" (1972, xvii).

Even though Benedict Anderson does not have cartoonists in mind, his observations about nationalism can be useful here. In his book *Imagined Communities* ([1983] 1991), his premise is that nationalism helps create an imagined community. Nationalism is not necessarily aligned with political ideology "but with the large cultural system that preceded it [and] out of which . . . it came into being" (12). This system would presumably include long-held prejudices. With regard to cartoonists, the denigration of minorities allowed white native-born or long-assimilated cartoonists and their viewers to think of themselves as sharing "remembered" experiences and therefore of belonging to an imagined community, wherever they might live in America. This view bolstered the sense of their American-ness and their difference from and superiority to recent immigrants (Anderson [1983] 1991, 22, 35).

Observations published in an article by sociologist Talcott Parsons in 1942 are pertinent here as well. Parsons understood anti-Semitism as "a manifestation of social disorganization" (114). Those so affected—and they included rich and poor, educated and uneducated—considered themselves victimized by the changes taking place in society. As a result, they grew increasingly insecure, developed a sense of injustice imposed upon them, were frustrated, and therefore developed aggressive tendencies. These tendencies, often based on overreactions to various conditions and circumstances—economic, social, cultural, nationalistic—led to attacks on certain symbols found in society. "From this point of view," Parsons stated, "anti-Semitism [was] undoubtedly an expression of this situation. . . . Psychologically, speaking, the Jew may, therefore, be considered as an appropriate symbolic object for aggressive sentiments, if not for any other reason than that they constituted an out-group as far as Gentile society [was] concerned" (114). He then concluded that "the most important source of virulent anti-Semitism is probably the projection on the Jew, as a symbol, of free-floating aggression, springing from insecurities and social disorganization" (121). And, we might add, as noted earlier, it is a Christian projection of failing to live up to ethical behavior norms found in the Hebrew Bible, of thinking of Jews as living symbols of aggressive capitalism, and of failing to acknowledge one's own complicity in promoting such economic activity.

In the end, it is the pictorial image that counts. And here art historian Ernst Gombrich's observations about caricatures are relevant. He has noted that "we respond to a face as a whole. . . . What is given us is the global impression and our reaction to it" (2000, 333–34).

And what might that reaction be? Caricature "offers a visual inter-pretation of a physiognomy which we can never forget and which the victim will always seem to carry around with him" (344). As applied to images of Jews in cartoons, this caricaturization might very well lead viewers who see monstrous noses, thick lips, fat bellies, and bowed legs and who then read the captions to respond in ways that reinforce their prejudices. In fact, in 1942 sociologist Carleton Coon described the entire Jewish face, not just the nose, as popularly "the combination of a relatively wide head and narrow face, with a slant-ing axis to the ears; a narrow lower jaw; a narrow interocular dis-tance; and a considerable nose length, with convexity of profile and a tip depression" (33).

The language of cartoon captions also seems to be a marker of "free-floating aggression," as Parsons put it, because virtually all were written in accented, imperfect English, implying that correct use and pronunciation of the language was the property of main-stream Americans. Or, to say it another way, people who spoke with accents were—pick any or all—the Other, not welcome as equals, not welcome at all, not well bred, permanently inferior persons. As Anderson reminds his readers, language is the personal property of specific groups ([1983] 1991, 84). So captions given in accented Eng-lish reminded the Others that they were truly Other and could be kept at a distance through language.

Perhaps there might also be some value in the thoughts of those few authors who in the late nineteenth century attempted to describe the American sense of humor. However, they were obviously edu-cated persons whose language was guarded, representative of their social class, and perhaps disinclined to enjoy fully the comic aspects others found in the cartoons. In 1875, Samuel S. Cox, for example, found that in absorbing other nations' characteristics through immi-gration, American society was "the most incongruous, grotesque, angular, outré, and peculiar ever yet known in history" (1875, 697). Without mentioning immigrants, Cox found that people laughed at the "oddities, whims, and the angularities of the other man, his out-of-the-way talk and conduct, and made these human ficklenesses the source of jocularity" (691). He did not always find this sense of humor a desirable quality insofar as "the worst men often use it." For him, "wit cuts," but "humor tickles" (691), a distinction blurred by a huge gray area of imprecision.

One social observer, Edmund Kirke, believed that "Americans are the most humorous of people" (1889, 43), and another, Hjalmar Boyesen, found jocularity to be "the most pervasive trait in the American national character" because Americans tended to take "a facetious view of life and extract the greatest possible amount of amusement out of every situation" (1895, 529). Boyesen went on to say that "all things . . . are with us legitimate subjects for jokes" because America's "all-leveling democracy has tended to destroy the sense of reserve which hedges certain subjects with sanctity, guarding them against the shafts of wit" (529). But he also pointed out that some French friends found American humor to be "grotesque rather than funny" and that another European friend found that reaching for the jocular "is essentially juvenile and barbaric" (533). Finally, Boyesen determined that humor blotted out tolerance of the views of others, tolerance being an essential condition for conversation (535).

In an article published in 1894, Oscar Fay Adams analyzed more deeply the nature of American humor. He divided humor into two categories—literary humor and day-to-day humor, the latter being the humor of the "comic papers, of the funny columns of papers that are not professedly comic, and of comic books that make no pretense to be considered as literature" (961). Adams immediately pointed out that refined persons would see no humor in tragic events or disasters. "Not one of them would delight in holding up to general ridicule the possibly Jewish profile of one neighbor or the large mouth and irregular teeth of another" (691). But such refined persons, he felt, are not competent to judge day-to-day humor based on vulgar conceptions of family life, shaky morals, and police-court news. Nevertheless, he said, his prejudices peeking out, "the persistent regularity [of] the ever-delightsome jest that has, in more or less offensive fashion, the Hebrew for its theme" remains popular (691). In effect, then, one might be a refined person but not be opposed to "ever-delightsome" anti-Semitic jests. Sniff, sniff.

Adams invented an imaginary English person as a foil for testing American humor. Said English person found that American humor "is for the most part the levity, the flippant bad taste, of a people for whom nothing in heaven or on earth is sacred" (1894, 692). Adams then admitted that American humor "substitutes flippancy and smartness for wit; that esteems nothing too high for its theme, as it considers nothing too low; that jests at scars, and runs riot among all the obligations of life" (692). Making no judgments about appropriateness or parameters, he ended his exploration of American humor with a question: Is such humor "our glory or our shame"? (692). However one answers that question, such humor did appeal to many Americans. In 1901, for example, *Judge's Library* had 114,000 subscribers, and the other humor magazines, as mentioned in chapter 1, had equally large numbers of subscribers in addition to an untold number of newsstand purchases (Dormon 1985, 490).

In the mid–twentieth century, at least one observer also tried to explain American humor. He found in it "a touch of brutality, perhaps[.] Anger rather than humor" (Morley 1933, ix). And he described its overall character as "sardonic, extravagant, macabre" and suggested that it pointed "to some essential hardness and sharpness of spirit" (ix). He found a sense of bitterness in American humor as well, so that, as he stated, "a history of Humor could be called a History of Ill Humor." He also found that the American spirit inhabited "a morose, unhappy people" (x), so I guess it was OK to take out that ill humor on the Jews and other minorities.

Although, as one observer has noted, "there is no acceptable way to document the motivation for cartoonists" (Dormon 1985, 494), a few contemporary (late-twentieth- and early-twenty-first-century) cartoonists have offered some clues to their mindsets. For example, Mike Peters, a cartoonist for the *Dayton Daily News*, has called cartooning "not a fair art. You can never treat anyone justly . . . [and] most cartoonists like me—who like to attack—are like loaded guns." Jules Feiffer has stated that, "outside of basic intelligence, there is nothing more important to a good political cartoonist than ill will." And *Chicago Tribune* artist Jeff MacNelly has said, "Many cartoonists would be hired assassins if they couldn't draw." Others have called cartooning an "offensive" and "destructive art." The idea is to "circle and stab, circle and stab" (all qtd. in Fischer 1996, 16, 17).

Several other observations are relevant to the late-nineteenth-century cartoonists' state of mind. First, hostile cartoons were created and revolved around "continuing domination of the culture and society by its existing hegemonic structure. . . . They argued for WASP America at a time that WASP America seemed most threatened by its ethnic blight" (Dormon 1985, 496). Second, "a source does not emit humorous statements unless he expects to achieve some interpersonal purpose by doing so" (S. Cohen 1985, 204). And third, "humor is a tool, sometimes a weapon. Quite possibly, that is as precise a definition as one can give of racial and ethnic humor" (S. Cohen 1985, 203; see also Boshim and Dorinson 1987 and Fischer 1996, 70–72).

The few contemporaneous responses by Jews to the visual and verbal attacks mentioned in the previous chapter were in general relatively mild and usually written in an apologetic, self-critical, and a bend-over-backwards-to-seem-objective stance. Uncertain of their status in America, Jewish respondents assumed the subservient tone commonly associated with Jews in Europe rather than a more confrontational American tone. As a result, their responses were probably ignored, or they left themselves open to all sorts of negative comments that played right into the cartoonists' hands. All in all, harsh criticisms in both articles and cartoons were answered with mild excuses and occasionally with praiseworthy statements about Jews.

A few examples. W. M. Rosenblatt realized that all Jews were judged as if they came from the Lower East Side and were immediately identifiable by their European-style clothing. So he concluded that the most backward and worst members of the community, those just off the boat who came from the most traditional and religious towns and villages, were considered to be representative of all Jews (1872, 47). Rosenblatt then apologized for the manner of Orthodox religious services, which, he admitted, are noisy and "exaggerated like the devotion of barbarous people, which substitutes physical demonstrations for the repose which they cannot comprehend, and which renders hideous and senseless the most beautiful and significant ceremonies" (49).

This passage very much sounds as if it comes from a German Jew who preferred a Protestant-like service and who probably disdained eastern European Jews, who would compromise his standing in society. (To this day, among ultra-Orthodox men piety and religious feeling are expressed through swaying and other bodily movements as well as by randomly and spontaneously speaking and audibly singing certain passages in the prayer books, their movements and sounds invigorating to them. Such movement and spontaneity are not anarchy or barbarism but expressions of spiritual exaltation and piety.)

Rosenblatt also noted that Polish Jews were knaves and swindlers. Finally, he got around to mentioning some redeeming features, stating that Jews were not dangerous, that they usually made good soldiers, and that they helped each other in moments of crisis, a characteristic that especially frightened Christians because it suggested clannishness and group loyalty rather than loyalty to the country (1872, 49). But then reassuming an apologetic tone, Rosenblatt ended his article by saying that Russian Jews in comparison to Polish Jews, although bigoted and ignorant, were learning to love America, and they were humanitarians and liberal in politics (48, 58).

Nina Morais also took a middle-of-the-road position rather than mount a stout attack against the cartoons or a defense of Jews. She acknowledged that aversion to foreigners was instinctive but could not understand why Jews were "excluded from human brotherhood" (1881, 265). She then proceeded to list why Jews were disliked. They were too shrewd, immoral in business, and noisy; they had poor command of English and talked only about money; they remained clannish, were Christ killers, had no sense of the "higher feelings" or for "the proprieties and amenities of cultured life." They remained totally foreign (265). So "to dislike the Jew per se is natural" (272).

Morais also realized that Jews wanted to be accepted or rejected as individuals, and she therefore discovered "no virtue in the reasoning which finds Christianity unwilling to typify itself in its Veneerings, yet which sees a just illustration of Judaism in the columns of a comic paper" (1881, 275).

After listing and discussing negative features, Morais then offered that Jews were peaceful people who rarely complained, were rarely imprisoned or sent to an almshouse, and were temperate as well as moral. They supported other Jews and would fight for America (1881, 266). But then she undercut her praise by adding that Jews in general did not show a sense of culture commensurate with their wealth because it was acquired too quickly. In other words, their poor social etiquette disqualified them from socializing with Christians of equal income.

Alice Hyneman Rhine gave one of the best summaries of the feelings against Jews in her article "Race Prejudice at Summer Resorts" (1887). Her list includes the following: Jews were at present too numerous; they lacked social refinement, proper table manners, and good taste; they were social climbers and were too obtrusive; they denied Jesus's divinity and were responsible for the Crucifixion; they shunned Christians and ignored the Christian Sabbath; and they spent less money than Christians at resorts, among other defects of character.

But then Rhine mentioned the obvious. The issue was not just a lack of reverence for American values and customs; rather, it was "an inborn prejudice against the Jews [that] brings the brunt of criticism to bear against them. Their pronounced racial characteristics betray them wherever they go." The refusal to accept Jesus "is an ever-present ground of dislike to the Christian mind" (1887, 528, 529). She then praised the Jewish character as well as Jewish morality and virtue but assumed that even though Jews might become as refined as Christians, they will never assimilate Christian culture. The best she could hope for was that Christians would not remain prejudiced. (For further discussion, see also Higham 1984, 123–30.)

Rhine did not mention clannishness by name, but that characteristic, considered a defect, appeared in other accounts and was used as an excuse for avoiding and turning away Jews. Otherwise, it would have been understood or at least might have generated some sympathy that immigrants who were brutalized by Christians in the Old Country and who did not yet speak English well or speak it at all in the New Country would not choose out of sheer perversity to remain among their own kind.

In a rare balanced account of Russian Jews in *Frank Leslie's Illustrated Newspaper* for August 29, 1891, its author, Charles Gross (who might or might not have been Jewish), emphasized at least one reasonable counterargument. "It is . . . ridiculous to ask the Jew of the Muscovite realm to be like other men, when the law of the land forces him to be different from them[,] or to mingle with other men, when the law keeps him apart from them, isolates him, and treats him as an outcast of society" (50). Gross then described the various laws and customs that isolated Russian Jews by restricting places of residence and economic opportunities. (For another positive view, see Peters 1910, discussed in Slezkine 2004, 56. For another negative opinion, see "Russian Jews and Gentiles" 1882.)

Since the end of the Second World War, there have been two separate kinds of responses to American anti-Semitism that can affect the way one chooses to read the cartoons. One response is based on the work of consensus historians such as Oscar Handlin (1951a, 1951b), who held moderate views, and the other is a less-forgiving type characterized by the writings of Michael N. Dobkowski (1977, 1979). I side with Dobkowski.

John Appel and Selma Appel, major collectors of magazine and newspaper cartoons published from the 1870s to the 1910s, follow Handlin's point of view in their writings (Appel 1981; Appel and Appel 1984, 1986; see also Mayo 1988, 16–19, 83, 91). The Appels, to their credit, call attention to the paradoxical fact that *Puck* simultaneously published articles both in favor of and against acts of anti-Semitism in America and abroad. But, overall, these authors are too easy-going, too generous, and too tolerant toward the cartoonists and their editors, even though they do acknowledge the vicious stereotyping seen in many cartoons. For example, John Appel states,

> This democratic editorial outlook of *Puck* was joined to a caricature "language" that employed and deepened attitudes and symbols inimical to Jews. This split-personality of *Puck* accounts for the appearance of cartoons and editorials attacking noted anti-Semites at home and abroad [along] with others picturing politicians and public figures as Wandering Jews, Shylocks, and Fagins, without intentional malice toward Jews, but without considering the negative implications carried by these types figures [*sic*] about Jews generally. (1981, 113).

Granted, the printed record shows that occasional philo-Semitic articles and books were published, and we know that anti-Semitism in America has never risen to the levels of intensity that existed and still exist in Europe. Nevertheless, "negative implications," whether in texts or images, remain negative implications. Because so many derogatory images appeared in so many magazine issues over so many years, I cannot accept the Appels' (or anybody's) excuses concerning the *Puck* editors' intentions. Nor do I believe that the editors of other publications were innocent or naïve—if they were, they were in serious denial—especially not after reading several accounts of the evidently nonstop hostility to Jews in public and private spheres, in literary works, in theatrical productions, and in government immigration policies (see Dobkowski 1977; N. Cohen 1979; the entire issue of *American Jewish History* for September 1981, in which Appel 1981 is given; Sarna 1981; Feingold 1982; and Michael 2005).

I do not consider the cartoons light-hearted or funny or genial ways to let off steam by the mainstream public or by immigrants from countries such as Ireland and Poland who, plainly and simply, brought their hatred of Jews with them. (To be sure, cartoonists did not spare the Irish either.) Rather, the anti-Semitic cartoons strike me as persistent reminders of the Otherness of Jews, who were and often still are criticized simply because they were or are Jews, and as evidence that, given the ignorance of and lack of familiarity with individual Jews, Christians had and have lumped them together as a race or a nation or a religion without any regard for individual variation. Alice Hyneman Rhine's words in 1887 are still applicable today: "For centuries it has been impossible to say a man is a Jew without the intention to reproach him for being a Jew" (525). Such victimization cannot be justified by allowing it to become a moral position. Rather, it sets social, cultural, and psychological barriers around an individual and denies or certainly inhibits choice or power to that individual.

The paradox mentioned by the Appels according to which the magazine editors could simultaneously condone and condemn anti-Semitism or writers in the late nineteenth century could say that they respected the religion but disliked the people or even modern scholars can argue over degrees of anti-Semitic behavior indicates how tricky the issue of Jew hatred was and is and how difficult it was and is to parse religious, cultural, social, political, and economic factors when discussing attitudes toward Jews.

One might also question the assumptions, perhaps unexamined, of scholars who no doubt have the best of intentions. A case in point. Roger A. Fischer, whom I have quoted affirmatively and with whom I would certainly agree regarding his observation that the anti-immigrant cartoons were "raucously unapologetically elitist in [their] ethnicity," nevertheless has stated without comment that the cartoonists were "poking fun at the stereotypical shortcomings of ethnic immigrants and racial minorities" (1996, 70). Well, fun for whom? And are "stereotypical shortcomings" really shortcomings, which imply deficiencies, or do they only reflect elitist attitudes that have been assigned to minorities with no basis in fact other than to point out differences in manner and language? I would not call, for instance, somebody struggling to communicate in English, which for immigrants is a foreign language, a stereotypical shortcoming unless one wants to say that speaking imperfect English is a shortcoming. In my mind, making fun of such a person is a shortcoming.

The possibility of accepting stereotypical shortcomings as actual shortcomings can also lead to internalizing hostile feelings toward any group. For example, literary historian Donald Pizer has noted that turn-of-the-twentieth-century authors such as Willa Cather, Theodore Dreiser, Hamlin Garland, Jack London, Frank Norris, and Edith Wharton held what he calls "regressive" anti-Semitic attitudes at the same time that they supported feminist values, social improvements, aid to the poor, and opposition to corporate greed (2008, ix; see also Hindus 1947 on F. Scot Fitzgerald). Pizer allows that the authors thought of themselves as advanced thinkers, "yet they failed to perceive a relationship between their frame of mind [seeking social justice and personal freedom] and the average Jew seeking the same justice and freedom in the face of immense hurdles and handicaps" (66). As the historian Michael N. Dobkowski astutely and wryly notes, "Antisemitism [sic] erupted even in those sections of American society that were reformist and libertarian" (1976, 27).

Pizer, however, chooses not to explore these authors' inconsistent positions, whether they were based on a deeply rooted personal dislike of Jews or simply on a lack of awareness of the implications of their own word choices. He instead prefers to heed the words of Czeslaw Milosz (1911–2004), the Polish poet, who thought that those who emphasize the personal in examining the bases of anti-Semitism, "rarely get to the heart of the matter because they overlook those peculiar traits that belong to geography and history rather than to psychology" (1981, 84, qtd. in Pizer 2008, xi). In other words, anti-Semitism is best studied as a bland response to social and political movements of the time as well as to stereotypical shortcomings rather than to the personal interests and desires of anti-Semites or the concerns of the victims.

This point of view boils down simply to saying "stuff happens." To blame the place and the zeitgeist is to exonerate or excuse individuals. Language is thought, after all, and if you think anti-Semitism, you might make a remark or make a cartoon about it. Dobkowski summed up this point of view well in 1977 at a time when debates about degrees of anti-Semitism in late-nineteenth-century America bounced back and forth among scholars of the subject. He found a "pervasive negative image of the Jew propagated by the popular culture of the period [and transmitted] through flagrant stereotyped expressions that appeared in literature, on stage, and in the press" (166). He did not accept "the pejorative portraits" of Jews as literary and visual conventions or figures of speech but rather asked, "Would it not be more accurate to surmise that the recurrence of the stereotype is itself an index of the continued presence of anti-Semitism in society?" (180). My answer would be a resounding "yes" insofar as, according to Dobkowski, "traditional prejudice is implanted in language as an index of popular attitudes" (181). One need only page through Eduard Fuchs's book *Die Juden in der Karikatur* (1921), which includes examples of *hundreds of years* of anti-Semitic images printed in a variety of languages and formats, to grasp Dobkowski's words fully. Fuchs's book was published years before the rise of Nazism and its effects.

In our own time, various explanations have been offered to justify such responses. One recent commentator trying to explain Jews' self-criticalness theorized that it stemmed ultimately from the prophetic tradition, which, coupled with worldwide hatred of Jews through the centuries, led to an internalized anti-Semitism and, ultimately, self-hatred (Reiter 2012, 114–15, Kindle ed.). Perhaps more to the point, in an essay titled "Self-Hatred among Jews" (1941), sociologist Kurt Lewin noted that "members of the lower social strata tend to accept the fashions, values, and ideals of the higher strata. In the case of the underprivileged group, it means that their opinions about themselves are greatly influenced by the low esteem the majority has for them" (226; see also Marcus 2015, 186–90, Kindle ed.). Simply stated, in the era reviewed here Jews accepted criticism of their behavior patterns, and even when they tried to defend themselves, there was nevertheless an undercurrent of self-hatred in this defense because they had internalized the objections expressed by Gentiles.

But in 1940 another observer noted, "As anti-Semitism does not spring from Jewish vices, it is not to be cured by Jewish virtues. Rooted deep in the soil of unreason, it is immune to both logic and fact. . . . In dealing with such adversity, Jewish apologetics is from a misunderstanding somewhere: if only that be corrected, all will be well" (Sacher 1940, 243, 244).

Dobkowski thought that "the pervasive negative image of the Jew propagated by the popular culture of the period" played a key role insofar as in the literature, on the stage, and in the press flagrant stereotypes were a constant presence (1977, 166). By this reasoning, cartoons were part of that "pervasive negative image" to which there was not much objection. Or, to say it differently, one way to consider anti-Semitism is to assume that it was (is) so deeply ingrained in Western culture that it played (plays) some role in "maintaining social stability even if anti-Semitism is itself despicable" (Marcus 2015, 54, Kindle ed.).

Whatever the subject of a cartoon and in whatever context each was presented, what do these cartoons collectively tell us? In an overview as value free as possible, one might say that the cartoonists and their public did not really desire to learn about immigrants. They instead based their knowledge on what little information they already possessed and what they thought they already knew. In effect, they defined and worked within the narrow parameters of their beliefs and knowledge. The results led to the creation of stereotypical images allied with stereotypical opinions. If we can imagine stereotyped individuals brought to life for a moment or think of them as actual people, their activities, beliefs, and intentions as cartoon subjects were irrelevant and certainly beyond their control insofar as they could not define or limit the situations into which the cartoonists had placed them. They were defenseless, in essence abused, victims purposely distanced from mainstream society by the destructive, antisocial behaviors assigned to them. As a result, their moral rights, if that is a proper way to phrase what was at stake, were constantly violated, their imagined self-respect diminished, and their actions made the stuff of cheap comedy.

3 Positive Images and Negative Images

THE NUMBER of anti-Semitic cartoons in humor-magazine cartoons dwindled through the first decades of the twentieth century and largely disappeared by the 1930s, a fact noted but not explored by Rudolf Glanz (1973, 194). We can surmise, however, that as immigrants assimilated, became more American in habits and customs, and as their children spoke American English, hostile cartoons describing the activities, interests, and personalities of recently arrived immigrants grew increasingly anachronistic. But prejudices remained and were articulated primarily in books and articles that exhibited sheer, bigoted hatred of minorities, in particular East Asians and Jews (Smith 1891; Ross 1904; Grant 1916; Gould 1920; Stoddard 1920, 1927; Gibbons 1921; for analysis, see also Higham [1955] 1992 and Michaels 1995). In fact, hatred of Jews was widespread throughout the interwar period and grew increasingly strong and menacing right through the years of the Second World War (Dinnerstein 1994, chaps. 6 and 7).

Whereas earlier cartoons and articles tended more toward hostility to Jewish individuals and their presumed nefarious activities as well as to the religion itself, subsequent criticisms also turned on Jews as a race, a people apart, who could never be properly assimilated. The membrane separating the earlier and later criticisms, however, was very permeable. As has been pointed out, "In the end, anti-Semitism is not about race or religion. Rather, it is a process of working up Jews into a distorted image of 'the *Jews*'" (Marcus

2015, 191). So it is not a question of keeping a comparative scorecard about which aspects of the religion and the people were critiqued but of noticing changes and alterations in the ways Judaism and Jewish people were viewed. These changes and alterations reflected varying levels of anxiety brought about by the potential influences on the nation's character. The negative reaction to the First World War and the internationalization of America's isolationist foreign policy only increased the fears felt by those horrified by the overwhelming number of new immigrants still arriving in America daily. Questions were asked: Could the immigrants be assimilated? Would the heretofore hegemonic Anglo-Saxon culture that had defined whatever was termed the American character be compromised or totally overrun? Would the American gene pool be jeopardized, contaminated, and polluted by immigrants considered to be biologically inferior? Many immigrants settled in large cities, and industrialization had become the driving force of the nation's economy, so would the growth of urban populations as well as an industrialized workforce replace and ultimately destroy long-held (but mythic) rural values that were thought to underlay so much of American culture?

Calling people, especially Jews, permanent "aliens" also suggests that something more was in the air around the turn of the century than just the usual list of objections—Jews' clannishness, strange customs, parvenu social climbing, criminal behavior, and commercial aggressiveness. The entire Jewish people, whether considered a race, a nation, or an ethnicity, came under scrutiny. Perhaps, many Americans thought, they really did not belong in America and were a peril to the country. Too many of them were already here, and more were on their way. Other negative opinions began to grow stronger, including the belief that Jews could not be assimilated because of their supposed lack of patriotism, civic loyalty, and national feeling as well as because of their presumed Asian origins, their mongrelized inferior racial status, their political radicalism, their desire to control world markets, as well as their supposed membership in the vaguely termed "Jewish international conspiracy." That is, many Americans believed that for historical, cultural, social, ethnic, and biological reasons Jews were not to be welcomed any longer in America. As much as Jews individually were disliked, hostility to the entire Jewish community now became a common theme.

Just as racial bigots mounted a defense of what they considered to be American core values, in the art world a similar defensive pattern began to emerge. Strong reaction to modern European art both before and after the First World War grew exponentially in the 1920s not only because most of it was incomprehensible and based on theories many rejected or simply misunderstood but also because it represented another kind of European invasion of American culture that, along with increasing urbanization and the corresponding loss of rural values, was thought to undermine the American character and spirit. I will not argue that cartoons played a key role in the development of a pro-America, anti-immigrant movement in the arts, but it is within reason to say that the general attitude of hostility that encouraged the negative cartoons—the climate of opinion that emboldened the cartoonists—merged with fears generated by the urbanizing and Europeanizing of an America increasingly governed by and controlled from the eastern big cities.

These fears contributed to the growth of American Scene art, a powerful force in the art world during the 1920s and 1930s, which to my way of thinking was part of a rear-guard activity in defense of an older and out-of-date America. Furthermore, anti-Semitism was quite openly expressed in the art world in the 1920s and 1930s. Jews as a group, in particular those who lived in New York, came to symbolize the changes taking place in the art world. The American Scene movement thus might be viewed less as a positive assertion of the American spirit than as a defensive ploy against the effects of demographic changes in the American population, the shift of power from rural to urban centers, and the challenge to if not the termination of Anglo-Saxon hegemony in the arts. Again, this is not to say that dislike and mistrust of Jews and other immigrants caused the rise of the American Scene movement but rather that mainstream attitudes need to be taken into account in any discussion of this movement as it relates to the climate of opinion in which the earlier cartoonists had flourished. Or, in historian Samuel P. Hays's pithy statement, "Americans could not separate the strangeness of the immigrant from the strangeness of industrial change, both seemed 'foreign'" (1957, 100).

As the number of malevolent hand-drawn images decreased but did not disappear, magazines began increasingly to use photographs as illustrative material. Rather than caricature, denigrate, or poke fun at immigrants, photographers showed the public what the new arrivals actually looked like and the kinds of activities that filled their days. Photographs could be primarily informational or documentary, or they could suggest something of the dynamic processes of immigrant assimilation. Photographers could also explore the "exotic" sights offered by the new arrivals without having to travel to the small towns of southern and eastern Europe. A major center of interest was New York's Lower East Side, where the majority of Jewish immigrants settled before moving on to other cities and states. The images produced from these varied points of view, contrary to the cartoonists' animosity, helped answer certain questions: What did the immigrants look like? What did they do? Where did they work? How did they worship?

At the same time, Jews began to take charge of their own image. Artists such as Jacob Epstein (1880–1959), Samuel Zagat (1890–1964), Max Weber (1881–1961), and Abraham Walkowitz (1878–1965) portrayed Jews in ways entirely remote from those employed by the cartoonists. Their works might even be viewed on some level as responses to the cartoons or, more positively, as community artists' own descriptions of their community. Exhibitions were held in settlement houses and in institutions such as the Educational Alliance. Alfred Stieglitz (1864–1946), the photographer and gallerist, became a leader of the modern art movement in mainstream American art. As a result, the pictorial record became less defamatory, but the written record became more so, a contradiction I outline here.

But before I look more closely at the negative written material and the decades between the wars, I want to go back to the start of the period in question to discuss on the positive side some favorable sets of illustrations—not cartoons—of Jewish contemporary life, two of which appeared in meticulously researched and thorough magazine accounts of Jewish secular and religious culture in America: the earlier an article in *Frank Leslie's Popular Monthly* (Trumbul 1877) and then later a two-article piece in *The Century* (Wheatley 1892a, 1892b).

The article in *Leslie's*, published just before the great migration from eastern Europe began, showed synagogue scenes, buildings, and portraits of respected members of what appears to be the German Jewish community. Its author, Alfred Trumbul, pointed out the importance of charity in Judaism, stating that no other faith extends "to their unfortunate fellows so liberal and ready a hand." But at the same time, stereotyping the entire Jewish community, he noted that Jews "are born traders and are found most numerously engaged in purely mercantile business" (1877, 142). He explained this circumstance by stating that because of restrictions on their activities in Europe, "they have been bankers and money lenders for centuries." Bankers such as the Rothschilds, for example, "may almost be said to hold in their hands the peace of Europe. They are creditors of most of the governments of the world" (143) (see fig. 23, p. 48).

Trumbul attributed the preponderance of Jewish bankers and brokers in America also to restrictions on Jewish activities in Europe that carried over to employment possibilities in America. But then, in words echoed by Jacob Riis in the 1890s (discussed later in this chapter), he stated that because of "the Jew's" immersion in money matters, "to him the most trivial coin figures in its full value. This generic trait of the race the storms of centuries have failed to eradicate" (144). To his credit, however, Trumbul suggested that partial blame should be assigned to Christians because of their willingness to bargain over prices of goods they purchased (144). Ending his article on a positive note, he considered Jews to be an "industrious, honest, and law-abiding people" (144), despite his playing of the money card as an inherently Jewish condition or trait.

The text and illustrations in *The Century* articles of 1892 provided a short but thorough history of Judaism, Jewish religious practices, and the bourgeois culture of an established, financially secure German Jewish family that conducted itself with appropriate American decorum. (The author omitted discussion of the lives of the recent immigrants from eastern Europe then pouring into New York's Lower East Side.) The illustrations depict the family's high-bourgeois tastes as well as a child's clean and spacious classroom, the celebration of lighting the Hanukkah candles, the dining-room table set for the Passover meal, in which the family servant participated, and views of synagogue services—all in contrast to contemporary magazine cartoons that scrutinized Jewish family life only in a derogatory manner. As we have seen in chapter 1, according to the cartoons, children were thought to be educated only to make money and to learn slippery business practices. Couples related to each other through sarcastic remarks, and social climbing was a significant activity. In contrast, the two *Century* articles described a family that very likely never experienced these kinds of activities in such gross ways, but it is also possible to imagine that the author intended to make implicit the point that German Jews were of a different sort and therefore more acceptable to Christians than those from eastern Europe, who were considered to be inferior beings.

In most of the illustrations for this article, the family, dressed in formal clothing and living in elegant quarters, are a unit in their actions and respectful of each other. Children study the religious texts in an environment conducive to learning (fig. 35); the *cohanim* (descendants of Aaron) bless the congregation during the Sabbath service (fig. 36), and the family, at home at the end of the Sabbath day, perform the *havdalah* ceremony separating the Sabbath from the rest of the days of the week, their servant looking on (fig. 37).

Some fourteen years later, in 1902, the then young artist Jacob Epstein illustrated Hutchins Hapgood's sympathetic account of everyday immigrant life on the Lower East Side in *The Spirit of the Ghetto*, first published in 1902 (Hapgood [1902] 1965). Epstein was born in that district and expatriated himself to Europe when he was twenty-two, settling permanently in England, so he knew the area and its inhabitants well. As he wrote in his two autobiographies, "I saw a great deal of Jewish orthodox [*sic*] life, traditional and

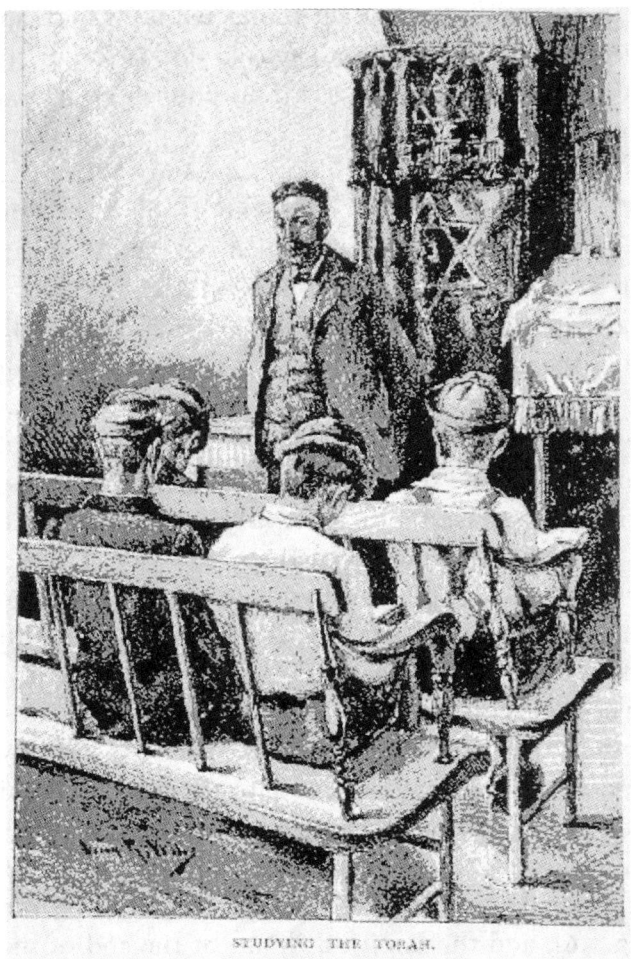

STUDYING THE TORAH.

35. Irving R. Wily, *Studying the Torah*, from *The Century*, February 1892, 519.

narrow. . . . This did not greatly influence me, but I imagine that the feeling I have for expressing a human point of view, giving human rather than abstract implications to my work, comes from these early formative years" (1940, 12; see similar thoughts in Epstein 1955, 9).

Because both Hapgood and Epstein were sensitive to the difficulties of creating a new life in a new country, their book was a

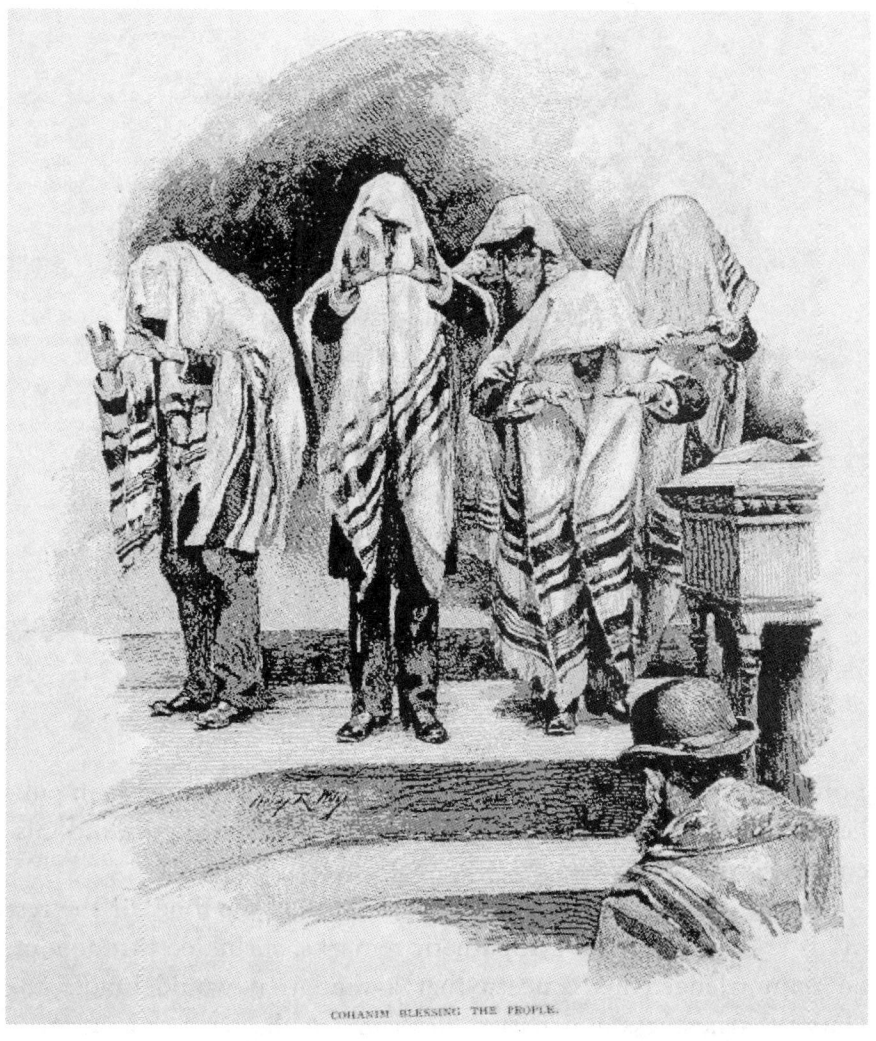

COHANIM BLESSING THE PEOPLE.

36. Irving R. Wily, *Cohanim Blessing the People*, from *The Century*, January 1892, 315.

rare publication in America at the time. Individuals were treated humanely, and the kinds of commerce conducted, the recreational possibilities available, and the different ways people led their lives in the business and art worlds were described and illustrated in a manner not seen before. For those who knew little about life in the

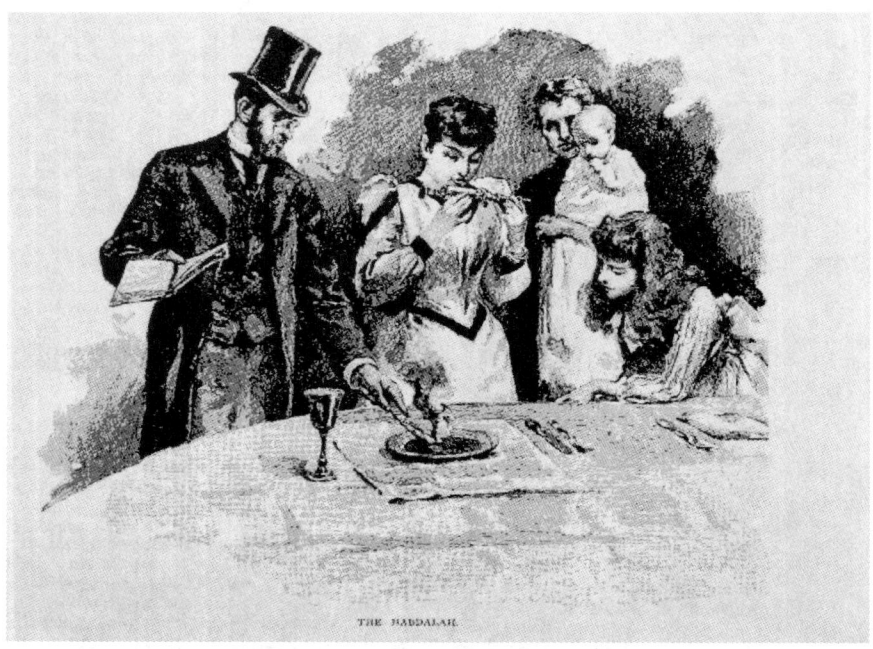

THE HAVDALAH.

37. Irving R. Wily, *The Havdalah*, from *The Century*, February 1892, 515.

Lower East Side and who learned about Jews from mainstream publications, Hapgood's book countered many negative myths and misconceptions about Jews.

In the opening pages, Hapgood established the tone for the rest of his book. Among his sympathetic remarks, sprinkled throughout, he acknowledged his concern that assimilation would hinder the "moral earnestness and native idealism" of the next generation, a rare combination of praise of Jewish morality and criticism of American, non-Jewish business ethics. He added that what is needed is "a spiritual unity . . . , something similar to the spirit and unity underlying the national and religious unity of Orthodox Jewish culture" ([1902] 1965, 46). The importance of the Jewish community, then, was in maintaining its values and traditions rather than in assimilating to American culture wholesale, as suggested by some writers mentioned in chapter 1.

Of workers and the havoc caused among them by immigrating to America, Hapgood wrote, "There are few more pathetic sights than an old man with a long beard, a little black cap on his head and a venerable face—a man who had been perhaps a Hebraic or Talmudic scholar in the old country—carrying or pressing piles of coats in the melancholy sweatshop, or standing for sixteen hours a day by his push cart in one of the dozen crowded streets of the ghetto ([1902] 1965, 7–8), a figure Epstein drew with compassion (fig. 38).

But cartoons themselves could be used to create favorable impressions. Sam Zagat, one of the most popular cartoonists of the day, was also sympathetic to the life-altering circumstances and hardships brought about by immigration. In his cartoon *Rival Newsboys* (1913) (fig. 39), one can only imagine the old man's humiliation in having to compete with a child young enough to be his grandson.

No cartoon jokes here about duping potential customers. Hapgood, Epstein, and Zagat also knew that Jewish children were not taught nefarious business practices from infancy. Hapgood, for instance, described the experiences of many youngsters in the following way: "Whether born in this country or in Russia, the son of Orthodox parents passes his earliest years in a family atmosphere, where the whole duty of man is to observe the religious Laws" ([1902] 1965, 23). Epstein illustrated this point by showing a father taking his son to synagogue (fig. 40). Because one is not allowed to carry anything on the Sabbath, we can deduce that the father, holding a bag containing his prayer shawl and his phylacteries, and the son, carrying a prayer book, are probably going to their synagogue for daily morning prayers. Both are dressed appropriately and will probably return home afterward to change into work and school clothing.

Perhaps the boy has taken a job after school or perhaps has dropped out entirely in order to help the family pay its bills, as many boys had to do (fig. 41). And when he has a spare moment, he devotes himself to his studies (fig. 42). And perhaps he might ultimately become one of those men who remain in their synagogue or in a yeshiva and spend their days studying the Bible, the Talmud, and other holy books (fig. 43).

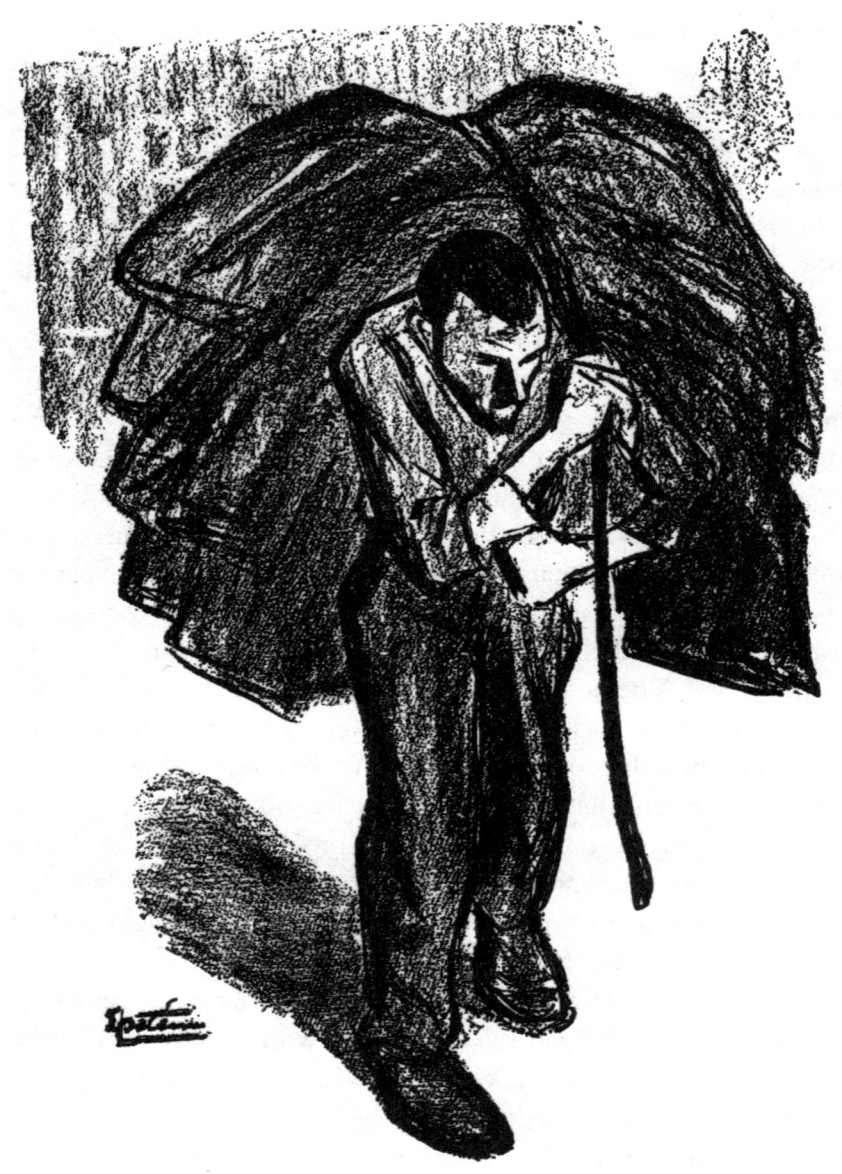

38. Jacob Epstein, *Man Carrying Bales*, from Hutchins Hapgood, *The Spirit of the Ghetto* (1902; reprint, New York: Funk and Wagnalls, 1965), 8.

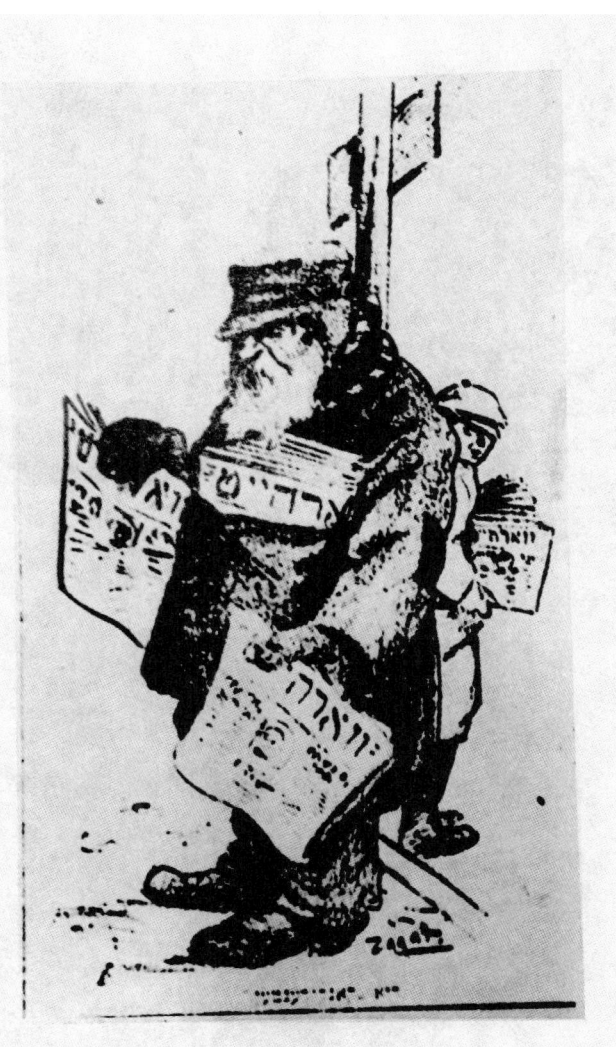

EAST SIDE STREET PROFESSIONS
Rival newsboys

1913

39. Samuel Zagat, *Rival Newsboys*, 1913, from Ida Zagat,
ed., *Drawings and Paintings: Jewish Life on New York's
Lower East Side, 1912–1962* (New York: Rogers Book Service, 1972), 29.

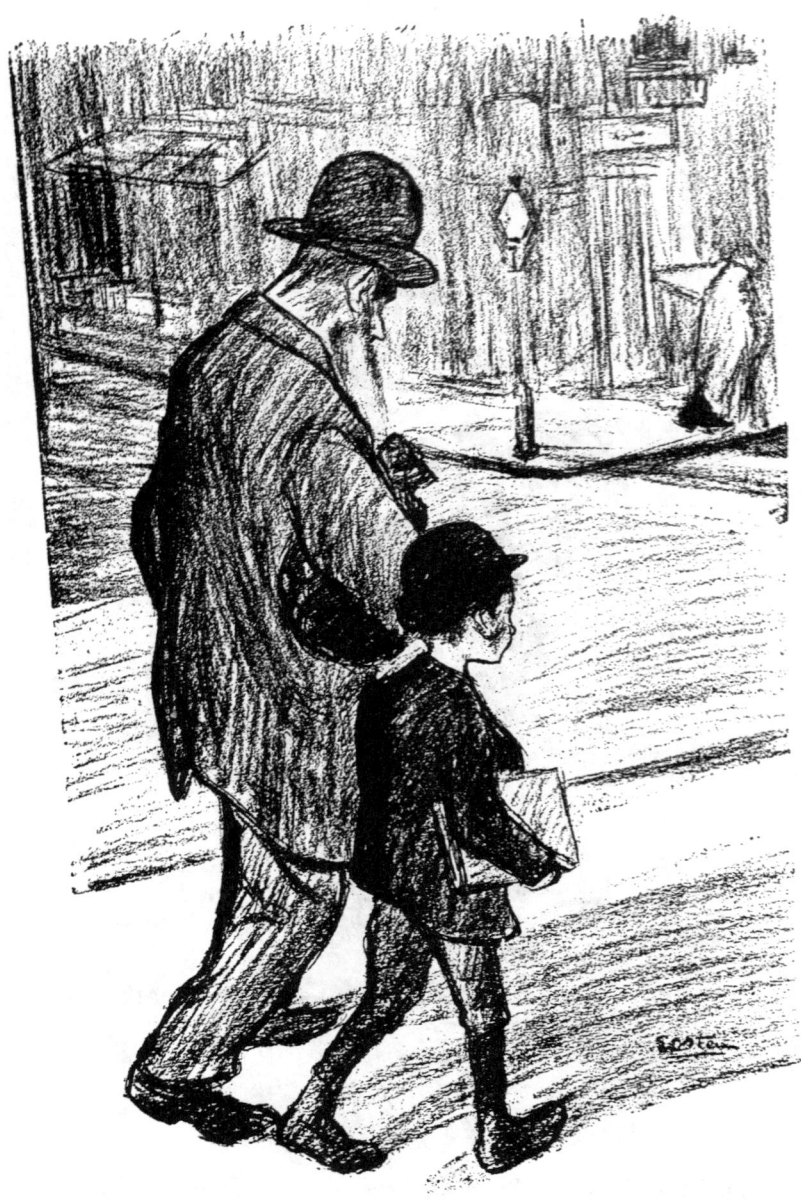

40. Jacob Epstein, *Going to Synagogue*, from Hutchins Hapgood, *The Spirit of the Ghetto* (1902; reprint, New York: Funk and Wagnalls, 1965), 23.

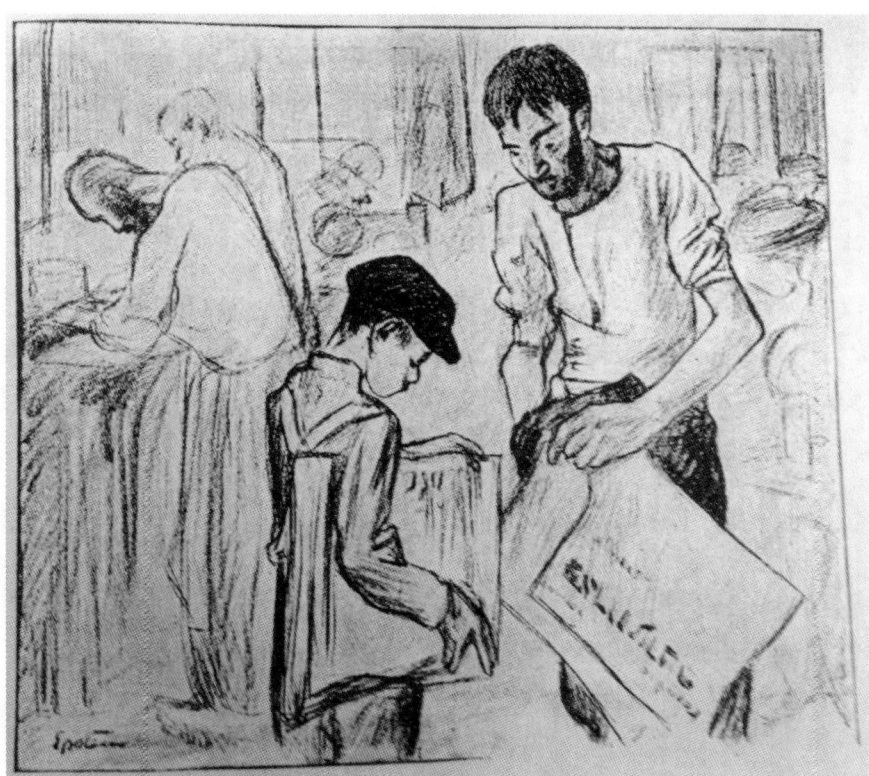

41. Jacob Epstein, *Buying a Newspaper*, from Hutchins Hapgood, *The Spirit of the Ghetto* (1902; reprint, New York: Funk and Wagnalls, 1965), 177.

Hapgood or Epstein titled the illustration in figure 43 *Submerged Scholars*, implying that these men are a remnant of those who had to abandon the tradition of long hours of daily religious study in face of the economic reality of making a living. In any event, the two men are seen studying together, a custom still alive today among the Orthodox, in which the men, perhaps life-long study companions, try to wrest as much meaning as possible from the text they are analyzing. Their pursuit of knowledge, part of their lifetime obligation of learning, despite whatever poverty they might endure, assured them a place of respect in their community.

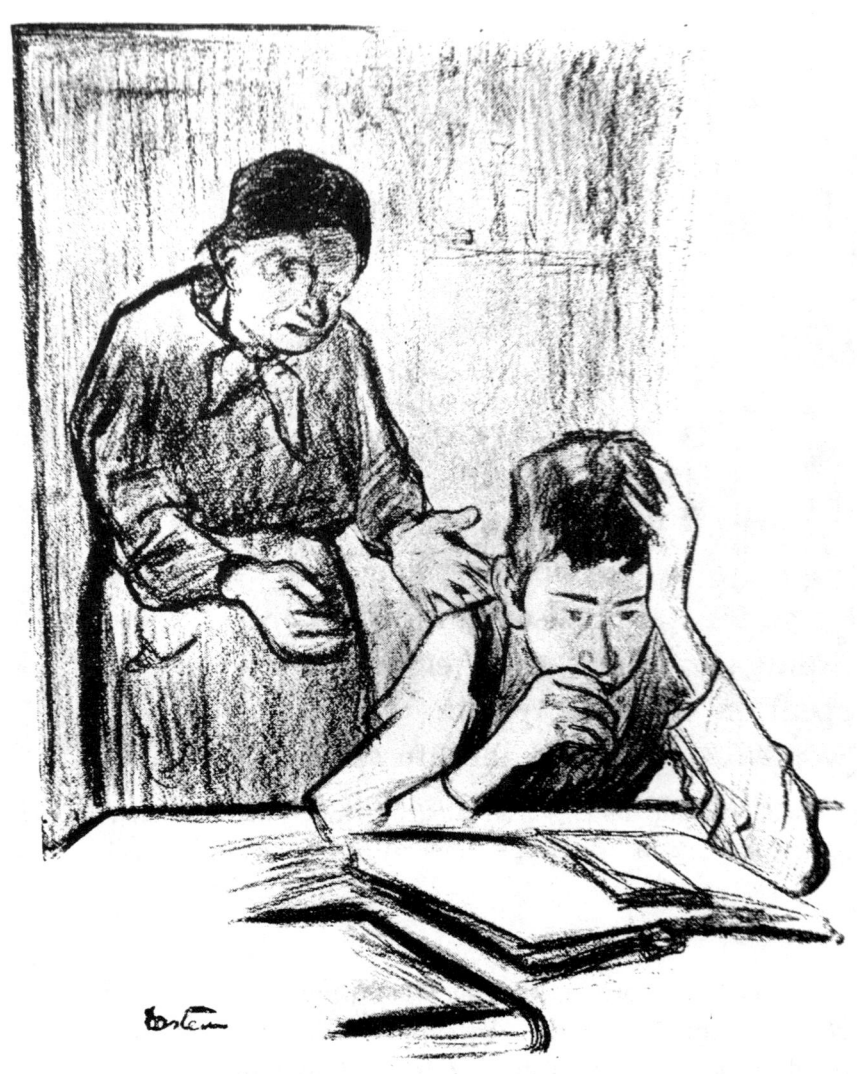

42. Jacob Epstein, *He Was Bewitched by Mathematics*, from Hutchins Hapgood, *The Spirit of the Ghetto* (1902; reprint, New York: Funk and Wagnalls, 1965), 207.

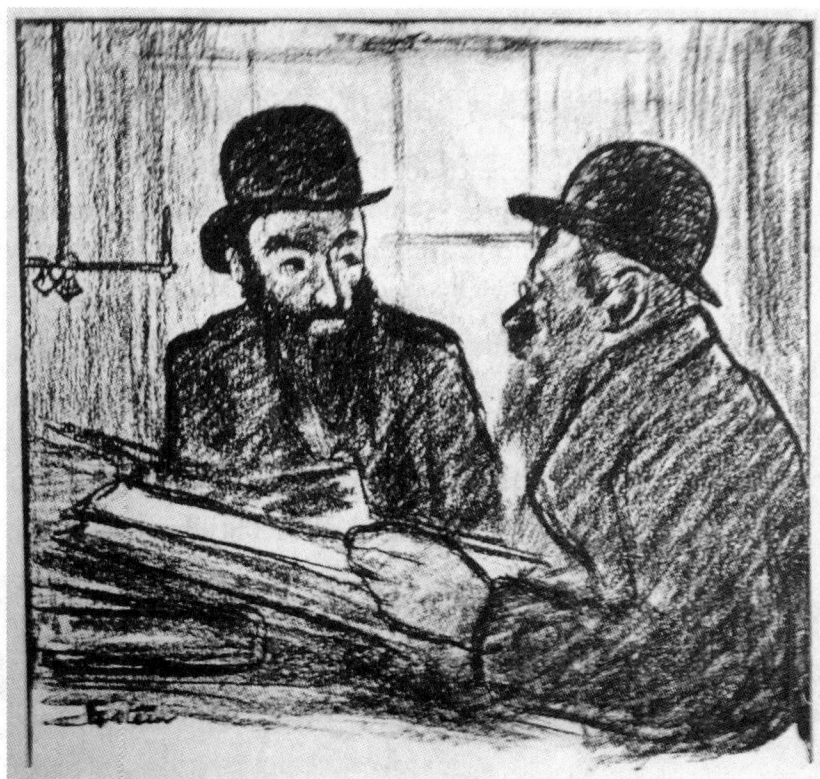

43. Jacob Epstein, *Submerged Scholars*, from Hutchins Hapgood, *The Spirit of the Ghetto* (1902; reprint, New York: Funk and Wagnalls, 1965), 65.

Epstein's illustrations for Hapgood's book portrayed common but also idealized situations that reveal modes of behavior concerning individual responsibility and the importance of education, to which Jews have aspired over the centuries, a fact demonstrated by the number of children of immigrants who by the 1910s and 1920s had entered the professions. In those decades, it had become obvious that Jews had become the most successful of all immigrant groups and were acknowledged as having arrived with the widest array of industrial skills (S. Steinberg 1989, 88–105). But their success as a group also created problems: to many, Jews posed a constant competitive threat as merchants, traders, and manufacturers to the extent that envy became another reason for Jew hatred. (For the links between envy and anti-Semitism in Germany, see Aly 2014.)

Other visual images also captured immigrant reality in ways totally foreign to most of the cartoonists of this era. For example, a photograph published by Byron Company around 1901 shows a peddler with his wares in midtown Manhattan (fig. 44; cf. fig. 31, p. 61).

Whether the peddler plied his trade in a city, small town, or rural areas, he was probably noted more for creating "a cultural bridge between people who seemingly had so little else in common" than as a rapacious swindler (Diner 2015, 5). Years later, in 1920, Sam Zagat, one of the most popular cartoonists who worked for various Yiddish-language publications, including *Warheit* (Truth, 1912–19) and *Forvitz* (Forward, 1919–62), created a series of prints depicting how

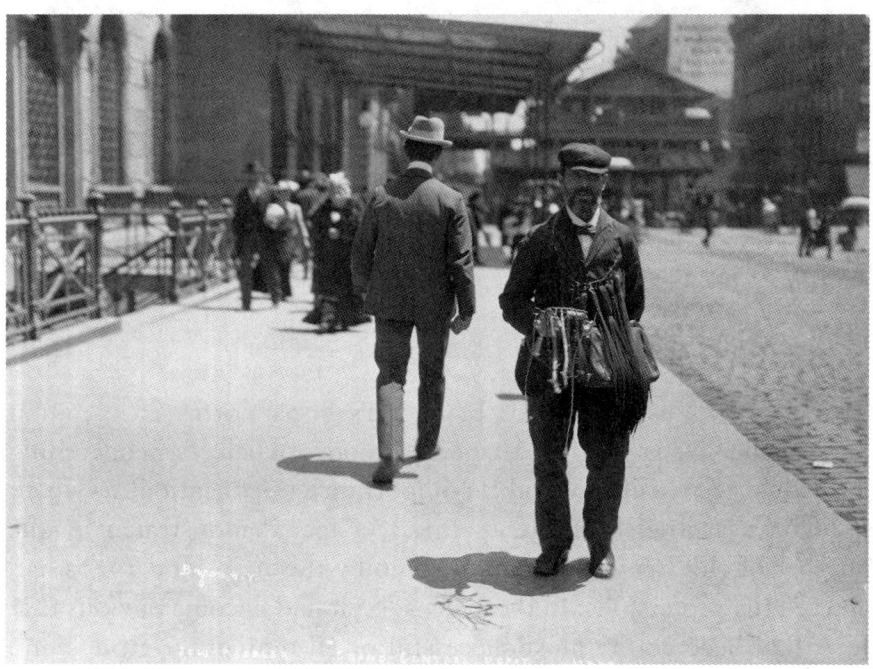

44. Unknown photographer, *Jew Peddler—Grand Central Depot*, 1901. Byron Company, New York. Courtesy of the Museum of the City of New York, 93.1.1.17211.

itinerant peddlers actually functioned in contrast to the stereotyped cartoon versions of Jewish business practices. I remember scenes in the late 1930s and the 1940s, as I was growing up, similar to Zagat's depiction of the cooking-pot repairman, whose most important days for fixing and cleaning pots and pans occurred just before Passover (see fig. 32, p. 62). Itinerant knife and scissor sharpeners, used-clothing buyers and sellers, and even singers of songs called out loud and clear from streets and inner courtyards so that apartment dwellers would hear them advertising their services and then bring down their knives or clothing as well as coins for the entertainers.

Through the first decades of the twentieth century, Jews were represented not just in prints and in magazine and book illustrations but also in other types of visual images—some relatively benign, others venomous. For example, Sadakichi Hartmann, an early writer on photography and painting, published in 1902 an article titled "Picturesque New York" under the pseudonym "Sidney Allen," in which he was concerned with the photographic possibilities of the Lower East Side. After mentioning that the Jewish quarter seemed like a medieval town, he said: "To the Gentile, the aristocratic uptowner, this scene is like a nightmare" (144). Having asserted that the Jews were certainly Other and that they had arrived in New York from another period in history, he then alerted his readers to the aesthetic side of the neighborhood. "The Hebrew quarter is undoubtedly the most picturesque part of New York City, the one which lends itself most easily to artistic interpretation. . . . Its very dinginess and squalor render it interesting" (144). Of course, this description was meant in an aesthetic, not a social worker, sense.

Whatever his actual experiences in the Lower East Side, Hartmann admitted that he viewed its inhabitants through figures in novels and in artworks by Rembrandt and Whistler. What he actually saw, he then transformed into images in his mind, removed from physical reality. Even garbage, he declared, "contains such a wealth of subtle values and warm color notes and such varieties of texture that it should send not only painters, but every person in search of the picturesque into ecstasies. . . . [The New York ghetto] promises more artistic possibilities for out-of-door photography" (Allen 1902, 145). He found that humorous and pathetic scenes followed each other in endless variety. Old men with beards and skullcaps "worship as in the days of Israel [and] whole chapters of the Bible seem to be personified in them" (144, 147), a scenario based on the sheerest fantasy and having no relation to actual life in the Lower East Side, let alone to ancient Israelites. (In this regard, see Hapgood's comments, given earlier, as well as Epstein's and Zagat's images.)

In truth, Hartmann was interested primarily in his aesthetic responses to the scenes before him, not in the scenes themselves. "The settings for a picture are really at every moment of the day. . . . You never need to wait for a composition. The crowd takes care of that. You only need to look into your finder and let the restless stream of humanity pass by" (Allen 1902, 146). Not surprisingly, he found sweatshop scenes too dreary insofar as "we are only in search of the picturesque" (146).

Before discussing sweatshops and clothing production (popularly called the "rag trade"), probably the most important industry in the Lower East Side at the century's turn and an essential part of the lives of many of its inhabitants, I want to mention some descriptions and word pictures by various authors that illuminate ways one can think about and visualize the immigrant population of this period. Like Hartmann, Mrs. Schuyler van Rensselaer (1892) was less inclined to see the new immigrants as people rather than as exotic creatures magically dropped down in New York. She viewed the Lower East Side inhabitants as sequences of picturesque images in whatever form she found them. She acknowledged that tenement districts were filthy and overcrowded but found pictorial pleasure in the vitality of the people, including the Jews on Hester Street. So enamored of the immigrants' dress and habits, Mrs. Van Rensselaer objected to the fact that they would soon lose their foreign ways and become good, ordinary-looking, and uninteresting New Yorkers.

One gathers from Mrs. Van Rensselaer's article that immigrants provided a kind of entertainment for her. They were not people who lived in often overcrowded quarters struggling to learn a new language, to find jobs, and to support their families, but foreign, strange people to be observed at one's pleasure, not unlike travelers visiting an Indian reservation in the American West to see how the natives lived—a human zoo, as it were—or visiting gypsy camps in the Balkans.

The writer Henry James's attitude was close to Mrs. van Rensselaer's. He did not indulge in Hartmann's visual exhilaration or display Hapgood's empathy when he wrote verbal pictures lamenting the days of his youth in *The American Scene* (1907), a book written about his visit to America after living abroad for several decades. Everything had changed so drastically, including the disappearance of his childhood home. Like other visitors to the Lower East Side, James found communication impossible with recent immigrants, and he was very reluctant to accept the fact that their presence would alter the character of the country and what he and others often called "the American Spirit" (86–87, 120).

Like the exaggerated fear of what a Jewish New York would appear to be in the future (as in figure 3, p. 9), James acknowledged "the Hebrew conquest of New York" (1907, 132). It was no longer his city, or at least it had become a city he now had to share with the Other, whom he actually described as less than human. In fact, he bestialized them. During a walk through the Lower East Side, he found himself "at the bottom of some vast sallow aquarium in which innumerable fish, of over-developed proboscis, were to bump together, forever, amid heaped spoils of the sea" (131). He also noticed the ubiquitous fire escapes and viewed them as "the spaciously organized cage for the humbler class of animals in some great zoological garden. This analogy is irresistible—it seems to offer, in each district, a little world of bars and perches and swings for human squirrels and monkeys," which allows the inhabitants to lead "like squirrels and monkeys all the merrier life" (134). (The word *merrier* is astonishingly vulgar in the context of immigrant poverty, illness, and struggle to survive.) During another visit, he happened upon a small square "in which an ant-like population darted to and fro" (134).

Because James might have been describing members of my father's family, whose stories of terrible poverty (seven people living in two rooms in a dumbwaiter tenement), their great desire to reinvent themselves as Americans, and their striving to make their way in their new country are etched in my mind, I find James's remarks not funny, lacking in minimal empathy, beyond condescension, and flat-out unacceptable even 110 years later. In this regard, his word pictures were not different from the cartoon images discussed in chapter 1; looked at from any angle, the fancy description "over-developed proboscis" still means "big nose."

Very likely, the sights James happened upon in the Lower East Side were much closer to the scenes recorded by Sam Zagat—that is, people working and shopping, children playing or attending to younger siblings while their parents were at work or honoring their religion. Had James visited on certain evenings, he might have seen, if he had had an open mind, Jewish men fulfilling the ritual of praying at first sight of the new moon (fig. 45), acting as ordinary humans honoring their culture and traditions rather than as animals scurrying around.

For many Americans, immigrants seemed so strange that they could only be considered as if another species. This is borne out by a passage in James Huneker's book New Cosmopolis (1915), in which he describes an imaginary tour of the Lower East Side. An acquaintance wanted to see the area as if through the eyes of the artist George Luks, who had painted single-figure portraits of very poor people as well as several immigrant group scenes (9, 20). The acquaintance spotted a small, thin, girl wearing a huge shawl and selling flowers. Huneker observed that the girl looked like "a regular Luks," meaning that she was very thin, looked tired and pale, and wore dirty, hand-me-down, ill-fitting clothing, probably somewhat like the young girl in figure 46. Having spotted a "Luks" figure, Huneker and his acquaintance considered the visit a success.

To Luks's credit, he did not limit himself to creating "Luks" portraits but also painted what might be termed informational group scenes of the different immigrant neighborhoods. Perhaps the most interesting of this type is Street Scene (Hester Street) (1905) (fig. 47).

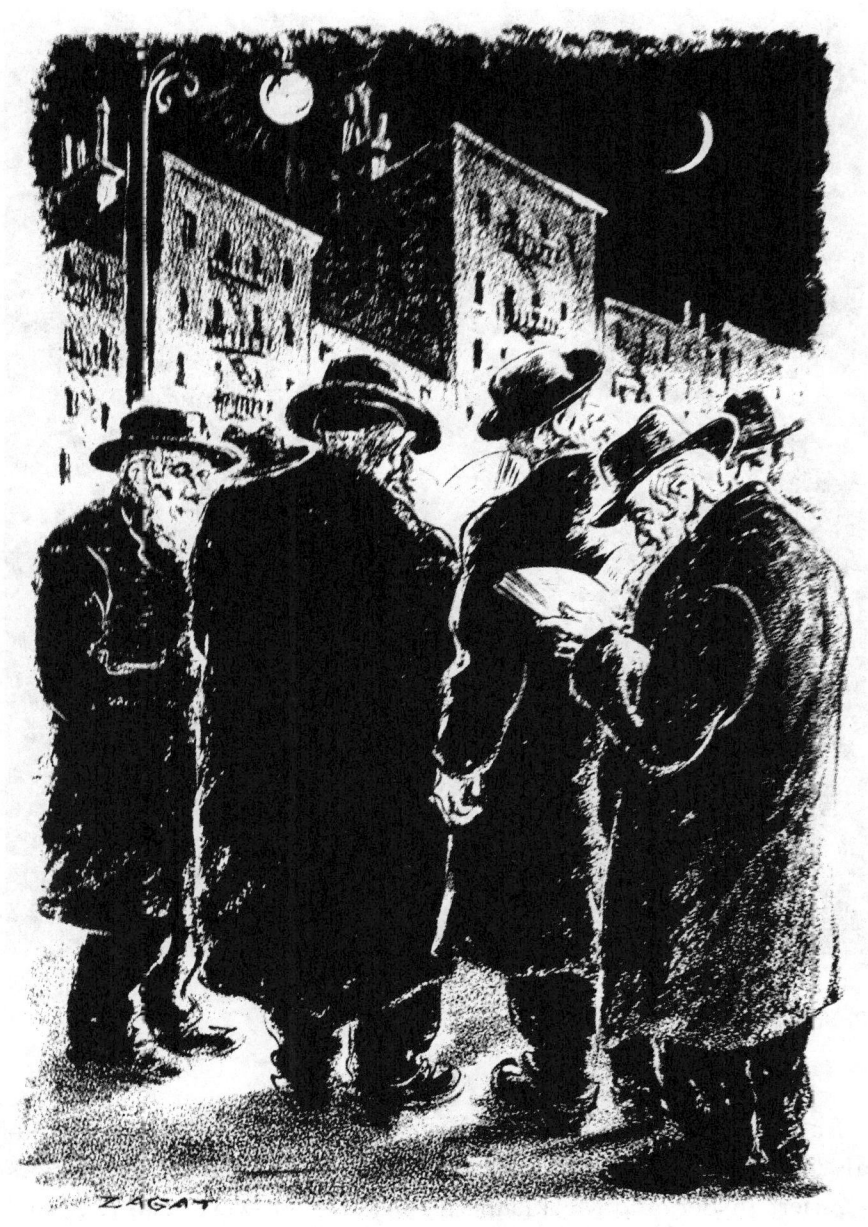

45. Samuel Zagat, *Men Praying to the New Moon*, c. 1920, from Ida Zagat, ed., *Drawings and Paintings: Jewish Life on New York's Lower East Side, 1912–1962* (New York: Rogers Book Service, 1972), 5.

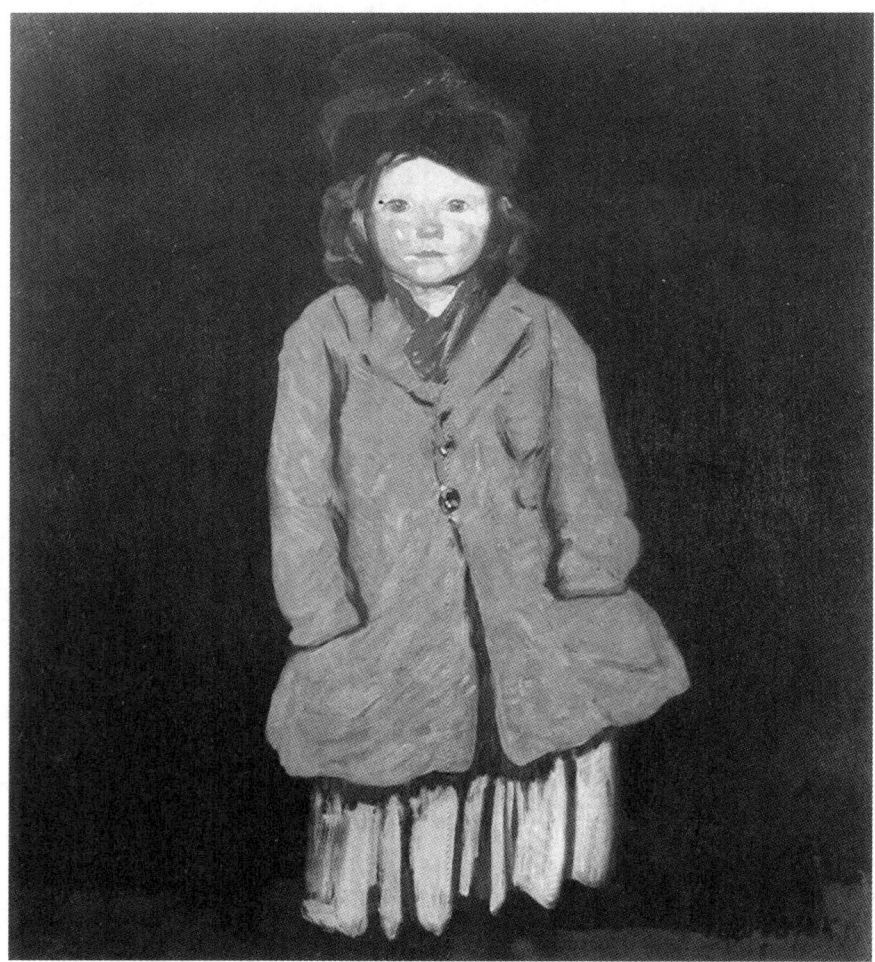

46. George Luks, *Lily Williams*, 1909. Oil on canvas, 15½ × 29½ inches. Private collection.

Of all his paintings of immigrant groups, this one shows individuals transforming themselves into Americans by their clothing styles (Zurier, Snyder, and Mecklenberg 1995, 26). However exotic or picturesque he might have found this busy Jewish shopping street, he revealed a community in process of reinventing itself as an American one. The man in the white fedora in the foreground might be a visitor

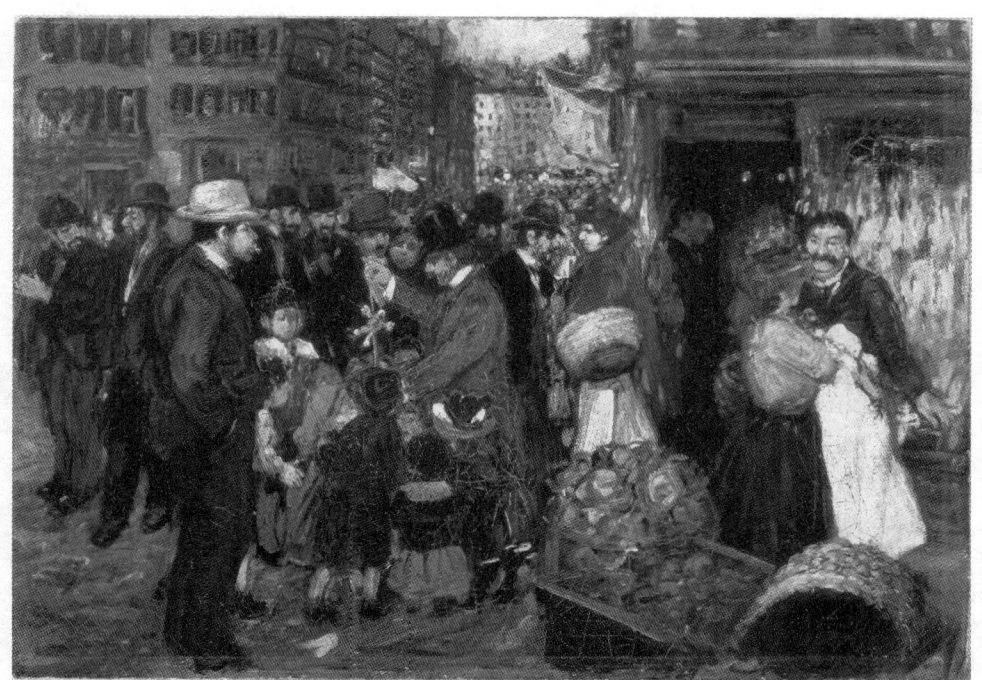

47. George Luks, *Street Scene (Hester Street)*, 1905. Oil on canvas, 26 13/16 × 35⅞ inches. Brooklyn Museum, 40.339, Dick S. Ramsey Fund.

because of his American-style clothing, or he might also be a person who still lived in but had already emotionally and psychologically left the Lower East Side. The men to the left behind him still wear European attire. And the modern clothing worn by the woman on the right contrasts with the old-fashioned red shawl of the woman behind her. In other words, the ghetto, although viewed with appalling condescension and as a picturesque photographic shooting gallery by some, was seen by its inhabitants as a dynamic place, fraught with difficulties but also filled with promise and dreams, which Luks acknowledged in this painting.

Luks was not the only one to notice individuals' desire to reinvent themselves as Americans. Years before he painted *Hester Street*, magazines such as the renamed *Frank Leslie's Illustrated Newspaper* ran photographic and artist-illustrated articles about immigrants.

One series, published in the paper's issues for May 14, September 12, September 26, December 12, December 19, and December 26, 1891, showed Russian Jews before their departure for America, on the ship, after landing in New York, shopping on the Lower East Side, and at work. Illustrations included scenes of being examined by a doctor onboard ship, eating the first meal on ship, waiting for entry upon arrival, and purchasing items from pushcarts (fig. 48).

This market scene, because of its great detail, provides the viewer with some idea of the crowded quarters and streets of the Lower East Side as well as the primitive, precapitalistic barter and bargaining economy of the sellers and buyers, but in the person of the young girl with her basket it also shows the almost immediate Americanization of youngsters, who had switched to modern dress in contrast to their elders. A view titled *Market Day in Jewish Quarter*

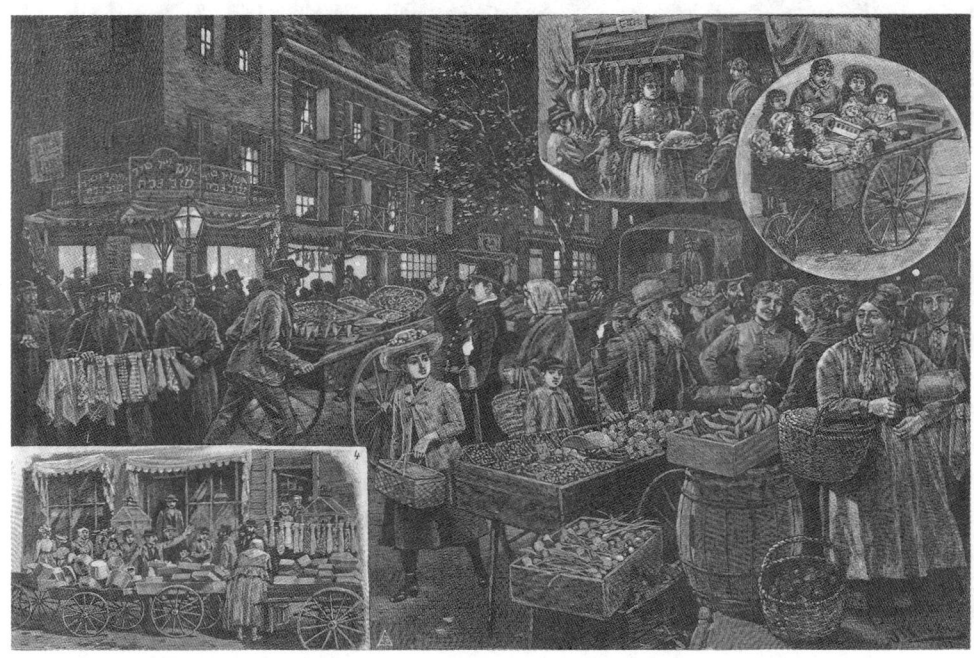

48. From a drawing by Durkin, *Market Scene*, from *Frank Leslie's Illustrated Newspaper*, September 12, 1891, 80. Courtesy of the New York Society Library, New York.

of Lower East Side, New York City (1912) by photographer Lewis Hine (1874–1940) also indicates how quickly immigrants discarded their Old Country clothing (fig. 49). Straw hats and dresses are much more common than beards and shawls in his photograph.

Jacob Riis (1849–1914), the most famous journalist-photographer of his time, published photographs that more than a century later provide us with compelling and truthful visual information about the Lower East Side, not excepting those photographs that are patently staged or posed. A Danish immigrant in 1870, Riis began to explore tenement life by the mid-1880s, less for its picturesque aspects than to point out the many social, workplace, and health problems faced by its inhabitants. Of his several books and articles, *How the Other Half Lives: Studies among the Tenements of New*

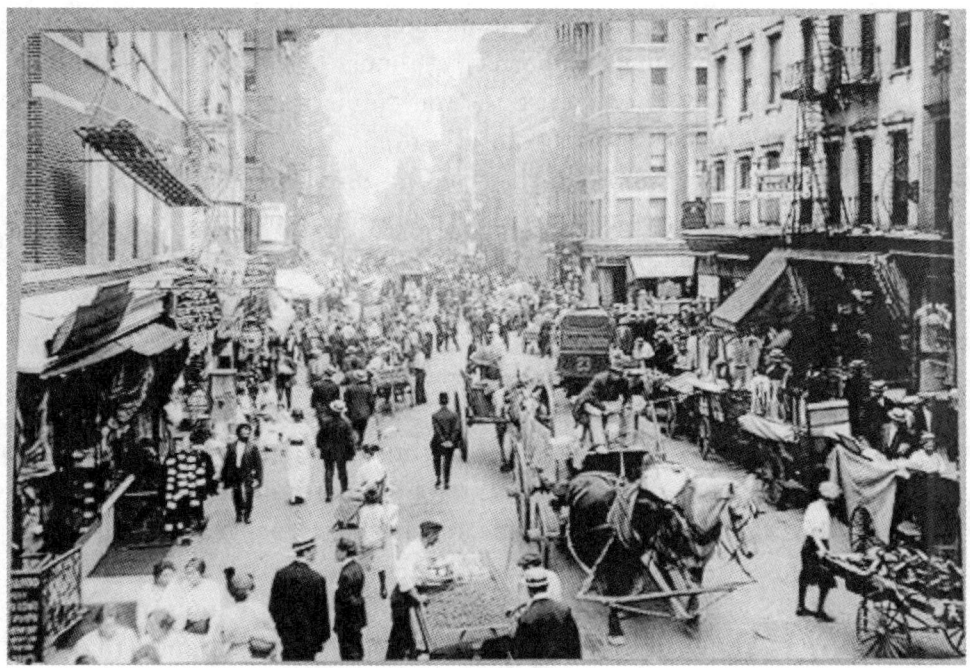

49. Lewis Hine, *Market Day in Jewish Quarter of Lower East Side, New York City,* 1912. Photography Collection, Miriam and Ira D. Wallach Division of Art, Prints, and Photographs, New York Public Library, Astor, Lenox, and Tilden Foundations.

York, first published in 1890, remains his best known. He devoted two entire chapters to Jews, titled "Jewtown" and "The Sweaters of Jewtown," *sweaters* being the then current word for sweatshops.

In the context of the language of his day, these titles were no more pejorative than the chapter titles "Little Italy" and "Chinatown." Even so, the verdict among scholars is that Riis was not a friend of the Jews (Ware 1938; Gurock 1981; Hales 1984, 191; Gandal 1997, 63–64; Trachtenberg 2010, xxvii). In fact, some of Riis's comments in both chapters on Jews in *How the Other Half Lives* could have served as captions for the humor-magazine cartoons of the day. For example, "Thrift is the watchword of Jewtown, as of its people the world over" (Riis [1890] 2010a, 103). "Money is their God. Life itself is of little value compared with even the leanest bank account. In no other spot does life wear so intensely bold and materialistic an aspect as in Ludlow Street" (104). "The instinct of dollars and cents is in them. They can count, and correctly, almost before they can talk" (110). And a chief characteristic is the "unhesitating mendacity of these people" (Riis [1890] 2010b, 115–16).

Of Riis's many photographs in *How the Other Half Lives*, at least two can be considered both complimentary and critical of Jews, although Riis might have had only the latter in mind. *Ludlow Street Hebrew Making Ready for Sabbath Eve in His Coal Cellar—Bread on His Table* shows a recently arrived immigrant who lives in a coal chute, his clothing hung on hooks and the table covered by a dirty cloth (fig. 50). He is seated alone for his Sabbath meal, which consists only of a loaf of challah bread. One might argue that this photo's purpose was to convince viewers that Jews did not mind living in filthy conditions, an opinion often repeated in magazine and newspaper articles (e.g., Van Rensselaer 1892, 172; Allen 1902, 145; Schoener 1967, 26, 58, 62). But the photo also perhaps contains an unintended countermessage, well summarized by Rabbi Judah L. Magnes (1877–1948) in a speech in 1909: "Strong roots in one's ethnic heritage would avoid the social disorganization caused by immigration and assure a sound integration into American society" (paraphrased in Goren 1982, 67). So one can read Riis's photograph as showing a

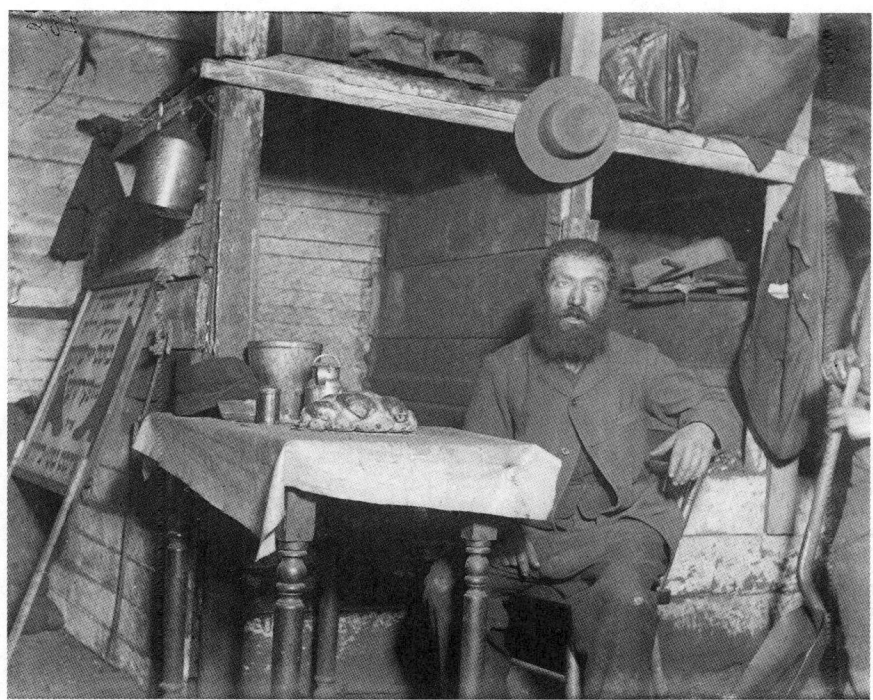

50. Jacob Riis, *Ludlow Street Hebrew Making Ready for Sabbath Eve in His Coal Cellar—Bread on His Table*, c. 1890. Jacob A. (Jacob August) Riis (1849–1914), Museum of the City of New York, 90.13.4.291.

person of considerable inner strength who found solace in traditional religious rituals despite terrible living and working conditions and the inevitable disruptions caused by immigration to a new country.

The second complimentary-critical photograph shows the airless, unkempt, and crowded conditions of a heder (religious school) quite different from the classroom illustrated contemporaneously in *The Century* in 1892 (fig. 51; cf. fig. 35, p. 98). Riis probably thought that the room he photographed was deleterious to the children's health and well-being. It might very well have been, but the fact of the school's existence, the determined look of the teacher at the far end of the room, and the placement of the children in the foreground reveal the community's continued meeting of its obligation

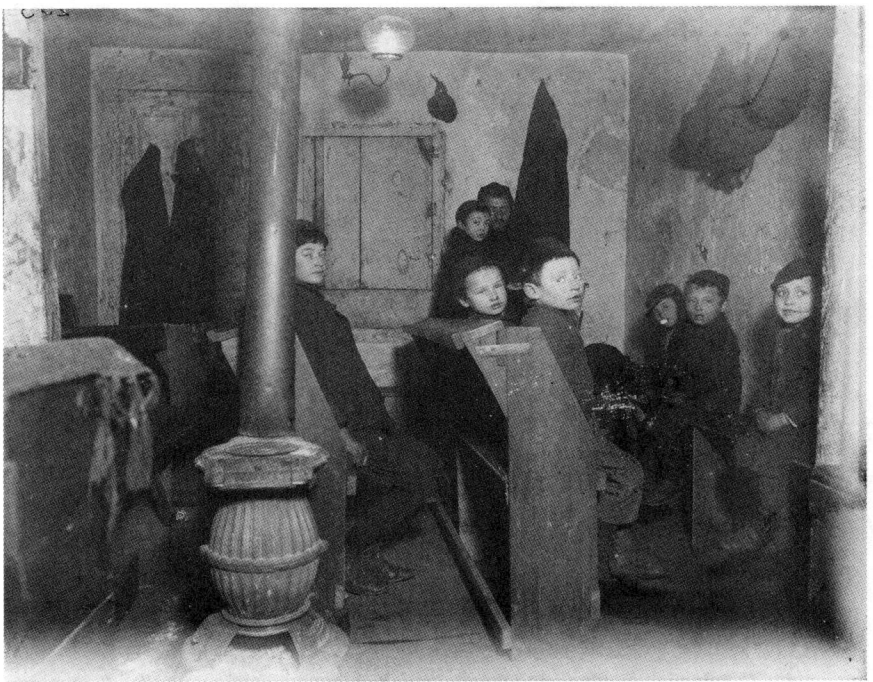

51. Jacob Riis, *Talmud School in a Hester Street Tenement*, c. 1890. Jacob A. (Jacob August) Riis (1849–1914), Museum of the City of New York, 90.13.4.257.

to provide a religious education for the next generation despite poverty and lack of decent facilities. In their different ways, the subjects of these two photographs by Riis call attention to the community's continued desire for religious observation and instruction as a way to ensure its survival and vitality.

Another of Riis's photographs provides some insights into the lives of those who worked in sweatshops, one of the mainstay occupations of Lower East Side residents (fig. 52). It shows a cluttered sweatshop apartment in which workers are finishing knee pants. It also tells another story. Like the two photographs just discussed, this scene of a family doing piece work at home also has a double meaning (Baigell 2009, 65–82). It shows impossible work and living conditions, but

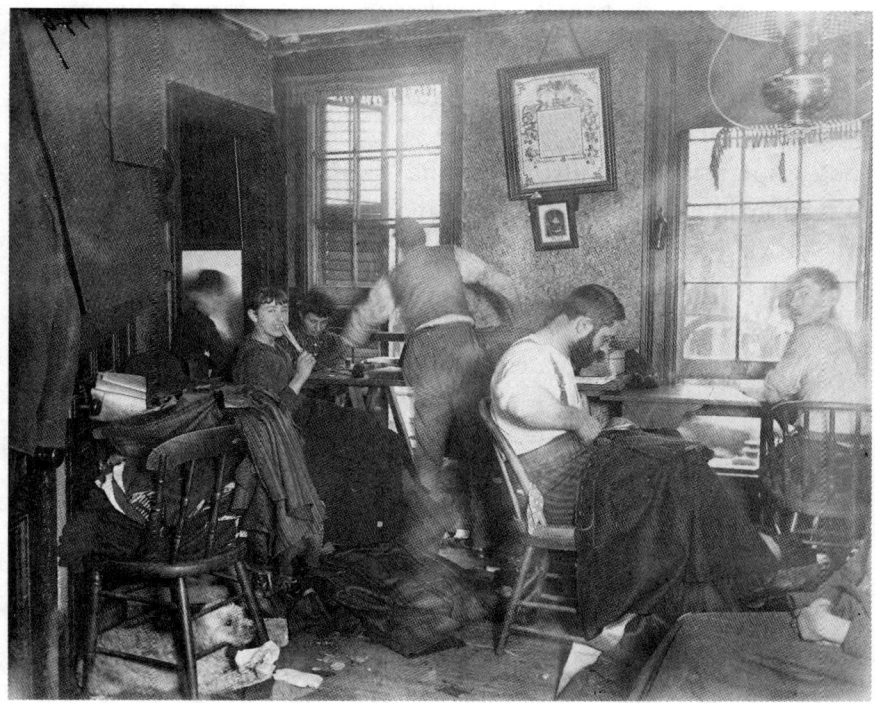

52. Jacob Riis, *"Knee Pants" at Forty-Five Cents a Dozen—a Ludlow Street Sweater's Shop*, 1889. Jacob A. (Jacob August) Riis (1849–1914), Museum of the City of New York, 2008.1.47.

a key object in this photograph, the framed picture on the far wall, focuses our attention on the family's desire to maintain close ties and traditional values despite the hardships it faced each day. The framed document is a *ketubah*, the Jewish marriage contract, often hung, then as now, on a living-room wall as both a reminder and a celebration of spousal and therefore familial responsibilities and obligations, suggesting spiritual and religious values completely absent from the depiction of Jews in the magazine cartoons.

The existence of sweatshops also focuses attention on aspects of Jewish life other than the purely commercial, although the commercial was clearly present as well. Government investigators and newspaper reporters described what they saw and smelled, and it was not pleasant. For example, the principle factory inspector for the Lower East Side said, without taking into account minimal sanitary facilities in overcrowded tenement buildings, that sweatshops "smell as powerfully and poisonously as the wretched toilers themselves" and that immigrant Jews were becoming "a race enfeebled by the strain of terribly long hours, lack of air, and bad sanitary conditions" (qtd. in Bender 2003, 24, 25). Another report asserted that Jews "seem to prefer to live in dirt" (Lennon 1901, qtd. in Bender 2004, 37). Commissioner General of Immigration Frank Sargent was quoted in a *New York Times* article in 1905 stating that, "today, there is an enormous alien population in our larger cities which is breeding crime and disease. . . . Unless something is done . . . it is my fear and belief . . . that the alien population of the country, or rather cities, will constitute a downright peril" ("Are We Facing an Immigrant Peril?" 1905, qtd. in Bender 2004, 5). That peril included the possibility that these immigrants would leave disease-laden germs on the clothing they slaved to make, which could infect "clean-living Americans" (Lennon 1901, qtd. in Bender 2004, 7).

It was also thought that immigrants might become a threat to the American gene pool and that they were undisciplined, too individualistic, and too physically weak to work under factory-regulated conditions. In an interesting application of reverse social Darwinism, it was also assumed that the longer Jews worked in sweatshops, the farther they and their offspring might slide down the human evolutionary scale because of lack of education, impossible working and living conditions, and poor sanitary habits. But the inspectors did not take into account the facts that because Jews had lived and survived in many countries and that in New York many had succeeded in surviving and prospering in the clothing industry, they were, in Darwinian evolutionary terms, very good adapters to the conditions at hand (Hart 2011, xxxi)!

Taken altogether, the varied attitudes of the writers and photographers of this era are important documentary tools to imagine the living and working conditions, educational and recreational opportunities, and aspirations of hundreds of thousands of new

Americans. But some of their reports alluded to the growing sense that Jews, whatever their individual characteristics, were as a group destructive to American values and to the gene pool, that they were biologically inferior and had no place in this country. By the 1890s and most certainly through the first three decades of the twentieth century, these notions became the common cant of bigots. Historian David Gerber observes that around 1900 Jews had to contend with the notion that they were different and alien not simply in "creed and faith, but in physiognomy and even more important in an inner nature or psychology" (1987, 3). Or to say the same thing in language that disparaged sweatshop workers, Jews were unassimilable "inferior immigrants" who, if any were producers rather than parasites, would raise little more than a "crop of pants" ("Studies in American Immigration" 1901, qtd. in Dobkowski 1979, 129).

It is not an exaggeration to say that around the century's turn ethnic and religious fear and hatred had grown more intense in this country as well as in Europe. In one of many articles in the American press on this subject, Henry Cabot Lodge (1850–1924), a leader of the anti-immigration movement, argued in the *North American Review* in 1891 that the number of immigrants from southern and eastern Europe as well as from eastern Asia allowed into the United States should be decreased dramatically. He noted that that the colonial settlers had by and large been from northwestern Europe and thus could easily be assimilated because of the "community of race or language" (30). But in the 1880s, he argued, immigrants from southern Italy and the Austro-Hungarian and Russian Empires were of a different sort. They were often illiterate and unclean, engaged in illegal activities, and worked for wages lower than those of "white" laborers, thus interfering with normal employer–employee relationships (31). In short, they were too alien to be assimilated easily, and therefore quotas were needed. In time, Lodge's concerns led to the immigration-restriction laws passed by Congress in 1924.

But in the same issue of the magazine in which Lodge's article was published, another author singled out Jews among the recent arrivals in a much more positive way, stressing their kindliness (Sanford

1891). And in yet another article, a surgeon in the army, marshalling a huge amount of data, concluded that the death and longevity rates of Jews were better than the rates for virtually all other groups and that they could handle adversity more easily (Billings 1891).

I mention these three articles published in a single issue of a magazine to make the point that although Jews were not universally condemned, they did seem to constitute "a problem." Nevertheless, by the second and third decades of the twentieth century, the various strands of anti-Semitic thought overcame positive comments and analyses in the highly discriminatory, if not to say unhinged, books and articles by figures such as Madison Grant (1916), Charles W. Gould (1920), and Lothrop Stoddard (1920, 1927), who opposed the increasing presence of non-Anglo-Saxon immigrants in America. These authors, it should be noted, were not people on society's fringe. Their works were published by major, mainstream publishers, such as Scribner's.

Among the most notorious books spouting hatred of Jews was the poisonous attack written and illustrated by the printmaker Joseph Pennell, *The Jew at Home: Impressions of a Summer and Autumn with Him*, published in 1892. It recorded his trip to eastern Europe the previous year. His was perhaps the earliest book put out by a mainstream publisher featuring the no-holds-barred, open-hatred-for-Jews discourse that replaced the discreet (by comparison) observations printed earlier. Stating that he would not consider why the eastern European Jew was "the most contemptible specimen of humanity in Europe" or "what makes him dreaded by the peasant" or "hated by the proprietor" or "loathed by people of every religion" or "despised by his fellow-religionists of the better class" or why Jews become "ten times worse" as soon as they leave Russia (6, 8), Pennell nevertheless preceded to excoriate Jews and scatter nasty criticisms throughout his book.

Pennell viewed Jews as an undifferentiated mass, and some of his stereotypical observations were commonplace—for example, that Jews always wanted more of whatever the item or issue of the moment was (1892, 9). To him, they looked consumptive, greasy, and degenerate and suggested "physical inadequacy" (23). In Austro-Hungary,

Jews, in contrast to the clean peasants, lived in filthy and crowded conditions (30). They worked hard, but not with their hands (32), and they were paradoxically also idle (41). "He [the Jew] produces nothing, he lives on nothing, and apparently wants nothing" (41). His sanitary habits were primitive (44). Blaming the victim, Pennell believed that Jews' sense of cleanliness, poverty, and ugliness were their own fault, not "as is usually supposed, forced upon them by Christian persecutors" (63). "They like dirt; they like to herd together in human pigsties" (95). And, of course, the old canard, "They are simply a race of middlemen and money changers" (96).

When in Brody, an Austro-Hungarian community, Pennell admitted that he had never visited a Jewish house of worship and included in his book an illustration of a crowded synagogue interior that calls to mind the witches' scene in *Macbeth* (fig. 53). (The same drawing is also given in a book about his travels published in 1925, where it is titled *Evening Service in a Synagogue. Berditchev. Seen through a Window* [Pennell 1925, 230]. Berditchev is now in north-central Ukraine.) In his illustration, Pennell chose to record a moment in the service when the bema is crowded with seemingly crazed-looking men. At best, it probably seemed disorganized to one familiar with Protestant services, but the Orthodox participants knew exactly the order of the ritual taking place, as they do now. In any event, Pennell's drawing presents a totally different aspect of Jewish ritual than the illustrations in *Century Magazine* in 1882 (see, e.g., fig. 36, p. 99).

Pennell did sympathize minimally with oppressed Jews, but he also sympathized with Hungarians, whom he claimed were sick of their Jews (1892, 7). Jews were bearable as individuals but not as a group (9). What was one to do? "Make him [the Jew] an Englishman or an American, break up his old customs, his clannishness, his dirt and his filth—or he will break you" (10). What Pennell failed to mention was that Jews were then in constant mass flight because of pogroms in eastern Europe and Russia (Sorin 1992, 43–44). As many as fifteen thousand refugees had descended on Brody, their numbers larger than the local population. Obviously, as accommodations grew increasingly limited, living and sanitary conditions grew increasingly

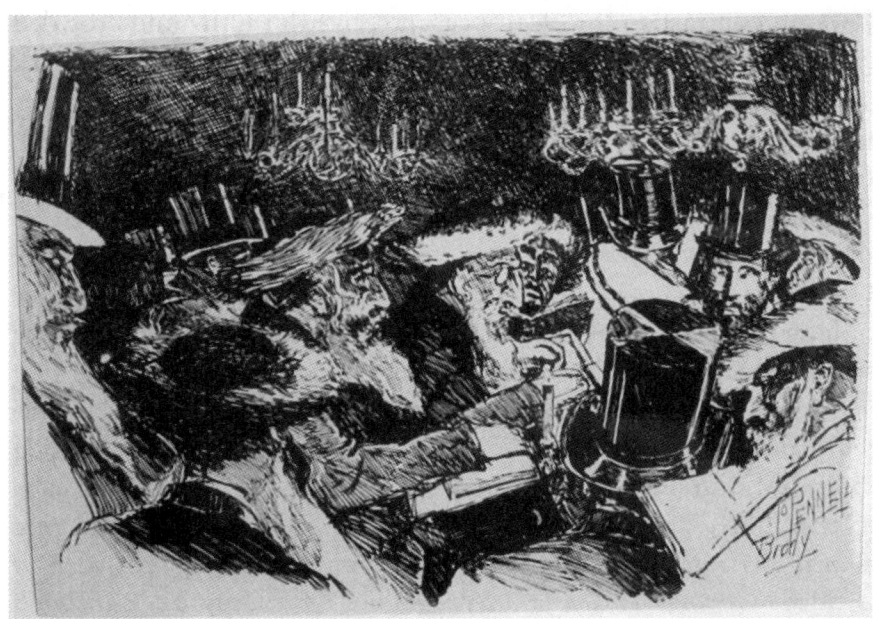

53. Joseph Pennell, *A Synagogue Interior*, from Joseph Pennell, *The Jew at Home: Impressions of a Summer and Autumn with Him* (New York: Appleton, 1892), 45.

intolerable. For Pennell, who lacked minimal empathy, the stereotyped thinking he brought with him was no doubt reinforced by the scenes he saw each day.

His rant against Jews in his later book was even more extreme. He found them to be "some appalling caricature of the human race" (1925, 223). In Transylvania, he "saw and heard that the entire country was in the clutch of these creatures," that they "swarmed like rats in the filthiest houses, or under them," that "the Jew of Russia, Hungry, Galicia, Slovakia, and Polakia is a blight and a plague," that prejudice against them is their fault (223, 224). Of Jews already in America, he said that "we are afraid of them. . . . I do not believe that any sane person who has seen the Jews in Russia and Hungary, and most of those who come to America, can think of anything else about them" (223).

Then Pennell, agreeing with those who insisted that eastern European Jews were descendants of Tarter Jews (a theory discussed later in this chapter), said incoherently: "We want our treatment of Tarter Jews, most aliens, elevators and uplifters, to go back to the great Dark Ages. We are now dictated to by fools, fanatics, and females. The life of the Russian, Polish, Rumanian Jews in all its filth and degradation, can be seen in 'this great Jew City [New York]'" (1925, 224). And then, linking Jews to the Russian Revolution, he stated: "We go on helping them 'idealistically' and ignorantly. Other nations have to endure them—for they are always with us, but never of us, and when the Bolshevist Jew tries to dominate us—remember Russia, for this sort of Jew does not forget and is out today for revenge" (1925, 236). (For similar commentary, see Boyesen 1897, 540; for analysis of such commentary, see Murphy 1964.)

In the art world, Pennell was not alone in his prejudices. Painter, illustrator, sculptor, and writer Frederick Remington (1861–1909) despised virtually all Others. Proud of his English heritage, he called himself an English American and spread his hatred around more broadly than Pennell (Nemerov 1995, 98–99). In addition to disparaging Native Americans, Remington bad-mouthed several immigrant groups openly and with a degree of animosity shocking to twenty-first-century sensibilities. For example, his description of a Native American he observed during a trip west in 1890 is appalling: "I sat near the fire and looked intently at one human brute opposite [a Native American]. He was a perfect animal, so far as I could see. Never was there a face so replete with human depravity, stolid, ferocious, arrogant, and all the rest. . . . As a picture, perfect; as a reality, horrible" (qtd. in McCracken 1947, 66).

At the same time, Remington, clearly an omnidirectional bigot, wrote articles and letters to friends of which the following letter to Poultney Bigelow is an example. Of a long labor strike in Chicago that Remington observed, he wrote, "Just back from Chicago—mob and soldiers—hot stuff. Got to have a big killing in this country. . . . You may have to come out here and help us lick the lice of Central Europe." He continued, calling the striking workers "un-American rats," and "anarchistic foreign trash" for perverting American labor practices (from Remington 1894a, 1894b, and Frederic Remington to Poultney Bigelow, July 27, 1894, in Splete and Splete 1988, 212, all qtd. in Dippie 2001, 96, 20). And just before the start of the Spanish-American War, Remington mentioned that he would be happy to see Spaniards killed rather than Anglo-Saxons (Frederick Remington to Owen Wister, April 1896, in Vorpahl 1972, 221, qtd. in Dippie 2001, 20).

A resident of New Rochelle, a suburb of New York, between 1890 and 1909, Remington observed with horror a shift in its population as the years progressed. He wrote in his diary for January 17, 1908, "New Rochelle is a d— crowded—Jew, Nigger—dry goods clerk European City and I wish I could get out of it. It was formerly a pretty little American Village—so time don't improve things hereabouts" (qtd. in Nemerov 1995, 100). And in a letter to a friend, he wrote, "Jews, Injuns, Chinamen, Italians, Huns—the rubbish of the Earth I hate—I've got some Winchesters and then the massacring begins. I can get my share of 'em, and what's more, I will" (Frederic Remington to Poultney Bigelow, May 1893, in Bigelow 1929, qtd. in White 1968, 109; see also Remington [1979] 1986, 152–59). Such brutal and ruthless words fantasizing murder of minority peoples clearly revealed Remington's disregard for these people as individuals, his view of them instead as a kind of subhuman element intent on destroying his universe. His was a closed mind in which power and force, the bellicose assertion of his belief system, trumped openness, understanding, and interchange.

Among his many illustrations accompanying articles, the three Remington provided for Poultney Bigelow's violently anti-Semitic tirade titled "The Russian and His Jew," published in *Harper's New Monthly Magazine* on December 1, 1893, match Bigelow's contempt. (In his article, Bigelow referred to Pennell's book *The Jew at Home* in favorable terms [603–4].) One of these illustrations, that of Jewish army recruits lined up in formation, suggests that they would not make good soldiers, a point Bigelow emphasized (610–12). Of the two others, Remington stressed the thieving nature of Jews: one shows a group of smugglers apprehended at the frontier, and the other shows Jewish smugglers and refugees in the hands of dragoons. Bigelow had not discussed Jewish smugglers, but Remington, probably believing that eastern European Jews possessed the same level of depravity as the hated American Indians, placed the former in a frontier situation that had no connection to the story.

A similar animus filled Madison Grant's writings. For example, fearful that Anglo-Saxon racial stock would be overwhelmed by immigrants, he found that "the Polish Jew, whose dwarf stature, peculiar mentality, and ruthless concentration on self-interest are being engrafted upon the stock of the nation" (1916, 14). Any offspring of a Jew and a non-Jew would always remain a Jew (16). Immigration had brought the weak, broken, and mentally crippled to America, including "hordes of the wretched, submerged populations of the Polish Ghettos" (80). Horror of horrors, "the man of the old stock . . . [is] to-day being literally driven off the streets of New York by the swarms of Polish Jews. . . . [They] adopt his language, they wear his clothes, they steal his name, and they are beginning to take his women, but they seldom adopt his religion or understand his ideals (81; for counterarguments given in the same period, see Brown 1933, 362). It was as if Grant in 1916 were providing a text for the cartoons of the entirely Jewish street published years earlier (see figs. 3 and 28, pp. 9 and 55).

Lothrop Stoddard, also highly critical of Jews, especially those from eastern Europe, found them to be "about as thoroughly 'alien' to America as it is possible to conceive." He stated further:

> To the mass of Eastern Jews the very phrase "national life" was not only meaningless but positively distasteful. They had never been a nation; nor had they ever formed part of a nation. . . . The only "national life" they knew was that of their hostile Polish and Russian neighbors. . . . Hence the Eastern Jews instinctively hated both nationality and government. This explains why international and radical revolutionary theories have gained such a hold upon the eastern Jewish element in America. (1927, 130–31)

The very important point missed by Stoddard and other like-minded individuals was that, as Daniel Elazar puts it, Jews looked upon politics as a "tool to advance moral ends rather than simply a means for material advancement or the maintenance of traditional ways of life" (1969, 215), meaning, in five words, better working and living conditions. But Stoddard believed that Jews had no concept of national loyalty and that they were susceptible to radical causes. Nor did explanations of their lack of loyalty to the czar based on descriptions of Russian anti-Semitic savagery change his mind (Gross 1891; "The Cause of Civilization 1916, 7; "NO TITLE" in *Life*, June 4, 1903, 510). As one among several scholars has pointed out, "Because Russia's version of capitalism was anti-Semitic in the extreme, modern Yiddish culture . . . had a strong anti-capitalist streak" (Brodkin 1998, 107; see also Dobkowski 1979, 219–23). (For more on Stoddard, see also Murphy 1964; Feingold 1982, 178; and Michaels 1995, 24.)

Two cartoons are pertinent to consider at this point, one in *Puck*, the other in *Der Groyse Kundes* (The Big Stick) (figs. 54 and 55). The former, published in the January 13, 1917, issue of *Puck* (p. 10), shows a Jewish Uncle Sam trying to raise money before a combative audience to aid those European Jews displaced from their homes by the First World War, especially in eastern Europe. At the top left, the arms of Jews reach out for the ten million dollars offered by American Jews to ameliorate conditions abroad. One conclusion might be that Jews were beggars. But at a time when Jewish patriotism was questioned, the cartoon also suggested that Jews were sending American money abroad because of their loyalty to other Jews rather than keeping it America. (One might note an additional reading of this cartoon. Uncle Sam seems aggrieved by the combative audience, perhaps because of public animosity to President Woodrow Wilson's mediation efforts in the European conflict before America declared war on April 6, 1917. Wilson appears behind Uncle Sam.)

Two years earlier, in the February 5, 1915, issue of *Der Groyse Kundes* (no page number), a cartoon titled *In Our Times* (fig. 55)

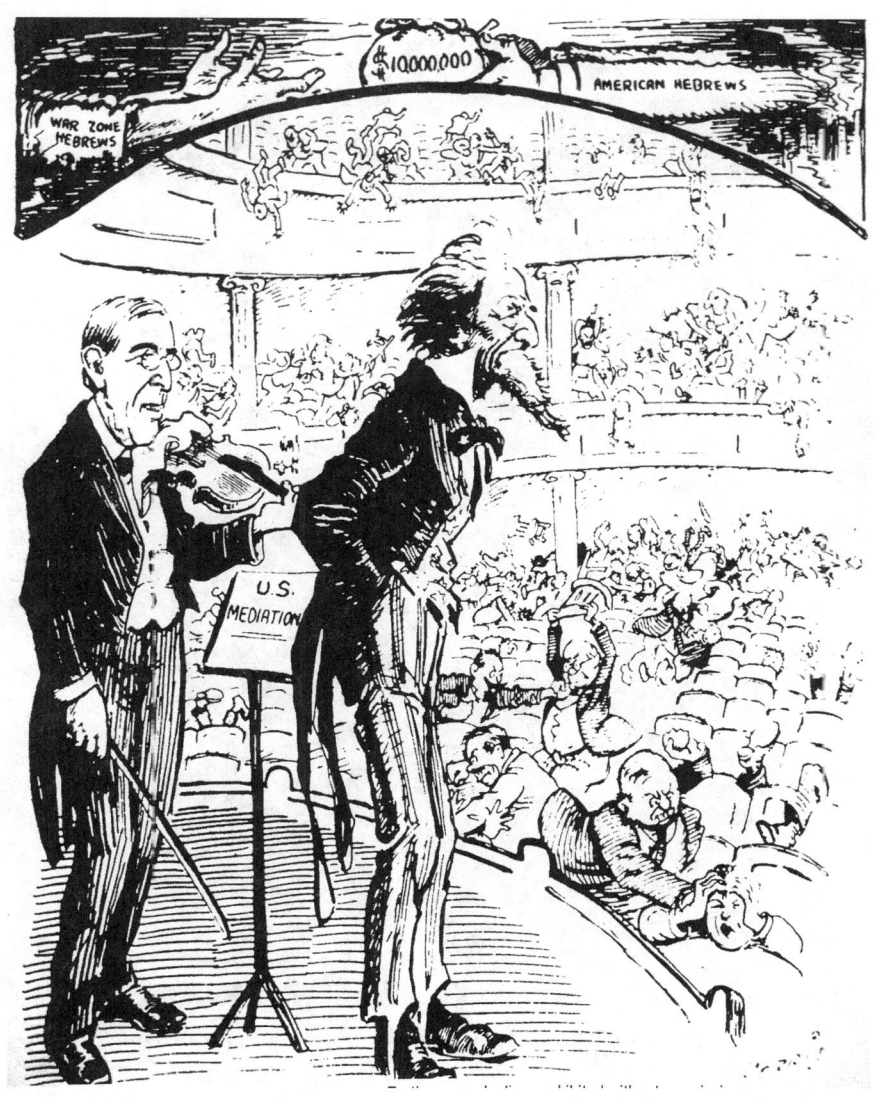

54. Unknown artist, *Untitled*, from *Puck*, January 13, 1917, 10.

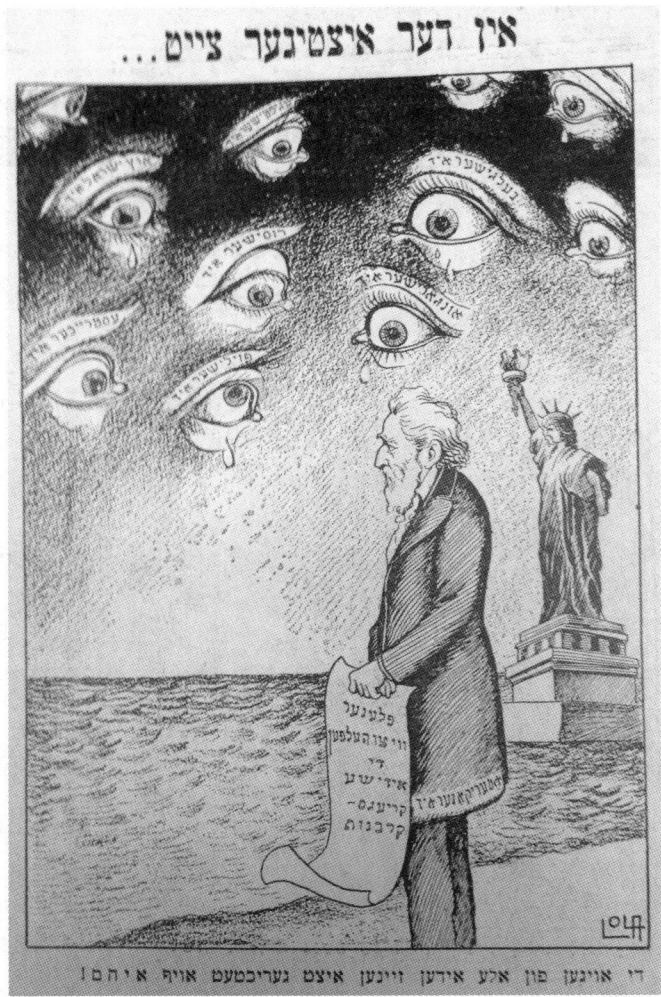

55. Leon Israel (LOLA), *In Our Times*, from *Der Groyse Kundes*, February 5, 1915, page number unavailable.

shows a conflation of Uncle Sam and an elderly Jewish man, standing before the Statue of Liberty and looking out into space. Surreal eyes in the sky looking down at him represent Jews in European countries, each labeled with a different name—"Belgian Jew," "Polish Jew," and so on. The caption at the bottom reads, "The eyes of all Jews are staring at him." The feeling that this cartoon projects is much more sympathetic to homeless refugees and those dislocated by warfare and pogroms, the issue being humanitarian charity not national loyalty.

One scholar has called the years between 1917 and the mid-1920s "probably unmatched in American history for xenophobia and paranoid suspicion" (Dobkowski 1979, 229). If one held such feelings at that time, then these two cartoons of Uncle Sam have some bearing on the matter of Jewish loyalties as it intensified during the First World War, especially after the publication of the Balfour Declaration in England on November 2, 1917, which called for a Jewish homeland in Palestine. Without getting into the very complicated issues of acceptance or rejection of Zionism by American Jews and their responses to the declaration as well as into the problems Zionism generated among non-Jews who did not trust Jewish patriotism, I will mention here only that the matter roughly boiled down to this: During the years around the time of the First World War, one could not be a hyphenated American. One could only be a 100 percent American or a 100 percent something else—in this instance, a 100 percent Zionist (Gibbons 1921, 791–92; Ribuffo 1983, 9; Higham 1984, 165; Hegman 1999, 52–57). On the national level, Jews who supported the establishment of a homeland in Palestine could be accused of challenging the concept of American unity insofar as they could not belong to or identify with two nations (the United States and a Jewish nation). Worse than that, on the international level Zionism as a worldwide movement lent itself to charges of encouraging an international community of Jews intent on dominating the world.

This reasoning was of course fallacious. Helping others in need is considered a basic Jewish value, and obligation for Jews everywhere is indicated in Leviticus and other religious texts. In the secular world, for example, virtually every issue of *The American Hebrew* in 1917 carried articles, or really updates, about pogroms in eastern Europe that served to remind its readers of their obligations. At one point, it was estimated that six hundred thousand Jews were made homeless in Galicia alone and that half of Russian Jews were without means of support because of the First World War ("Among Our Brethren Abroad" 1917; Feingold 1992, 27). One might argue that providing funds for refugees to settle in Palestine as a result of war and pogroms in Europe might be a species of Jewish nationalism, but most Jewish Americans who supported Zionist causes had no intention of moving there. America was their home, and the children of immigrants knew no other home (Zuckerman 1944; Urofsky 1975; Halpern 1979; N. Cohen 2003, 6–7, 64–94).

Nevertheless, Jewish loyalty to America was challenged in at least two ways around the turn of the century—as Jews loyal to their own kind and as political radicals. For example, in 1891, years before the Balfour Declaration, one author stated, "It is impossible that a man should be heartily loyal to two nationalities at once; and so long as a trace of Jewish nationality remains the Jew cannot be a thorough Englishman or American" (Smith 1891, 142). A short article in the June 20, 1918, issue of *Life* revealed a different kind of critical thought, especially at a time of great fear of communism (the "Red Scare") in America. It is about the trial of a Russian-born woman, Mrs. Rose Pastor Stokes, for violating the Espionage Act of 1917. She was an active socialist and an advocate for birth control. She was reported to have said, "Much as I love the Stars and Stripes, I love the red flag better." The article's author asserted that Russian Jews such as Mrs. Stokes "have no real national feeling. They are loyal to Socialism, to Internationalism, to whatever untried ideal of human welfare may be floating in their heads at a given time." Her "chief errand as a sojourner here has been to change what she could of what she found!" (E. S. M. 1918, 983).

The article's author, acknowledging that Jews were above average in intelligence, that they had great power in the newspaper world, and that many loved and worked hard for America, nevertheless insisted that "the Jewish mind is a totally different instrument from other minds that operate in these States. It has a different background, different racial instincts, [and] different traditions" that need constant monitoring. Alluding to President Woodrow Wilson's notion that America's entry into the First World War knitted the country together, the author concluded: "As the knitting goes on[,] shall they [the Jews] be part of the yarn, or are the rest of us to be the yarn and they the needles?" (E. S. M. 1918, 983). This was not a soft or quiet note at the end of the article but an orchestral blast about distrust based on race, religion, place of birth, state of mind, lack of national loyalty—of a piece with assertions by figures such as Madison Grant and Lothrop Stoddard.

Such thoughts must have insulted those Jews who served in the military during the First World War. It hardly mattered to those who were uninformed or had short memories or thought that Jews were uninterested in and perhaps congenitally unfit for military service, but the truth was that more than 150,000 Jewish soldiers served; 4 percent of the armed services were Jews even though Jews were only 3 percent of the general population; 48 percent of these Jewish soldiers were in the infantry, compared to 28 percent of all soldiers in the infantry; and 2,800 Jews died and 10,000 were wounded (Leavitt 1919, 142–43; McCall 1924, 126, 129, 131, 159).

The rejection, toleration, or acceptance of Jews within American culture, then, as revealed in statements by individuals in this chapter and earlier chapters suggests that, whatever else, Jews were seen as threatening and challenging to American social and economic structures but at the same time were looked upon as a business model to emulate. They might either be trusted or remain suspect, depending on the degree to which American values had tempered their acquisitive inclinations and group loyalties and proper cultural conditioning had modified their sense of aggressive self-interest.

4 Art and Politics

A SIMILAR AMBIVALENCE, not to say distrust, permeated the art world, especially when Jews began to assert their presence in that world in the years before and after the First World War. Alfred Stieglitz, photographer, gallerist, and the most important early proselytizer of modernist art in America, presided over the Little Galleries of the Photo-Secession (popularly known as 291 for its Fifth Avenue address) from 1905 to 1917. Artists such as Max Weber and Abraham Walkowitz began creating works with both religious and secular Jewish content and exhibiting them in mainstream venues. And authors such as James Oppenheim (1882–1932), Louis Untermeyer (1885–1977), Waldo Frank (1889–1967), and Paul Rosenfeld (1890–1946) wrote on aspects of American art and culture for magazines such as *The Seven Arts* and *The Dial*.

As in the world of business, the presence of these and other individuals did not go unnoticed or undisputed in the art world. As ideas about the nature of an art for Americans based on American experiences grew stronger through the early years of the twentieth century, questions arose about who was to decide the character of American art and culture and, more to the point, who was *not* to decide its character or challenge traditional Anglo-Saxon hegemony in such matters. For example, in an issue of *The Nation* in 1920, Mary Austin (1920) chided critics who confused New York with America. She singled out Jews as unable to interpret America, incapable of developing an American consciousness in the arts, and uncomprehending of the forces of American life.

In 1923, art critic Royal Cortissoz, usually categorized as an arch traditionalist who despised modernist art, might also be considered, like Mary Austin, in a strongly nationalistic light because his most famous pronouncement reads as if Madison Grant or Lothrop Stoddard could have written it, although there is no evidence of any connection between them.

> There is something in this [contemporary] art situation analogous to what has been so long going on in our racial melting pot. The United States is invaded by aliens, thousands of whom constitute so many acute perils to the health of the body politic. Modernism is of precisely the same heterogeneous alien origin and is imperiling the republic of art in the same way. . . . These movements have been promoted by types not yet fitted for their first papers in aesthetic naturalization—the makers of true Ellis Island art. (18)

And in the January 1930 issue of *The Arts*, art critic Forbes Watson questioned whether Japanese-born Yasuo Kuniyoshi, the American-born but German-identified Lionel Feininger, and the European-born Jews Jules Pascin, Bernard Karfoil, Maurice Sterne, and Max Weber should be included in a show entitled *The All American Nineteen*.

Short of including a full-dress review here of American Scene art, the most popular art movement of the interwar years, the following can be said. Art critic Thomas Craven, a xenophobe and anti-Semite closely associated with that movement, also grew increasingly hostile to artists with foreign-sounding names through the 1920s and early 1930s. He listed in his book *Modern Art* the following artists, not all Jewish, who exhibited in modernist styles: Ben Benn, Louis Bouché, Oscar Bluemner, Andrew Dasburg, Samuel Halpert, Walt Kuhn, Yasuo Kuniyoshi, Gaston Lachaise, Joseph Stella, Maurice Sterne, Max Weber, Abraham Walkowitz, and William Zorach. More venomously than sarcastically because intentionally exclusionary, he called them "scions of our colonial aristocracy" (1934, 315).

Craven's most famous blast concerned Alfred Stieglitz, about whom he said, "Stieglitz, a Hoboken Jew, without knowledge of, or interest in, the historical American background, was—quite apart from the doses of purified art he had swallowed—hardly equipped for the leadership of a genuine American expression: and it is a matter of record that none of the artists whose names and work he has exploited has been noticeably American in flavor" (1934, 312).

I want to digress for a moment in order to consider Stieglitz as an American and as a Jew insofar as Craven attacked him because he was a Jew, as if being Jewish were in and of itself something terrible. What Alice Hyneman Rhine said in 1887 applies here as well as to the depiction of Jews in cartoons discussed in chapter 1: "For centuries it has been impossible to say a man is a Jew without the intention to reproach him for being a Jew" (525). First, concerning Stieglitz as an American, one might respond to Craven's bigoted comments by calling to mind at least two positive statements. Critic C. J. Bulliet said that even though it was dangerous to be an art radical during World War I, Stieglitz was among "a few hardy souls" to carry on (1930, 216). And Elizabeth McCausland (1934) was magnanimous in her appreciation of Stieglitz in her contribution to the collection of praiseworthy essays *America and Alfred Stieglitz: A Collective Portrait*. In her comments, she asked if the American character was forged on the frontier and thus "welded into the spiritual unity by latter-day Americans" (229). She answered in the affirmative, not by suggesting the importance of environmental influences, favored by Craven, but by associating the intellectual and spiritual openness of the frontier attitude with Stieglitz, who favored freedom and liberty "of outward movement, of happiness, free speech, [and] no interference from the next man" (229). To make her point clear, she also connected Stieglitz's attitude to that of such luminaries as Ralph Waldo Emerson, Walt Whitman, and Emily Dickinson as well as to contemporary figures such as John Marin, Georgia O'Keeffe, and Arthur Dove. The kind of freedom they represented, McCausland insisted, "does not sacrifice universal or human truth for an easy nationalistic imprint" (229).

The written record suggests that Stieglitz had only a glancing knowledge of or special interest in Judaism but rather a much stronger interest in associating his thought and the art of the painters he favored with an open, exploratory idea about America. In her biography of Stieglitz, Dorothy Norman relates that he told her that during the 1890s he spent time walking New York's streets. His reactions were not unlike Sadakichi Hartmann's, mentioned in the previous chapter (see Allen 1902). Stieglitz said that he "loathed the dirty streets," but wherever he looked there were fascinating pictures that moved him, "the derelicts, the secondhand clothing shops, the rag pickers, the tattered and the torn." He said, "I felt that the people nearby, in spite of their poverty, were better off than I was" because "there was a reality about them lacking in the artificial world in which I found myself." In the streets, he found himself "in relationship to America" (qtd. in Norman 1973, 39). As an American, not as a Jew. (See also Kroiz 2012, 199 n. 43.)

Stieglitz's concern, then as later, was to find his place in America perhaps in part because the rise of nationalism during and after the First World War prompted many to proclaim themselves as a 100 percent American (Higham 1984, 204–12). As a Jew and the grand proselytizer for modern foreign art in America and therefore always vulnerable to criticism, Stieglitz, whatever else he was, was not a fool. As he said in 1921, "I was born in Hoboken [New Jersey]. I am an American" (Stieglitz [1921] 2000, 226, also qtd. in Norman 1973, 142; see also Baigell 1987, 32). And in 1924 a reporter for *The American Hebrew* noted that Stieglitz was "not consciously Jewish," an observation based on Stieglitz's own assertion: "Please note that I'm not proud of being a Jew—nor am I ashamed of being one, although I confess to no creed except my own" (qtd. in Freed 1924, 305, cited in Kroiz 2012, 221 n. 38).

As for his concern for American art, Stieglitz made several statements and assertions over the years that indicate America was very much on his mind. Bram Dijkstra notes that all of Stieglitz's activities after the opening of the Little Galleries in 1905 "were centered on his search for an art which would express itself in terms of the native context" (1969, 94). Stieglitz wrote, "I had been thinking of America constantly in the days before the war [First World War]. What was

'291' but a thinking of America?" (Stieglitz 1940–41, qtd. in Dijkstra 1969, 94).

In a letter to Paul Rosenfeld in 1923, Stieglitz wrote that he wanted to encourage an American art "without that damned French flavor. . . . That's why I'm really fighting for Georgia [O'Keeffe]. She *is* American. So is [John] Marin. So am I. Of course by American I mean something much more comprehensive than is usually understood" (qtd. in Greenough and Hamilton 1983, 212). To that end, he founded the Intimate Gallery in 1925 (1925–29), which replaced the Little Galleries of the Photo-Secession (1905–17), to concentrate his attention on the art of seven Americans—Marin, O'Keeffe, Arthur Dove, Charles Demuth, Paul Strand, Marsden Hartley, and himself (Hoffman 2011, 172). And in the announcement for an exhibition of Marin's work in 1927, Stieglitz wrote: "The Intimate Gallery is dedicated to an Idea and is an American Room" (qtd. in Norman 1973, 169).

Stieglitz is recorded to have said on April 21, 1926, "What I am doing here is to ask America, in the name of America, whether there is no place for her own" (qtd. in Seligmann 1966, 77). In a letter to the collector Duncan Phillips, Stieglitz clearly stated: "I have a passion for America and I feel, and have always felt, that if I could not believe in the worker in this country, not in the imitator of what is European, but in the originator, in the American himself, digging from within, pictures for me would have no significance" (qtd. in Newman 1981, 31).

And, finally, Stieglitz's efforts were gratefully acknowledged by artists. As Georgia O'Keeffe said, "His battle was principally for the American artist-photographer, sculptor, painter. In his time, the French were of much more interest than the Americans, but he thought that something of interest and importance must come out of America" (qtd. in Stieglitz 1978, not paginated).

Juxtaposing Craven's slanderous comment with Stieglitz's statements calls to mind Mark Twain's observation in 1899: "You [Jews] will always be by ways and habit and predilections substantially strangers—foreigners—wherever you are, and that will probably keep the race prejudice against you alive" (528). Or as Saul Bellow bluntly stated around one hundred years later, "As a Jew you are also an American, but somehow you are also not" (2000, 2, qtd. in N. Cohen 2003, 23). And Paul Krugman noted in 2016, "A rueful old line from my own heritage says that if you should happen to forget that you are Jewish, someone will remind you" (2016a, A27).

Craven's comments about a single individual, Stieglitz, are among the most straightforward of all those explicit and implicit comments previously mentioned. Whatever other anti-Semitic, antiurban, and antiforeign prejudices Craven harbored, these comments could not be held in check when his national, racial, religious community's century-long cultural control was challenged. Let me give one hypothetical example of what I mean. With respect to one term from the parlance of racism, *white privilege*, one can imagine an individual of the majority culture assuming without any forethought that his or her thoughts and actions are entirely normal and think or say them without any self-awareness that they are insulting examples of "majority privilege."

As noted elsewhere, Jewish artists had presented images of Jews in political, social, and religious scenes in the English- and Yiddish-language Jewish presses since the 1880s and in Lower East Side art galleries since the turn of the century (Baigell 2015, 61–82). But artists such as Max Weber and Abraham Walkowitz, by the early years of the twentieth century, had also become part of the mainstream art world, exhibiting modernist works in 291 and creating Jewish genre and religious scenes that might have been seen by both cartoonists and the general public (Norman 1973, 234).

Walkowitz especially made many prints and drawings of Lower East Side subjects. In comparison to works by cartoonists published in *Puck* and the other humor magazines, Walkowitz's work included portraits of individuals with normal-size noses, some of whom seemed fatigued, perhaps after putting in long hours in a sweatshop or standing behind a pushcart, but who invariably look alert, intelligent, and serious (fig. 56). Nor did Walkowitz create demeaning, stereotypical studies of individuals who sell goods on street corners;

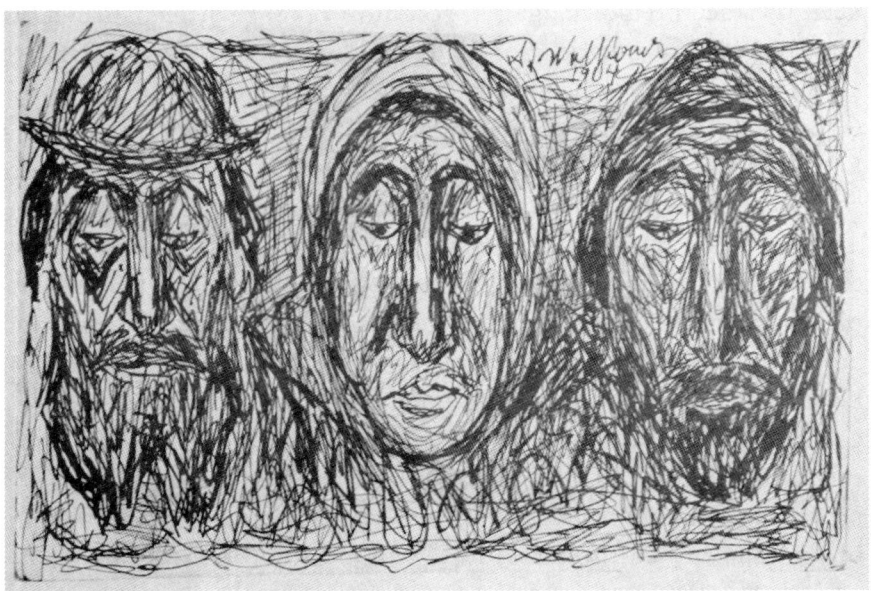

56. Abraham Walkowitz, *Untitled*, 1904, from Abraham Walkowitz, *Ghetto Motifs* (New York: Machmadin Art Editions, 1946), not paginated.

for instance, contrast his view of such individuals (fig. 57) with the stereotyped figure in *Consistency* by Joseph Keppler (fig. 31, p. 61). And like the illustrations in the article on Jewish life in New York in *The Century* in 1892 (Wheatley 1892a, 1892b; figs. 35–37, pp. 98–100), Jacob Riis's photograph of a living-room sweatshop (fig. 52, p. 121), and Jacob Epstein's illustrations for Hapgood's book *The Spirit of the Ghetto* ([1902] 1963) (figs. 40–43, pp. 104–7), Walkowitz acknowledged the centrality of religion and the importance of family coherence in Jewish life in his drawings of old men holding Torah scrolls tightly to their breasts and walking with their children or grandchildren (figs. 58–59).(For more of and on Walkowitz's work, see Walkowitz 1946a, 1946b, and Weinberg 1917, 410, 426.)

During these early years of the new century, Weber also emphasized these everyday concerns within the Jewish community when he drew rabbinic figures for Jewish publications and, by 1920, made paintings that included rabbis and others involved in religious rituals.

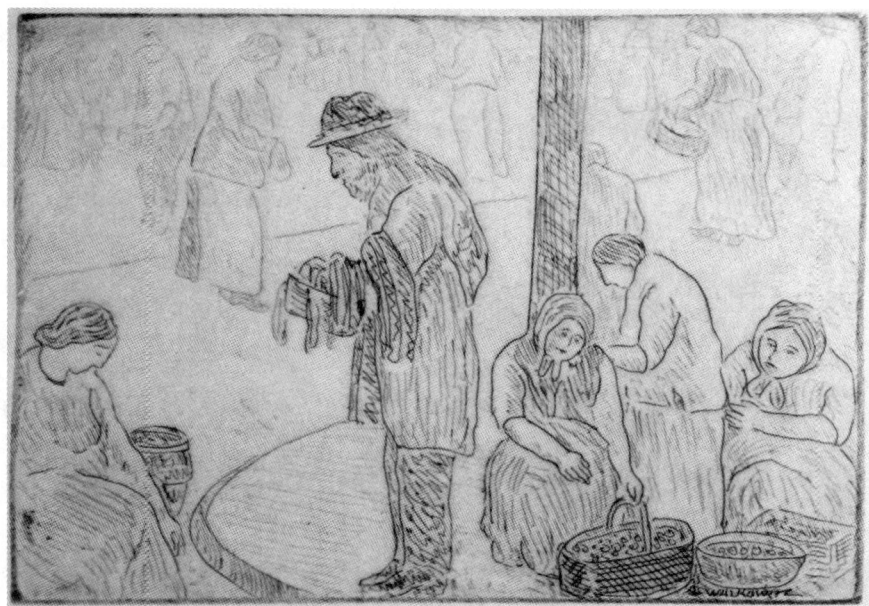

57. Abraham Walkowitz, *Untitled*, n.d., from Abraham Walkowitz, *Ghetto Motifs* (New York: Machmadin Art Editions, 1946), not paginated.

Of Weber's religious paintings, mainstream critics wrote about the culture they represented without condescension or hostility but rather with evident sympathy and curiosity (Baigell 2000). Illustrations Weber created for *Shriftn* (Writings) alternated between secular and religious images. The two shown here (fig. 60) are a portrait bust of a religious man and a portrait of a group of three men studying their holy books.

The portrait, its Cubist-style overtones evident, probably depicts a rabbi. Weber imbued the figure's face with sadness because of his belief, recorded perhaps around this time (the early 1920s), that the rabbi is a "symbol of spiritual leaders whose dignity, faith, and moral conviction surmounted pain and bitterness throughout history" (from an article in the Weber Clipping File, New York Public Library).

The second illustration shows three men, perhaps life-long study partners, a tradition continued to this day. The prayer shawl covering

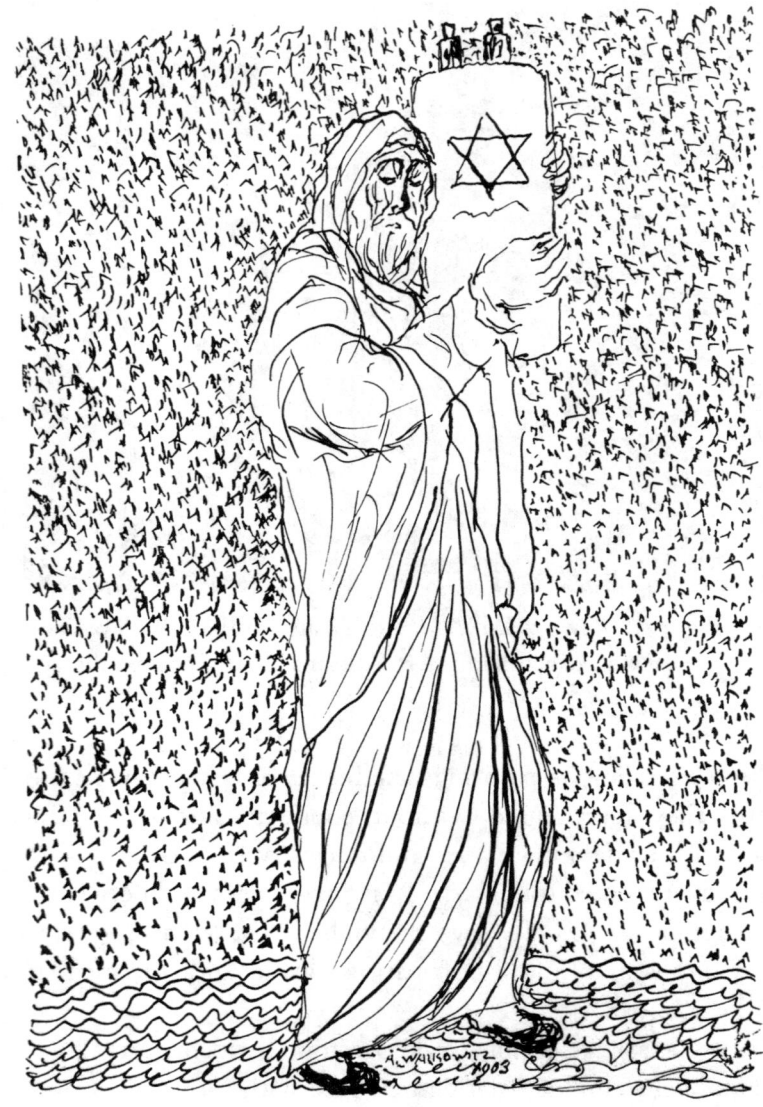

58. Abraham Walkowitz, *Untitled*, 1903, from Abraham Walkowitz, *Ghetto Motifs* (New York: Machmadin Art Editions, 1946), not paginated.

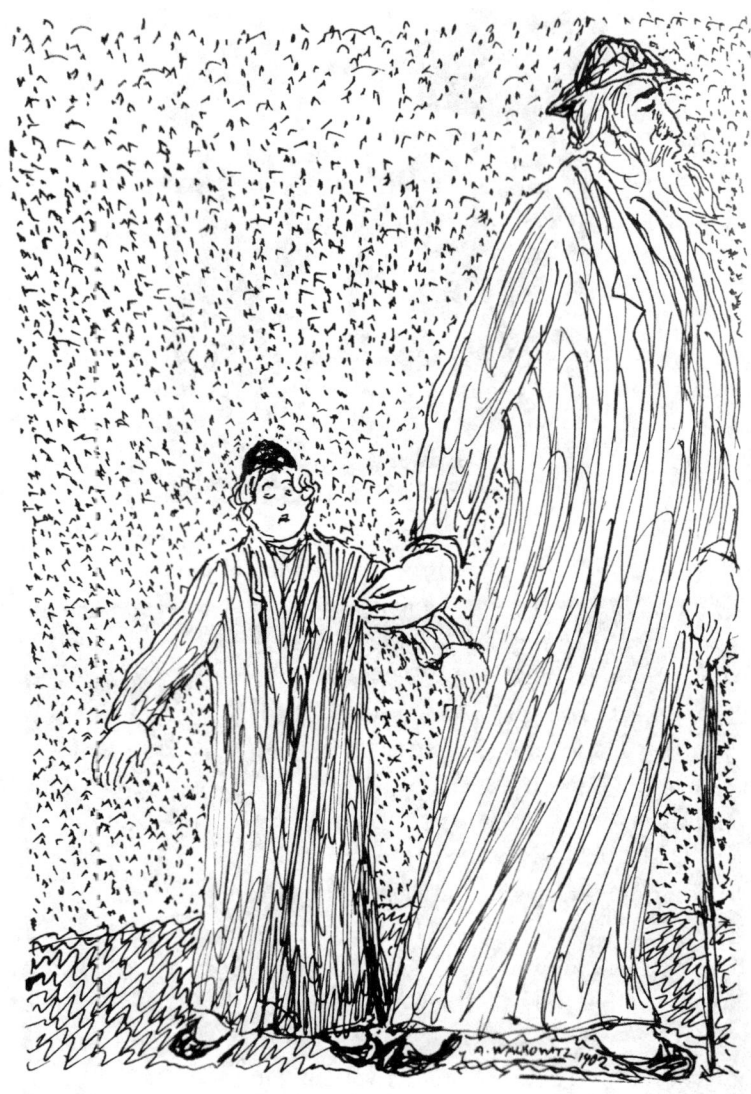

59. Abraham Walkowitz, *Untitled*, 1902, from Abraham Walkowitz, *Ghetto Motifs* (New York: Machmadin Art Editions, 1946),
not paginated.

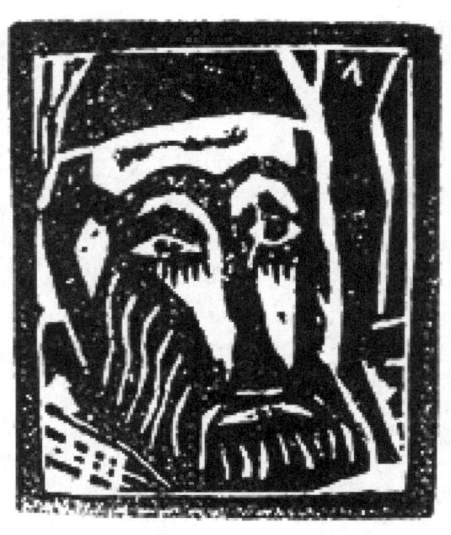

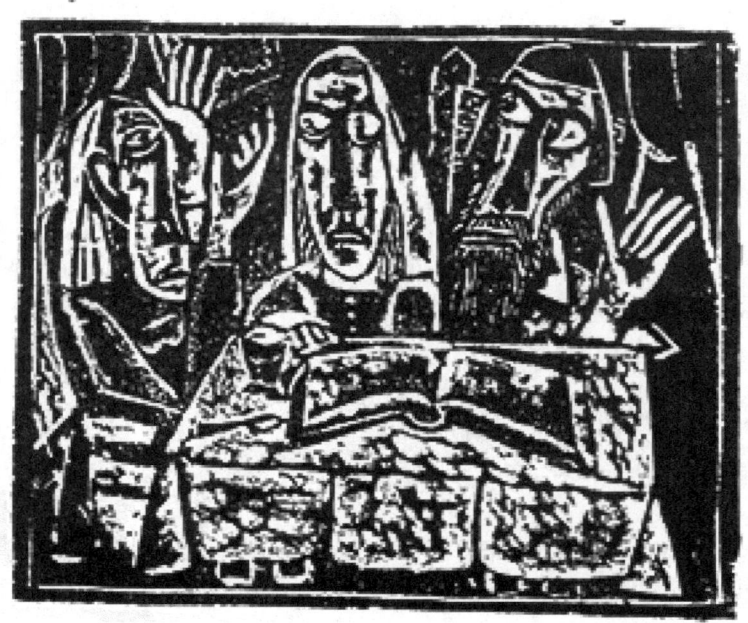

60. Max Weber, *Untitled* and *Untitled*, 1921, separate woodcuts in *Shriftn* 7, not paginated.

the central figure's head indicates that he is studying the religious texts with a sense of great piety. The men gesticulate, which is of no particular religious significance but which reinforces the idea that study is part of an oral tradition and often results in animated conversations as the men challenge each other's interpretations of passages in order to arrive at a better understanding of the text in question.

In the non-Jewish art world, negative images of Jews all but disappeared, but one major work by Thomas Hart Benton (1889–1975) requires comment here. The work in question includes a single figure in a panel in his mural series *The Arts of Life in America* (fig. 61), made for the Whitney Museum of American Art in 1932 (and now in the New Britain Museum of American Art in New Britain, Connecticut). Together with his writings, this work acts as a summary of

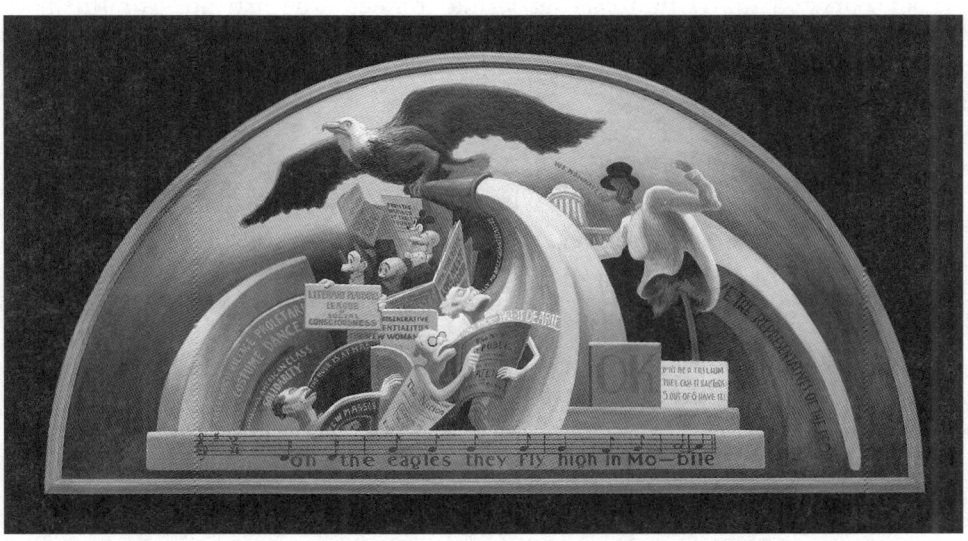

61. Thomas Hart Benton, *Political Business and Intellectual Ballyhoo*, 1932. Egg tempera and oil glaze on linen, 56½ × 113 inches. Courtesy of the New Britain Museum of American Art, Stanley Fund 1966.05. Art © T. H. Benton and R. B. Benton Testamentary Trusts, UMB Bank Trustee. Licensed by VAGA, New York, NY.

the various negative attitudes toward Jews in the early decades of the twentieth century.

The figure in question is the man behind the masthead of the Communist-controlled magazine *New Masses* in the lower left. Benton certainly knew that this figure, plainly and simply a gratuitous insult to Jews and placed in a prominent position in a mural intended for a New York museum, would be seen by many people. Recent comments about this figure have been largely muted. Art historian James M. Dennis refers to him as "a curly haired, bewhiskered, hook-nosed, and chinless radical bearing the Communist Party's *New Masses*. . . . From his mouth there issues the words 'THE HOUR IS AT HAND'" (1998, 55; for other comments, see also Doss 1991, 95, and Mazow 2012, 56). And although not referring directly to Benton's mural, Karal Ann Marling inadvertently links the image of the man to anti-Semitic cartoons by pointing out that in general Benton stereotyped many figures that would reflect "the attitudes of [his] audience" and to that audience's shared ideas (1982, 15).

Why would Benton have included such a caricatured figure in his mural? He completed the mural about two years before he got into public arguments with left-wing artists, so the figure could not have been painted as petty payback for such arguments. According to Benton's latest biographer, the artist wanted to contrast the "rigid worldview of hard-lined radicals, represented by the Jew," with "the busy goings-on of America. But his meaning backfired, as the caricature reveals his narrowness of mind rather than an appreciation of the myriad cultures that make up America" (Wolff 2012, 228). We might ask: What is the connection between rigid radicals and busy goings-on in America? Why a hateful caricature? Why pick a Jew to symbolize rigid thinking? Were all Jews rigid and part of the radical Left? Were there any left-wing Christians who might have been equally radical and equally rigid in their thinking? Or was the usual association of Jews with radical politics made because it was believed their loyalty to socialism and internationalism surpassed any national feeling for America? Or perhaps the figure reflected Benton's true attitude toward Jews. Some answers can be suggested by Benton's own writings, aspects of which might also help explain the cartoonists' hostility in the late nineteenth and early twentieth centuries.

As mentioned earlier, Jews had to contend with yet another stigma—the growing belief that they were descendants of middle-Asian peoples and therefore biologically mongrel and incapable of being assimilated into the American polity. In *Re-forging America* (1927), Lothrop Stoddard made certain to assert this "fact" three times: "East European Jews are not Semitic Hebrews but are descended from West Asiatic stock akin to the Armenian or from Central Asiatic (Mongoloid) folk—the Khazars" (121); Ashkenazic as opposed to Sephardic Jews came from the Caucasus and Armenia about one thousand years ago (128–30); modern Polish and Russian Jews are chiefly of West Asiatic Armenoid stock and also of Central Asiatic Khazar blood. This racial makeup, Stoddard argued, is "very alien to America" (130).

And this attitude became a staple of anti-Semitic rants. For example, in the 1880s a typical anti-Semitic article would describe— or, really, demonize—individuals for their shortcomings in character, morality, social graces, and aggressiveness, especially if they wanted to run for public office (see, e.g., "Jews in Congress" 1883). When nominated for the Supreme Court in 1916, Louis Brandeis (1856–1941) was vilified and thought unfit to be appointed because of his biological heritage (Gossett 1963, 207–8; Dobkowski 1979, 220; Dinnerstein 1994, 68–69). In a letter to Massachusetts senator Henry Cabot Lodge—as mentioned in chapter 3, a leader of the immigration-restriction movement—his nephew Ellerton James wrote that Brandeis "is a Hebrew and, therefore of Oriental race and his mind is an Oriental mind, and I think it very probable that some of his ideas of what were fair might not be the same as those of a man possessing an Anglo-Saxon mind" (qtd. in Todd 1964, 68–69, and Dinnerstein 1994, 69; on author Owen Wister's negative comments about Brandeis, see also Gossett 1963, 207). James's comments are another example of what the historian Samuel P. Hays termed "a desperate racial vindictiveness which stressed . . . race superiority"

(1957, 102). It is also worth noting here that in a planned official photograph of all of the justices in 1917, Justice James Clark Reynolds refused to sit next to Brandeis because he was Jewish (Millhiser 2015, 128).

The relevance to the art world of attitudes such as that described by Hays might well have influenced Benton's and Craven's hostility in the 1920s to the presence of many left-wing Jewish artists in New York and especially in the 1930s to the artists' Communist-controlled organizations, such as the John Reed Club (1929–35) and the American Artists' Congress (1935 to the early 1940s). Benton's words are relevant here. He found communism to be a monolithic system, universalist, internationalist, and absolutist—"nothing but a new oriental religion good only for people used to an authoritarian society" (1969, 171). Further, he did not seem to differentiate one artist from the next or acknowledge any variation of opinion about or commitment to communism (Baigell 2001b).

According to Benton, Karl Marx was rigid, not a compromiser. He was a German and thus authoritarian; he was also a Jew who was "addicted to ancient Jewish apocalyptic dreams." Benton insisted that "Marx was the savior of the people in Semitic or Asiatic style but he was to save them German style by authority—authority of the proletariat. Marx was 'the leader,' the Messiah of his savior cult." Absolute dictatorship by himself and his group was regarded as essential (Benton 1937, 7–9; Benton n.d.a).

At face value, such comments seemed to mark the limit of Benton's thinking in the 1930s. Marx, as we know, was not Jewish but of Jewish ancestry, so he could not escape his tainted biological heritage. Nor could he escape the German environmental heritage in which he grew up. In Anglo-Saxon America, then, according to Anglo-Saxon Americans, Jews who followed Marx were unable to grasp the principles of democracy and would therefore always be considered permanent aliens, regardless of citizenship.

In an undated manuscript that Benton probably wrote in the 1960s in language reminiscent of Stoddard's, he determined that Jews were conditioned by their background to make "radical changes in our social order" (Benton n.d.b). He obviously had consistently held this view over a lifetime, arguing in the late 1930s that because New York City was home to many Europeans, who brought their European ideas with them, artists in that city could easily mix "political and aesthetic doctrines drawn from middle European philosophizing on the function of the proletariat in the cultural and political world of the future." He believed that New York "harbor[ed] the attenuated, political, artistic, and economic ideas of Europe" ([1937] 1983, 262)—ideas that were anathema to him.

Remembering the heyday of American Scene art, Benton could not help but mention that artists of the Communist-controlled John Reed Club "couldn't paint anything *real* about America because their European-derived Communist preconceptions wouldn't permit real experiences of American situations," meaning rural and pioneer situations dating back to the eighteenth century ([1937] 1983, 169, 171). According to this line of reasoning, Jews were rigid and, as Benton no doubt believed, were best visualized like the man in the Whitney mural as staunch left-wingers who followed Marx.

As pointed out earlier in this chapter, Lothrop Stoddard thought in a similar manner when he determined that "radical revolutionary theories . . . gained such a hold upon the eastern Jewish element in America" because they experienced Polish and Russian hostility (1927, 130).

Benton's figure in the mural was of a piece as well with the written contents of anti-Semitic publications of the period. Surprisingly, no such illustrations appeared in the venomous periodical *Social Justice* (1936–42), presided over by Father Charles E. Coughlin (1891–1979). Between 1940 and 1942, for example, Coughlin published 102 anti-Jewish articles but no hostile illustrations (Dinnerstein 1994, 132).

Oddly enough, however, such stereotypical figures appeared from time to time in the Yiddish- and English-language Jewish press. One such very popular but apolitical figure was the short and stocky Gimpl Beinish, everybody's favorite uncle who brought people together in the cartoon series *Gimpl Beinish der Shadchen* (Gimpl Beinish the Matchmaker), created by Samuel Zagat and published in *Warheit* (Truth) from 1912 to 1919 (Zagat 1972, 7). And through the 1920s and early 1930s, obvious Jewish types appeared in Communist-controlled publications, especially in the Yiddish-language daily *Frayhayt* (Freedom, 1922–88) and the monthly *New Masses* (1926–48). The artist William Gropper (1897–1977) is most closely associated with these images. Benton, then, was not alone in his portrayal of the leftist as a caricatured Jew.

Why Jewish cartoonists and writers would caricature their religious cohorts so unfavorably is an open question. Even Freud had no answers: "The occurrence of self-criticism as a determinant may explain how it is that a number of the most apt jokes . . . have grown up on the soil of Jewish popular life. They are stories created by Jews and directed against Jewish characteristics. . . . I do not know whether there are many other instances of a people making fun to such a degree of its own character" (1960, 111–12).

Given the issues of assimilation and political preferences at the time, literary historian Louis Harap suggests one possible answer to this question. He makes a distinction between those Jews who wish to distance themselves from all Jews because of their desire to identify with the majority culture and those Jews who dislike certain groups of Jews because of their social class and political differences (1987, 152, 156). In the 1920s and 1930s, political differences were more important, and cartoons presented, according to Charles Press, "the social (including religious), political, and economic leaders as inhuman monsters while conjuring up pictures of the atrocities that flow from their malevolence. The rules and symbols of that system are to be regarded with contempt at every opportunity, while those who oppose it, domestic or foreign, are feted as heroes" (1981, 136).

Those pilloried in *Frayhayt* and *New Masses* were non-Communist Jewish leftists as well as Zionists. The irony is that at the same time that anti-Semites were condemning Jews as Communists, Bolsheviks, and un-American radicals, Communist Party stalwarts were attacking certain Jewish union officials in publications, at lectures, and in meetings as not Communist enough and for not following party policies, which they felt weakened and undermined the Communist movement. At this far-left end of the political spectrum, political motivation also trumped religious loyalty by pitting Jew against Jew in battles that ultimately nobody won. By my imperfect count, Gropper created more cartoons of this political type than any other artist in the 1920s and 1930s, those of the late 1920s being especially vicious.

A child of the sweatshops, Gropper opposed rapacious bosses and businessmen, and as early as 1919 he began to make "proletarian cartoons" (Salpeter [1937] 1973). Although he and others asserted that he never joined the Communist Party, he was certainly sympathetic to its aims, became involved in its affairs, and created many cartoons that followed the party line (M. Epstein 1959, 228). Gropper became a staff cartoonist for *Frayhayt* in 1924 and was a founder of *New Masses* in 1926. He visited the Soviet Union and attended the First World Plenum of the International Bureau of Revolutionary Literature in Kharkov in the Soviet Union in 1927, upon his return writing a letter to a friend in which he stated that "if the delegates to all countries don't go back with revolution in their hearts, then there must be something I cannot understand" (William Gropper to Kalman Marmor, 1927, qtd. in Strauss 2004, 255). He was a founder of the John Reed Club in 1929, a party-controlled organization of artists; he attended the Second World Plenum in 1930 as one of six John Reed Club delegates; and he signed the manifesto of the International Bureau of Revolutionary Artists to promote class struggle and proletarian culture (Aaron 1961, 236; Gahn 1966, 53, 54, 61, 64, 66, 126–27; Salpeter [1937] 1973, 199; Phagan 2000, 216, 219–20). In short, whatever reservations Gropper might have held about Communist Party activities in America or in the Soviet Union, he was involved with and trusted by both.

A somewhat baffling point concerns Gropper's cavalier attitude toward those he mocked and pilloried. He was evidently not as politically aware as his cartoons seemed to indicate, nor, it is said, could he read Yiddish. He presumably was responding to ideas and suggestions of others on the *Frayhayt* staff, especially Paul Yuditch for labor affairs, Paul Novick and Melech Epstein for political materials, and

Moishe Katz for Jewish themes (M. Epstein 1959, 228; Gahn 1966, 53–55). But we will probably never know the extent to which Gropper's cartoons expressed his own feelings or the feelings of those who advised him. There is no scholarly monograph on Gropper's entire career, although two appreciative monographs (Freundlich 1968; Lozowick 1983) and two dissertations (Gahn 1966; Phagan 2000) have been written on aspects of his work. None of the authors, however, breaks down Gropper's Jewish works (cartoons, prints, and paintings) into their three chronological periods: those hostile to Jewish businessmen as well as to religious and anti-Communist figures (1921–c. 1935); those hostile to Hitler and sympathetic to the victims of the Holocaust (c. 1930–c. 1950); and those devoted to Jewish genre scenes (c. 1950–1977), often *Fiddler on the Roof* and eastern European in tone and subject matter.

Needless to say, Gropper's cartoons of the late 1920s and early 1930s followed Communist Party concerns and should be considered in context with certain events at the time. In 1924, the Fifth Communist International (Comintern) World Congress called for the capture of labor unions, and in 1928, at the Sixth Comintern World Congress, the so-called Third Period was announced, according to which certain union leaders and others on the left such as socialists of any stripe and Social Democrats were considered to be counterrevolutionary or social fascists or both, the latter term never being clearly defined. The first extended analysis of the leftist anti-Communist policies of various organizations took place at the Tenth Plenum in October 1929. These organizations included the American Federation of Labor and the International Ladies Garment Workers Union. Throughout the latter half of the 1920s and into the early 1930s, then, American cartoonists such as Gropper were given free rein to attack those union leaders, many of whom were Jewish, who disagreed with party diktats.

In 1935, however, at the Seventh Comintern World Congress, the Popular Front was instituted: its purpose—to invite all organizations, including the Socialist Party, to form a united front and join in the fight against war and fascism, meaning Hitler's Nazi regime in

Germany. As a result, the Popular Front replaced the Third Period's program of revolutionary activity. Cartoon subjects that pilloried the non-Communist Left were no longer acceptable ("On the Immediate Tasks of the CUSA" 1935; Gahn 1966, 94–99; Pells 1973, 293–99; Klehr 1984, 11–17; Phagan 2000, 232–67).

Looking back at the Third Period, it is difficult to parse precisely what was on the minds of many Jewish leftists concerning Judaism. The Communist Party emphasized union organizing in order to strengthen the party and played down ethnic issues. Yet it also sponsored Yiddish-language organizations, and Jewish members certainly spoke Yiddish, among other eastern European languages, to each other. By whatever means of self-justification, they wanted to maintain a Yiddishist secular culture as part of promoting a universal proletarian culture. This meant attacking Jewish religious institutions (Baigell 2015, 90–91). Rabbis were accused of "poisoning the minds of working class children," and Jewish capitalists were thought capable of acting like Germans under Hitler's rule by harming Jews if it were in their interests to do so (qtd. in Sokolsky 1935, 27; see also Gerber 1987, 43).

However the "enemy" was rationalized in the Communist press, Gropper attacked members of the non-Communist Left and business figures by freely associating them with religion and capitalism. His cartoon *Capital Embraces Religion* (1934) not only reveals contempt for both religion and rapacious capitalist Jewish businessmen but also suggests their close relationship (fig. 62). The words *Simchas Torah* appear above the obese man who holds a Torah scroll and a bag of money. Simchas Torah is the holiday that marks the end of the annual reading of the Torah and is usually accompanied by a celebration that includes members of the congregation dancing with a Torah scroll. Gropper might have intended to show a rapacious, prosperous businessman who wants to believe that God rather than shady business practices grants him wealth or that wealth buys religious sanctification. Whatever Gropper intended, a person who dances with a Torah scroll does so not to celebrate wealth but to show piety, love, and reverence for the Torah, the principle text of Judaism. Gropper's

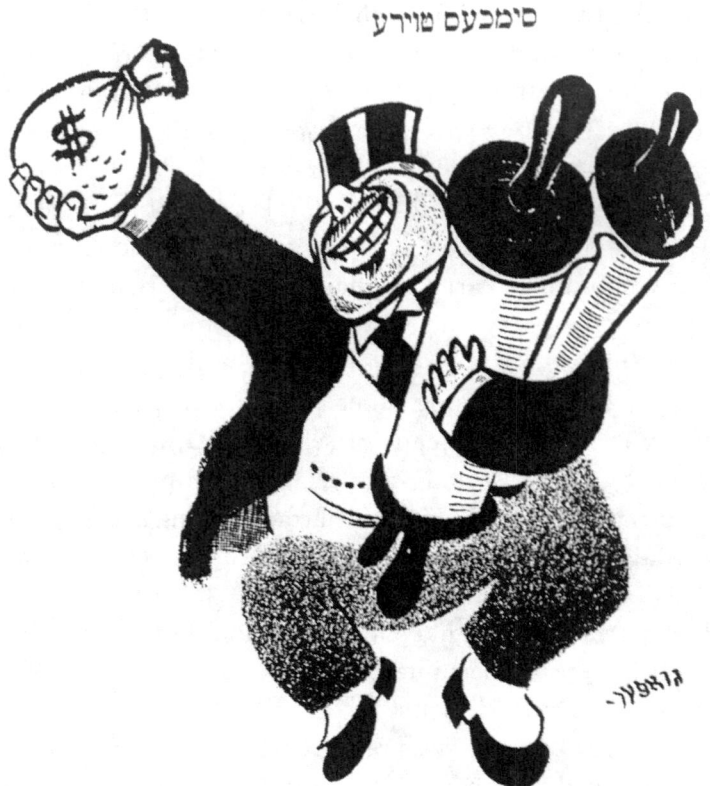

"Capital Embraces Religion." by William Gropper. Der Apikeures (1934).

62. William Gropper, *Capital Embraces Religion*, from *Der Apikeures*, 1934. Reprinted in Peter Buhle, "Jews and American Communism: The Cultural Question," *Radical History Review* 23 (Spring 1980): 19. © Estate of William Gropper. Courtesy of ACA Galleries, New York.

ecstatic dancer seems instead to be an offspring of the fat Jewish businessman in the cartoon *Vulgar Display* from the February 21, 1894, issue of *Puck* (fig. 63). The businessman's friend, Mr. Rosenbaum, says, "So hellup me! How Goldstein worships der almighty dollar! Shoost look at dot sofa!" At least the older cartoonist did not connect Jewish businessmen with religious practices.

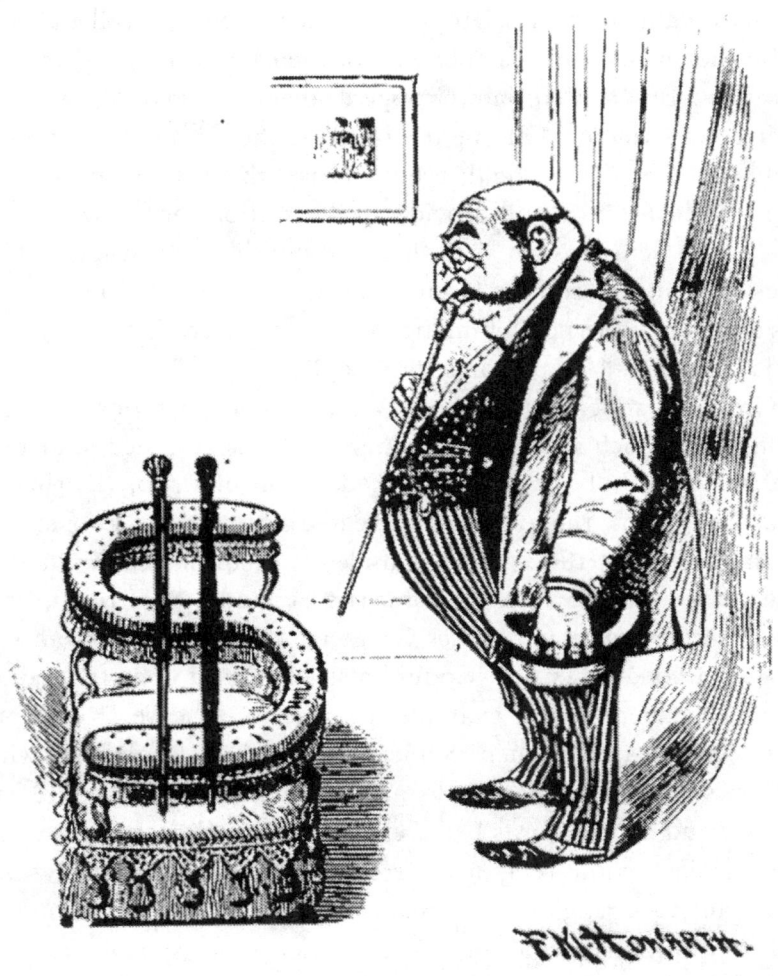

VULGAR DISPLAY.

Rosenbaum — So hellup me! How Goldstein worships
der almighty tollar! Shoost look at dot sofa!

63. F. K. Hovarth, *Vulgar Display*, from *Puck*, February 21, 1894, 3.

One might infer that Gropper meant to condemn all rich Jewish businessmen in his cartoon. If so, then his ideological blinkers were as narrow as Benton's. Gropper, however, could be even more outrageously vicious. On one occasion—although probably on others as well—he could equal, even surpass, the animosity of earlier magazine cartoonists and provide an illustration for the worst fears held by anti-Semites such as Lothrop Stoddard: a Polish Jew holding a sack of coins and smiling lasciviously at the American businessman he is crushing underneath him (fig. 64). On the victor's clothing is the ironic statement "A handsome [or nice] Polish Jew."

Gropper, at least since 1919, had created cartoons attacking union leaders such as Samuel Gompers (1850–1924), the founder and longtime leader of the American Federation of Labor. During the 1920s and 1930s, the artist often created scurrilous cartoons about Abraham Cahan (1860–1951), founder and editor of *Forvitz* (Forward) from 1887 to 1946, and Morris Sigman (1880–1931), president of the International Ladies Garment Workers Union from 1923 to 1929, among other anti-Communist leftist and nonleftist editors and labor leaders. A few examples provide some sense of Gropper's attitude toward these men. Some of his many cartoons in which they are subjected to his attacks are composed of single figures, the captions and added words being essential to catch Gropper's intent. Some invoke obvious religious references; others are secular in theme but might have religious references obvious to Jews. The multifigured compositions containing narrative elements also need texts and labels to explain Gropper's intentions and meanings.

In a cartoon in *Frayhayt* for July 10, 1927 (p. 10), condemning Morris Sigman's use of nonunion labor, Gropper shows Sigman as a carny barker calling attention to the freak show at his amusement park in Iowa, where Sigman had a home (fig. 65) (M. Epstein 1950–53, 2:139; Gahn 1966, 98 n. 68). The text at the top reads, "Marisky [a Russian diminutive for 'Morris'] says buy cheap, everything at my place is cheap, books, hot dogs, workers, hot mamas, and more, and more, and more." On the left is a "hot mama," and on the right is

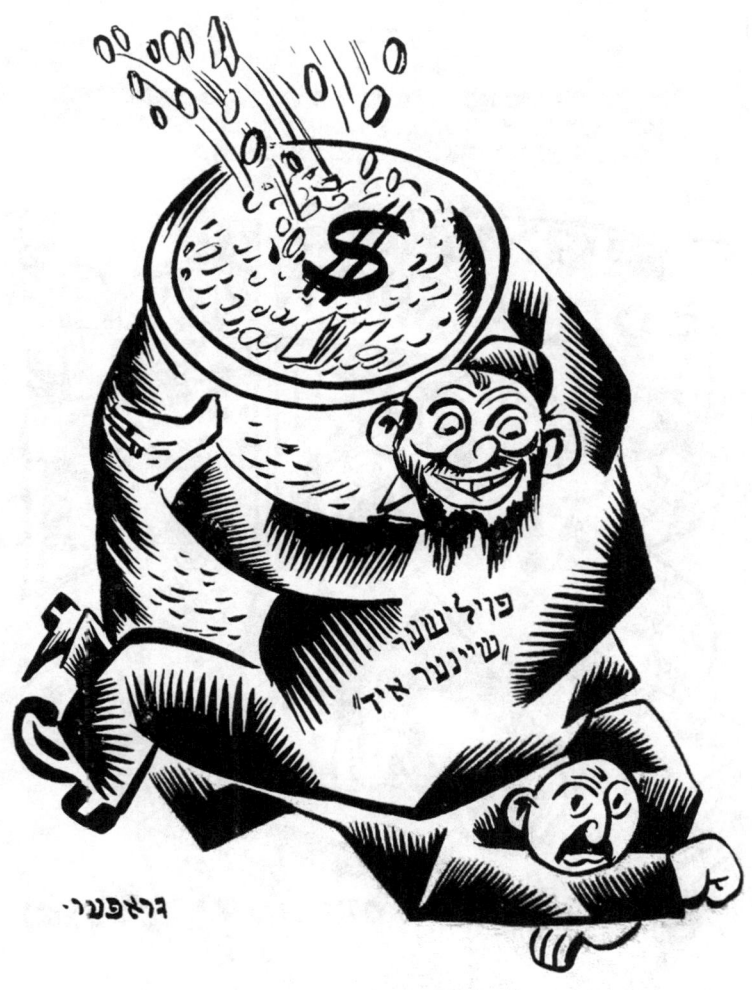

64. William Gropper, *A Handsome Polish Jew*, from Melech
Epstein, *Di Goldene Medineh fun Vilyam Groper* (The Golden
Country by William Gropper) (New York: Farlag "Frayhayt,"
1927), reproduced as *Di Goldene Medineh: William Gropper*
(Amherst, MA: National Yiddish Book Center, Steven Spielberg
Digital Yiddish Library No. 13818, 1927), not paginated. © Estate
of William Gropper. Courtesy of ACA Galleries, New York.

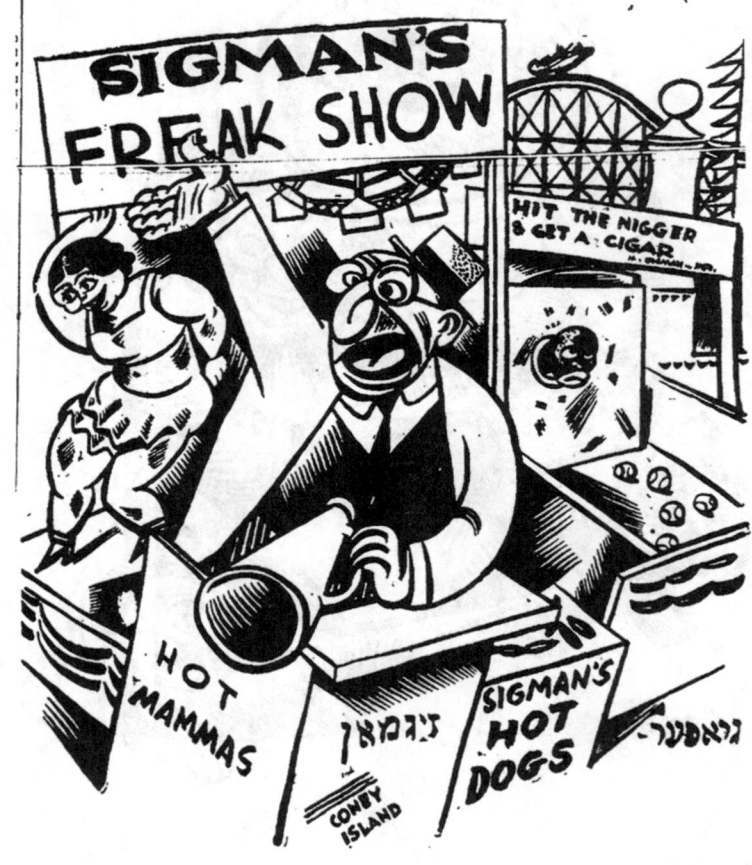

65. William Gropper, *Sigman's Freak Show*, from *Frayhayt*, July 10, 1927, 10. © Estate of William Gropper. Courtesy of ACA Galleries, New York.

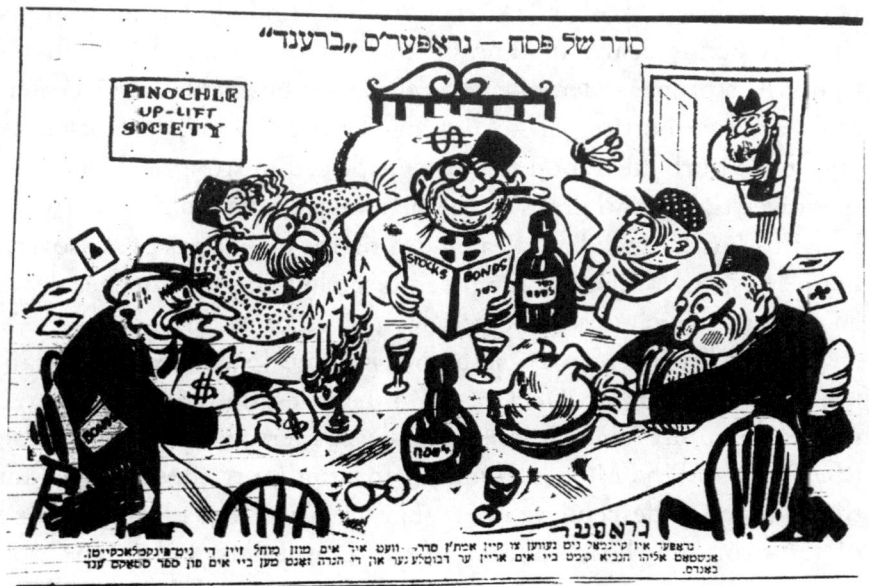

66. William Gropper, *Red Poison Ivy*, from *Frayhayt*, April 28, 1929, 8. © Estate of William Gropper. Courtesy of ACA Galleries, New York.

a caricatured African American, his head poking through a screen, dodging balls thrown at him.

The cartoon titled *Red Poison Ivy* was to a traditional Jew about as blasphemous as a cartoon could be (fig. 66). One reads just beneath the title, "Passover Seder—Gropper's Brand." The text at the bottom reads, "Gropper has never been to a real seder. You have to forgive his idiosyncrasies. Instead, for him, the Prophet Elijah comes as a bootlegger[, and] the Haggadah is a book of taxes." The Haggadah is the book read at a seder, and Elijah is traditionally invited at a prescribed moment by every host to his or her seder by opening the front door and reciting a traditional text.

Morris Sigmund, propped up by a sack filled with money, conducts the seder at the "Pinochle Up-lift Society." (One is supposed to recline at a seder.) He reads from the "Book of Stocks and Bonds," which is labeled "kosher." A recognizable Abraham Cahan is at his right. A bonds dealer holding on to bags of money is to Cahan's right. (At a proper seder, one never discusses business.) In the center, there are two bottles of "kosher-for-Passover" wine, so labeled. A pig's head (forbidden food for Jews) is placed in front of the man in the lower right, who grabs at the plate as he holds matzos between his arms (unleavened bread eaten during the eight days of Passover), but he has either a loaf of rye bread or a challah in his pocket (leavened bread, which is not allowed during Passover).

For the April 14, 1929, issue of *Frayhayt* (p. 8), Gropper's cartoon *East Broadway Declares War* belittles the editors of three non-Communist Yiddish-language newspapers, *Forward*, *Der Tog* (the Day), and the *Morgn Zhunal* (Morning Journal), so labeled on the cannons in descending order (fig. 67). (East Broadway was one of the principle thoroughfares of the Lower East Side.) The cartoon, published during the month in the Jewish calendar in which Passover is celebrated, shows the editors attacking the Soviet Union with matzos. The weapons shot from the cannons are individual sheets of matzos and matzo balls, or *knaydlach*. The man at the top, Abraham Cahan, editor of *Forward*, is flinging some kind of gooey mess at the "enemy," probably a tasty dish served during a seder. The editor of the *Day* fires matzos from the middle canon, and the editor of the *Morning Journal* is ready to launch a huge matzo ball or *knaydle* from a fork. In descending order, the words on the right are *trust*, *matzo*, and *knaydlach*, and the box labeled "Kosher for Passover" contains the matzo missiles. The caption at the bottom reads, "Passover is approaching, and the black and yellow artillery begins an offensive against the Soviet Union." (I could not find out what the "black and yellow artillery" refers to, but of the many black-and-yellow flags shown on *Wikipedia* one represents anarchocapitalism.)

It was, then, the Communist-controlled press that prolonged the use of stereotypical images of Jews into the 1930s. But, as mentioned, with the creation of the Popular Front in 1935 to combat the threat to Europe by Hitler, cartoonists "quickly switched from portraying

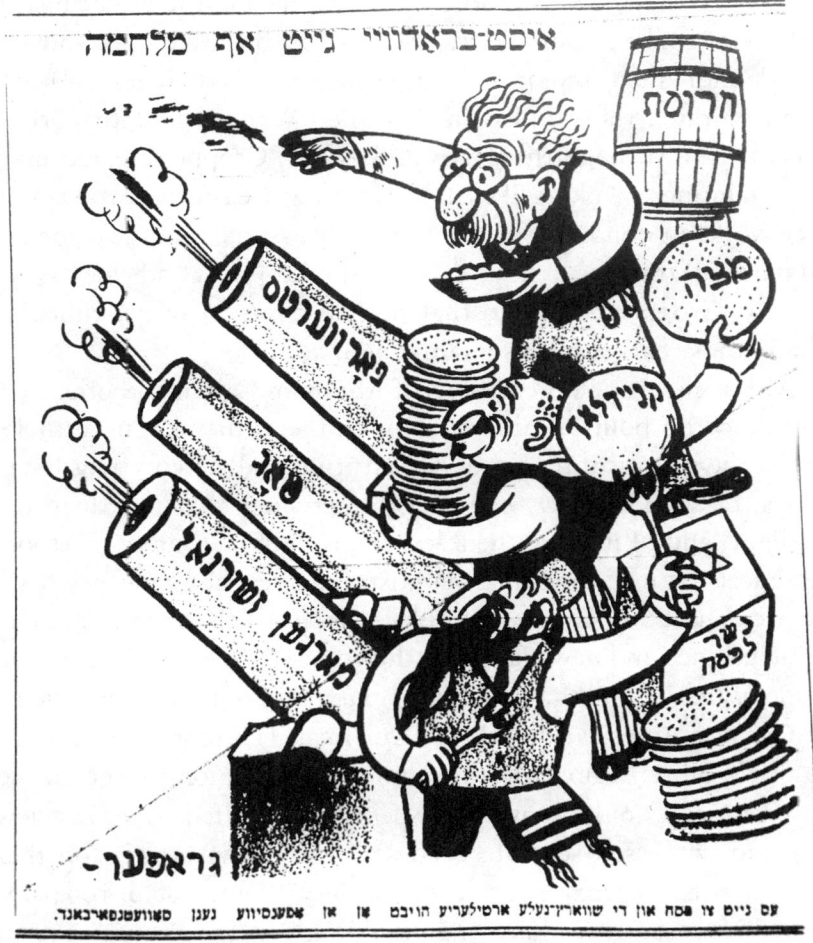

67. William Gropper, *East Broadway Declares War*, from *Frayhayt*, April 14, 1929, 8. © Estate of William Gropper. Courtesy of ACA Galleries, New York.

exploited workers, fat capitalists, leftist non-Communist organizations to attacking fascists and racists at home and abroad" (Fitzgerald 1973, 23). To Gropper's credit, he had already begun in 1931 to create cartoons attacking Hitler and subsequently made numerous cartoons sympathetic to Jewish victims of German anti-Semitism and, during the 1940s, to those murdered during the Holocaust. In the late 1940s, he began a series of paintings, one each year, showing a single individual imploring or arguing with God. These paintings commemorated those killed in the failed Warsaw Ghetto uprising of 1943. And through the 1950s and 1960s, Gropper created many genre paintings invoking Jewish life in prewar eastern Europe. With these works in mind, one would not easily assume that the same person made all those scurrilous cartoons in the 1920s and early 1930s. In 1965, Gropper confessed that he had come to regret ridiculing Jews in those earlier works (Gahn 1966, 56, 119).

Although Gropper's cartoons of Abraham Cahan and other Jews were based on political differences with them, they are nevertheless part of the historical record of caricaturing and stereotyping Jewish bodies, of showing Jews engaging in activities that put them in a bad light, and of making them look ridiculous. Gropper's cartoons, created at a time when anti-Semitism had reached new heights in America and Europe, take their place alongside the earlier cartoons; the magazines and newspapers of the 1920s, 1930s, and 1940s, such as *Social Justice* and the *Brooklyn Tablet*; and organizations such as the German American Bund, the American Fellowship Forum, and the Silver Shirt Legion. As one commentator among several noted at that time, a "quiet sense of desperation engulfed American Jews who had witnessed several decades of increasing attacks on them from almost every major segment of society" (Dinnerstein 1994, 127, also 78–104; see also Masserman and Baker 1932, 224–26, 233–35, 344–58; Waldman 1932, 9; Strong 1941; Adler 1961, 266–68; Levinger [1925] 1972, 13–15, 71–73, 117; Higham 1984, 278–86; Wenger 1996, 224). And, as demonstrated here, those attacks included ones by the American Communist Party.

In subsequent years, cartoons of caricatured Jews largely disappeared from the mainstream and Jewish presses. But to this day, horrific ones appear occasionally in European publications and on the Internet and remain a staple in Muslim countries, where distortions, misperceptions, and sheer hatred can be read into virtually every cartoon that includes a Jewish symbol or, more usually, an image of a physically repellant Jewish person. As for America, it was encouraging to read in a *New York Times* report in November 2014 that the *Indianapolis Star*, prompted by protests, removed from its website a racist cartoon "depicting an Hispanic immigrant family climbing through a window to crash a white family's Thanksgiving dinner" (Fitzsimmmons 2014, A15). The white father tells his family that the extra guests showed up thanks to President Obama's immigration policies. Despite its recent date, this cartoon reveals that neither the cartoonist nor his editor, their apologetic statements to the contrary, had any understanding of the president's policies let alone of the insults or bruised feelings generated by the cartoon. It is evidently still acceptable in some quarters to stereotype members of minority groups, in this instance Hispanics, as moochers and takers. This notion would have been red meat to late-nineteenth-century cartoonists, and the thought of issuing an apology for its contents would never have entered their minds or those of their editors.

Caricatures, whether written or imaged, would not be necessary if all Jews (or Hispanics) of whatever political stripe actually looked and acted like their caricatures. But they don't. So caricatures are and remain necessary to give credence to all of those discriminatory beliefs about Jews and other minorities. Literary critic Geoffrey Hartman has called this necessity "the finiteness of human empathy" (1992, 332, 330), according to which caricatures and other such negative representations reflect fantasies that have little or nothing to do with actual, living human individuals. John Sifton has reached the same conclusion a bit differently. He finds such hostility to be a result of empathy directed only toward one's own kind, "whether ethnic, national, religious, or political" (Sifton 2015, qtd. in Packer 2015, 73).

It is the point of this book that of all minority groups not of one's own kind, one might ask, Which group has been caricatured so continually as being nonspiritual, materialistic, aggrandizing, corrupt, and self-blinkered ideologues? Which outsider group, among many such groups, has been so consistently portrayed as the most Other of the Others, the most insulted and reviled collective body of individuals to show the Otherness of the Others? An enormous visual and written record makes a strong case for the Jews, but without implying that other groups have not also been treated with great contempt and hatred.

Conclusion

EVEN THOUGH JEWISH CARTOONISTS flourished in the Yiddish- and English-language Jewish press and Jewish painters and sculptors began to play a role in mainstream American art in the years before and after the turn of the twentieth century, both written and visual anti-Semitic materials were ever present in the art, cultural, and political worlds. In the previous chapters, I reproduced several cartoon images, hostile in nature, that visualized for readers of American humor magazines the presumed physical features and social attitudes of Jewish people, and I cited opinions that indicated in broad terms the general climate of opinion that encouraged such negative attitudes to be expressed so openly. Of the larger issue of worldwide and centuries-long anti-Semitism, I addressed only one small aspect and maintained my focus on a very restricted chronological period of what is obviously a long and troubling history. But in a study such as this one, it is impossible to avoid considerations of anti-Semitism, so further thoughts are necessary here.

The first point I discovered in all the books and articles I consulted is that no succinct, single definition of anti-Semitism exists. Throughout his book *The Definition of Anti-Semitism* (2015), Kenneth Marcus makes this point very clear. After discussing the issue from many points of view, he finds anti-Semitism to be an amalgam of attitudes, conduct, ideology, and pathology along with general considerations of race and religion by an individual, a group, or a national entity. But in one passage in his book, he nails the matter succinctly. He argues that anti-Semites' perceptions "are based neither on actual experience nor on a fixed set of stereotypes, but on a term [*anti-Semitism*] that yields a fluid range of attributes. That is to say, the signifier for anti-Semitism, 'Jew,' always means more than the set of properties with which it is associated at any particular time" (142, Kindle ed.). In the course of reviewing the cartoons illustrated in the previous pages and in sampling the opinions of a variety of authors, I have pointed out a host of reasons (some mutually contradictory) that anti-Semites offer for their Jew hatred, such as Jews' supposed social climbing, clannishness, unsocial behavior, unscrupulous business practices, enviable business tactics and acumen, divided national loyalties, low interest in hard work, high interest in hard work, and other negative traits.

The causes, reasons, and persistence of anti-Semitism, then, are numerous, varied, and, in the end, incomprehensible. However, Marcus cites an observation by Berel Lang appropriate to cartoon imagery: among all the varied explanations of anti-Semitism, it is better to focus on acts and conduct—that is, on the immediate event or occurrence—rather than on theoretical and historical considerations. "Where anti-Semitism matters, is in the acts or conduct of which the concept (and term) stands" (Lang [1999] 2004, 91, 95, qtd. in Marcus 2015, 39, Kindle ed.). And it is the anti-Semitic images by cartoonists and at least one artist included here as well as the anti-Semitic writings of various authors that form the substance of this book.

One notion became clear as the book took shape. Images and especially opinions developed a tautological aspect in that by masquerading as facts about Jews, they became explanations and answers for Jewish behavior, which in turn led to more opinions masquerading as facts. For this kind of circular reasoning to make sense, ideas to which the cartoonists and their viewers were previously predisposed became factual conclusions that had already been reached, whether done consciously or unconsciously (Nirenberg 2013, 461–71, Kindle).

One example of this kind of circular reasoning, considered previously, combines the notion that Jews might never be considered 100 percent decent, fair-minded Americans because of the belief in their

proclivity for rapacious capitalism. This insatiable predatory quality, considered different from and independent of the belief in the
American sense of fair play that helped define the national character
and spirit, was believed to be a Jewish cultural and biological characteristic. Around the turn of the twentieth century, a person with
little or no knowledge of Jews might look at a cartoon that depicted
this trait and perhaps without thinking allow it to reinforce his or
her belief that Jews were genetically disposed to engage in nefarious business practices, even despite that person's knowledge of the
activities of such non-Jewish figures as the Rockefellers, the Mor-
gens, the Carnegies, and other robber barons of the past and present,
whose actions could be described as manipulative, dishonest, and
ethically disgraceful. So an anti-Semitic posture was perhaps more
central in American thought than we would like to imagine in that
it helped non-Jewish Americans define themselves as good, decent
people rather than as persons committed to enriching themselves in
sometimes underhanded (read: Jewish) ways.

Another notion became clear to me as I did my research. Jews
were often described in the abstract and in the most general terms as
a group rather than as individuals. True, other groups have also been
characterized in this manner. Scots are thrifty, Germans are hard-
working, the Dutch are sturdy. Generalizations are still with us, but
generalizations about Jews were inevitably described in overwhelm-
ingly pejorative terms. As Mark Nirenberg observes, anti-Judaism is
"a powerful theoretical framework for making sense of the world"
based on critical concepts "produced by a history of criticizing Judaism, and hampered by that history when it comes to producing a
critique of the anti-Jewish critique" (2013, 464, Kindle ed.). For the
period under discussion as well as of earlier and later decades, I
found few critiques that took serious issue with anti-Jewish critiques.

For example, Marx so completely associated Jews with capitalism and money-making endeavors that he raised the issue of the
emancipation of Jews from their greedy, inborn nature in his essay
on the Jewish question. But such "huckstering" (his word, repeated
three times) had spread to Christians, and they, too, needed to be

emancipated from their financially acquisitive instincts (Marx 1972, 46). As he stated, "The practical Jewish spirit—Judaism or commerce—has perpetuated itself in Christian society and has even attained its highest development there. . . . The god of practical need and self-interest is money. . . . The god of the Jews has been secularized and has become the god of the world" (48, 49).

This is a very crude reduction of Marx's thesis, but for as many times as I have read his essay, trying to fathom as fully as possible its varied social, political, and religious implications, however subtle or obvious they might be, I always come to the same conclusion: for Marx, *Judaism* is a synonym for the powerful instinct of acquisition; it is a state of mind not necessarily limited to Jews, but it is central to their being. Whatever else is part of his argument, he reduced *Judaism* to a lowercase descriptive adjective of acquisitive tendencies rather than understanding it as an uppercase noun designating the religion and culture of a certain people.

Closer to our own time, in *Anti-Semite and Jew* (1948) Jean-Paul Sartre defined the Jew differently. Although acknowledging that Jews had a history of their own, he nevertheless held "that it is the anti-Semite who creates the Jew" and that "the situation of the Jew is such that everything he does turns against him" (143, 141). What is to be done? he asked. Wait for the classless society in which anti-Semitism would disappear? (150). That would probably place a heavy burden on Jews and result in even more hatred for upsetting the organization of society. Or, as Sartre suggested, it should be "point[ed] out to each [Frenchman] that the fate of the Jews is *his* fate. Not one Frenchman will be free so long as the Jews do not enjoy the fullness of their rights" (153). A nice idea, but it sounds as if Jews should just sit around more or less passively waiting for the French to change their minds. But how did Sartre intend to convince those anti-Semites who "create[] Jews" to abandon their hatred? And how would Jews change (or disappear) once anti-Semites stop defining them?

Closer to home and in a different key, opposition to Jews as well as to Italians, Slavs, and East Asians increased radically as a result of the huge numbers of immigrants who arrived in the United States in the decades before and after the turn of the twentieth century. So many foreigners legally invading the country, challenging Anglo-Saxon cultural hegemony, polluting the American gene pool, taking advantage of American business practices, contributing to urbanization and industrialization, destroying rural values, fomenting radical discord. But as has often been pointed out, the number of new arrivals exacerbated a nativism that had existed as early as the turn of the nineteenth century and reached an initial high point in the 1850s with the Know Nothing movement in reaction to the high numbers of Irish and German immigrants and then another high point during the 1920s and 1930s (Higham 1984, 3–11). John Higham defines nativism as "intense opposition [by the Anglo-Saxon majority] to an internal minority on the ground of its foreign (i.e., 'un-American') connections" and the possibility that "a distinctively American way of life" (1984, 4) will be destroyed, as I have noted in the writings of Joseph Pennell, Grant Madison, Lothrop Stoddard, and others. As a result, the insistence of a strong American identity, which implied an Anglo-Saxon cultural identity, distanced the foreign born and their children from being considered as completely American even if they held citizenship, participated in elections, and served in the military (Michaels 1995, 15).

Rhetoric to that effect has never disappeared from public discourse in America, and we can see it even in our own times. To telescope what would be another kind of study into a few sentences, one can point to several outbursts of nativist rhetoric especially during presidential election campaigns over the past thirty years. For example, in 1986 Pat Robertson, then a presidential aspirant and television preacher (and sounding much like Thomas Craven), attacked Norman Lear, a Jew and founder of the liberal group People for the American Way, in the following manner: "I have a fairly good idea of what the American way is because it was my ancestors who helped make the country. Regretfully, Norman Lear does not have the same sense of history that somebody of my heritage has" (qtd. in Baigell 2001a, 78).

Or when campaigning as John McCain's running mate in the presidential election in 2008, Sarah Palin is known to have said in a small town in the South that its inhabitants represented the "real America" (qtd. in Krugman 2016b, A27). Or I heard the following line several times from various presidential aspirants during the campaign in 2012: "We must take back America." The response to that assertive demand is to ask, From whom? From other Americans? More recently, various presidential aspirants' desire to build a wall between the United States and Mexico and to police neighborhoods where people of the Muslim faith live is part of the same rhetoric.

As in the past, the implications of this kind of language and the behavior of those who agree with it suggest that the barest scratch on the veneer of good manners and the expressed desire to welcome strangers to the country would reveal the same old nativist rage of the past two centuries, and for members of minority groups there is always concern if not outright fear of that rage.

Although anti-Semitic acts occur in America today, I do not know of any anti-Semitic cartoons published in reputable magazines. But truly hostile and the worst kind of stereotypical cartoons published in Muslim countries are very easy to find and in great abundance on the Internet. A glance at a few examples make the point that anti-Israel rhetoric is no different from and conflated with anti-Jewish rant. Given the history of anti-Semitic activity, including wholesale murder of Jews, in the past hundred-odd years, at least one magazine, the *Journal for the Study of Anti-Semitism*, continuing the tradition of magazines such as *Contemporary Jewish Record* and others during the 1930s and 1940s, has documented anti-Semitic acts around the world as well as in the United States in every issue since its inception in 2009. (It has also published two articles on political cartoons ["Jew Cartoons" 2009; F. Cohen 2012].) In addition, organizations such as the World Jewish Congress have provided data both in print and online on acts of anti-Semitism throughout the world. Such journals and organizations, had they existed around the turn of the twentieth century, would undoubtedly have publically condemned every hostile cartoon, cartoonist, and magazine editor.

Today, objections to Latinos and Muslims rather than to other immigrant groups are more common in America, but overt hatred of Jews is never far from Jews' consciousness—especially the hatred that emanates from the Muslim world—as the editors of the *Journal for the Study of Anti-Semitism* know so well. Memory prods us to remember past events and to be watchful of contemporary activities, as recent art exhibitions attest. In 2016 alone, two exhibitions—one in the United States and the other in Germany—and the second Iranian Holocaust Cartoon Exhibition invoke the worst aspects of twentieth-century and contemporary anti-Semitism (see Medoff and Yoe 2015; Rendell and Heywood 2016; Rosen 2016; Thaoor 2016); and "UNESCO Condemns Iran's Holocaust Cartoon Contest" 2016).

The importance of such exhibitions and publications is clear: they remind us that hostile cartoons and other similar materials have over the years helped visualize and organize thoughts, feelings, and opinions, however misguided or false they might be. In this regard, one of the great ironies of the 1930s is that the beautiful Aryan child selected to represent Nazi youth, whose face appeared on postcards and in magazines through the Third Reich, was a Jewish infant, six-month-old Hessy Taft (née Levensons) (Nemes 2014).

That factoid aside, the cartoons and comments noted in these pages and those concerning other minority groups not discussed here are part of the history of American art and culture. There is no question that the period between roughly 1880 and 1940 is fertile ground for further study. As Otto Frank, Anne Frank's father, wrote, "We have to know the past to understand the perils of today" (qtd. in Rendell and Heywood 2016, 10).

Works Cited

Index

Works Cited

Aaron, Daniel. 1961. *Writers on the Left.* New York: Avon.

Adams, Oscar Fay. 1894. "Is 'American Humor' Humorous?" *Outlook* 49 (June 2): 961–62.

Adler, Selig. 1961. *The Isolationist Impulse: Its Twentieth Century Reaction.* New York: Collier Books.

"Alas! Poor Hilton." 1878. *Puck*, Dec. 25, 2.

Allen, Sidney [Sadakichi Hartmann]. 1902. "Picturesque New York in Four Papers: The Esthetic Side of Jewtown." *Camera Notes* 6 (Oct.): 143–48.

Aly, Götz. 2014. *Why the Germans? Why the Jews? Envy, Race Hatred, and the Prehistory of the Holocaust.* New York: Metropolitan Books.

Amishai-Maisels, Ziva. 1999. "The Demonization of the 'Other' in the Visual Arts." In *Demonizing the Other: Antisemitism, Racism, and Xenophobia*, edited by Robert S. Wistrich, 44–72. Amsterdam: Harwood Academic.

"Among Our Brethren Abroad." 1917. *The American Hebrew* 101 (June 15): 148, 168.

Anderson, Benedict. [1983] 1991. *Imagined Communities: Reflections on the Origin and Spread of Nationalism.* Rev. ed. London: Verso.

"Anti-Semitic Life." 1908. *B'nai B'rith News*, Nov. 10, 3.

Appel, John. 1981. "Jews in American Caricature, 1820–1914." *American Jewish History* 71 (Sept.): 103–33.

Appel, John, and Selma Appel. 1984. "Jews in American Graphic Satire and Humor." In *Jews in American Graphic Humor and Satire* (exhibit catalog), 3–23. Cincinnati: Hebrew Union College–Jewish Institute of Religion.

———. 1986. "Anti-Semitism in American Caricature." *Society* 24 (Nov.–Dec.): 78–83.

"Are We Facing an Immigrant Peril?" 1905. *New York Times*, Jan. 29, no page numbers.

Ash, Stephen V. 1982. "Civil War Exodus: The Jews and Grant's General Order No. 11." *The Historian* 44 (Aug. 1): 505–23.

Austin, Mary. 1920. "New York: Dictator of American Criticism." *The Nation* 111 (July 31): 129–30.

Baigell, Matthew. 1987. "American Landscape Painting and National Identity: The Stieglitz Circle and Emerson." *Art Criticism* 4:27–47.

———. 2000. "Max Weber's Jewish Paintings." *American Jewish History* 88 (Sept.): 341–60.

———. 2001a. "American Art and National Identity: The 1920s." In *Artist and Identity in Twentieth-Century America*, 60–79. New York: Cambridge Univ. Press.

———. 2001b. "Benton and the Left." In *Artist and Identity in Twentieth-Century America*, 117–41. New York: Cambridge Univ. Press.

———. 2009. "Sweatshop Images: History and Memory." *Images* 2:65–82.

———. 2015. *Social Concern and Left Politics in Jewish American Art, 1880–1940*. Syracuse, NY: Syracuse Univ. Press.

Banta, Martha. 2003. *Barbaric Intercourse: Caricature and the Culture of Conduct*. Chicago: Univ. of Chicago Press.

Bellow, Saul. 2000. *Revelstein*. New York: Viking.

Bender, Daniel. 2003. "A Foreign Method of Working: Racial Degeneration, Gender Disorder, and the Sweatshop Danger in America." In *Sweatshop USA: The American Sweatshop in Global and Historical Perspective*, edited by Daniel Bender and Richard Greenwald, 19–55. New York: Routledge.

———. 2004. *Sweated Work, Weak Bodies: Anti-sweatshop Campaigns and Language of Labor*. New Brunswick, NJ: Rutgers Univ. Press.

Benton, Thomas Hart. 1937. "Confessions of an American, Part l." *Common Sense* 6 (Sept.): 7–9.

———. 1969. "American Regionalism: A Personal History of the Movement." In *An American in Art: A Professional and Technical Autobiography*, 147–92. Lawrence: Univ. Press of Kansas.

———. [1937] 1983. *An Artist in America*. 4th ed. Columbia: Univ. of Missouri Press.

———. n.d.a. "Dilemma." Microfilm roll 2327, frame 162. Archives of American Art, Smithsonian Institution, Washington, DC.

———. n.d.b. "Thirties." Microfilm roll 2327, frame 5. Archives of American Art, Smithsonian Institution, Washington, DC.

Bergson, Henri. 1956. *Laughter*. In *Comedy*, 61–190. New York: Doubleday.

Bernheimer, Charles S. 1908. "Prejudice against Jews in the United States." *Independent* 65 (Nov. 12): 1105–8.

Bigelow, Poultney. 1893. "The Russian and His Jew." *Harper's New Monthly Magazine* 88 (Dec. 1): 603–14.

———. 1929. "Frederic Remington: With Extracts from Unpublished Letters." *New York Historical Association Quarterly Journal* 10 (Jan.): 45–52.

Billings, John S. 1891. "Vital Statistics of the Jews." *North American Review* 152 (Jan.): 70–84.

Bourne, Randolph. [1916] 1992. "Trans-national America." *Atlantic Monthly* 118 (July): 86–97. Reprinted in *Randolph Bourne: The Radical Will, Selected Writings 1911–1918*, edited by Olaf Hanson, 248–64. Berkeley: Univ. of California Press.

Boshim, Joseph, and Joseph Dorinson. 1987. "Ethnic Humor: Subversion and Survival." In *American Humor*, edited by Arthur Power Dudden, 97–117. New York: Oxford Univ. Press.

Boyarin, Daniel. 1997. *Unheroic Conduct: The Rise of Heterosexuality and the Invention of the Jewish Man*. Berkeley: Univ. of California Press.

Boyesen, Hjalmar Hjorth. 1895. "The Plague of Jocularity." *North American Review* 161 (Nov.): 528–35.

———. 1897. "Danger of Unrestricted Immigration." *Forum* 3 (July): 532–42.

Brodkin, Karen. 1998. *How Jews Became White Folks and What That Says about Race in America*. New Brunswick, NJ: Rutgers Univ. Press.

Brown, Lawrence Guy. 1933. *Immigration: Cultural Conflicts and Social Adjustments*. New York: Longmans, Green.

Browne, Julius Henri. 1874. "The Knights of the Red Shield." *Harper's New Monthly Magazine* 48 (Jan.): 209–24.

Buhle, Peter. 1980. "Jews and American Communism: The Cultural Question." *Radical History Review* 23 (Spring): 9–33.

Bulliet, C. J. 1930. *Apples and Madonnas: Emotional Expression in Modern Art*. Rev. ed. New York: Covici-Friede.

"The Cause of Civilization as First Heard by the Allies." 1916. *Puck*, Feb. 26, 7.

Chicago American. 1908. Untitled article, 1 (Oct. 14): no page numbers.

"Christian and Hebrew." 1888. *Jewish Messenger*, Aug. 31, 4.

Cohen, Ben. 2012. "The Big Lie." *Commentary* 133 (Feb.): 13–19.

Cohen, Florette. 2012. "Do Political Cartoons Reflect Anti-Semitism?" *Journal for the Study of Anti-Semitism* 4 (June): 41–64.

Cohen, Naomi W. 1979. "Anti-Semitism in the Gilded Age: The Jewish View." *Jewish Social Studies* 1 (Summer–Autumn): 187–210.

———. 2003. *The Americanization of Zionism, 1897–1948*. Hanover, NH: Brandeis Univ. Press.

Cohen, Rich. 2015. "Ebb Tide in the Golden Century." *Tablet*, June 1. At http://www.tabletmag.com/jewish-news-and-politics/191087/ebb-tide -in-the-golden-country.

Cohen, Sandy. 1985. "Racial and Ethnic Humor in the United States." *Amerikastudien / American Studies* 30, no. 2: 203–11.

Coon, Carleton Stevens. 1942. "Have the Jews a Racial Identity?" In *Jews in a Gentile World*, edited by Jacques Graeber and Steuart Britt Henderson, 20–37. New York: MacMillan.

Cortissoz, Royal. 1923. *American Artists*. New York: Scribner's.

Cox, Samuel. 1875. "American Humor." *Harper's New Monthly Magazine* 50 (Apr.): 690–701.

Craven, Thomas. 1934. *Modern Art*. New York: Simon and Shuster.

Dennis, James. 1998. *Renegade Regionalists: The Modern Independence of Grant Wood, Thomas Hart Benton, and John Steuart Curry*. Madison: Univ. of Wisconsin Press.

Dewey, Donald. 2007. *The Art of Ill Will: The Story of American Political Cartoons*. New York: New York Univ. Press.

Dijkstra, Bram. 1969. *Cubism, Stieglitz, and the Early Poetry of William Carlos Williams: The Hieroglyphics of a New Speech*. Princeton, NJ: Princeton Univ. Press.

Diner, Hasia R. 2015. *Roads Taken: The Great Jewish Migration to the New World and the Peddlers Who Forged the Way*. New Haven, CT: Yale Univ. Press.

Dinnerstein, Leonard. 1994. *Anti-Semitism in American History*. New York: Oxford Univ. Press.

Dippie, Brian W. 2001. *The Frederic Remington Art Museum Collection*. New York: Abrams.

Dobkowski, Michael N. 1976. "Populist Antisemitism in U.S. Literature." *Patterns of Prejudice* 10 (May–June): 19–27.

———. 1977. "American Anti-Semitism: A Reinterpretation." *American Quarterly* 29 (Summer): 166–81.

———. 1979. *The Tarnished Dream: The Basis of American Anti-Semitism.* Westport, CT: Greenwood.

Dormon, James H. 1985. "Ethnic Stereotyping in American Popular Culture: The Depiction of American Ethnics in the Cartoon Periodicals of the Golden Age." *Amerikastudien / American Studies* 4: 489–507.

Doss, Erica. 1991. *Benton, Pollock, and the Politics of Modernism: From Regionalism to Abstract Expressionism.* Chicago: Univ. of Chicago Press.

Dundes, Alan. 1971. "A Study of Ethnic Slurs: The Jew and the Polack in the United States." *Journal of American Folklore* 84 (Apr.–June): 186–203.

Elazar, Daniel. 1969. "American Political Theory and the Political Notions of American Jews." In *The Ghetto and Beyond: Essays on Jewish Life in America,* edited by Peter I. Rose, 203–27. New York: Random House.

Epstein, Jacob. 1940. *Let There Be Sculpture.* New York: Putnam's.

———. 1955. *Jacob Epstein: An Autobiography.* New York: Dutton.

Epstein, Melech. 1950–53. *Jewish Labor in the United States: An Industrial, Political, and Cultural History of the Jewish Labor Movement.* 2 vols. New York: Trade Union Sponsoring Committee.

———. 1959. *The Jew and Communism, 1919–1941: The Story of the Early Communist Victories and Ultimate Defeats in the Jewish Community, USA.* New York: Trade Union Sponsoring Committee.

"Escape of Daniel Emanuel from Capt. Brantley's Party of Loyalists." 1917. *Puck,* Jan. 6, 20–21.

E. S. M. 1918. "The Jewish Mind in These States." *Life,* June 20, 983.

Evans, Harold, Sir. 2012. Foreword to *A Convenient Hatred: The History of Anti-Semitism,* edited by Phyllis Goldstein, iii–x. Brookline, MA: Facing History and Ourselves National Foundation.

Feingold, Henry L. 1982. "Anti-Semitism and the Anti-Semitic Imagination in America: Case Study—the Twenties." In *A Midrash on American History,* 177–206. Albany: State Univ. of New York Press.

———. 1992. *A Time for Searching: Entering the Mainstream, 1920–1945.* Baltimore: Johns Hopkins Univ. Press.

Fischer, Roger A. 1996. *Them Damned Pictures: Explorations in American Political Cartoon Art.* North Haven, CT: Archon.

Fitzgerald, Richard. 1973. *Art and Politics: Cartoonists of the Masses and Liberator.* Westport, CT: Greenwood Press.

Fitzsimmons, Emma G. 2014. "Newspaper Apologizes for Cartoon on Immigrants." *New York Times,* Nov. 24, A15.

Forman, Jerome J. 2014. *Graphic History of Anti-Semitism.* Atglen, PA: Shiffer.

Freed, Clarence I. 1924. "Alfred Stieglitz—Genius of the Camera." *American Hebrew,* Jan. 18, 305.

Freud, Sigmund. 1938. *Wit and Its Relation to the Unconscious.* In *The Basic Writings of Sigmund Freud,* edited and translated by A. A. Brill, 633–806. New York: Random House.

———. 1960. *Jokes and Their Relation to the Unconscious.* Translated by James Strachey. New York: Norton.

———. 1967. *Moses and Monotheism.* Edited by Katharine Jones. New York: Vintage.

Freundlich, August L. 1968. *William Gropper: Retrospective.* Los Angeles: Richie Press.

Fuchs, Eduard. 1921. *Die Juden in der Karikatur.* Munich: Langen.

Gahn, Joseph Anthony. 1966. "The Art of William Gropper, Radical Cartoonist." Ph.D. diss., Syracuse Univ.

Gandal, Keith. 1997. *The Virtues of the Vicious: Jacob Riis, Stephen Crane, and the Spectacle of the Slum.* New York: Oxford Univ. Press.

Geertz, Clifford. 1976. "Art as a Cultural System." *Modern Language Notes* 91 (Dec.): 1473–99.

Gellner, Ernest. 1997. *Nationalism.* New York: New York Univ. Press.

Gerber, David A. 1987. "Anti-Semitic and Jewish–Gentile Relations in American Historiography and the American Past." In *Anti-Semitism in American History,* edited by David A. Gerber, 3–54. Urbana: Univ. of Illinois Press.

Gibbons, Herbert Adams. 1921. "The Jewish Problem: Its Relation to American Ideals and Interests." *Century Magazine* 102 (Sept.): 785–92.

Gilman, Sander. 1991. *The Jew's Body.* New York: Routledge.

————. 1998. *Love + Marriage = Death and Other Essays Representing Difference*. Stanford, CA: Stanford Univ. Press.

Glanz, Rudolf. 1973. *The Jew in Early American Wit and Graphic Humor*. New York: KTAV.

Glassman, Bernard. 1979. *Anti-Semitic Stereotypes without Jews: Images of Jews in England, 1290–1700*. Detroit: Wayne State Univ. Press.

Gold, Herbert. 1972. Introduction to *Kike: Anti-Semitism in America*, edited by Michael Selzer, ix–xvii. New York: World Publishing.

Gombrich, Ernst H. 1960. *Art and Illusion: A Study in the Psychology of Pictorial Representation*. Princeton, NJ: Princeton Univ. Press.

Goren, Arthur. 1982. *The American Jews*. Cambridge, MA: Harvard Univ. Press.

Gossett, Thomas F. 1963. *Race: The History of an Idea in America*. Dallas: Southern Methodist Univ. Press.

Gould, Charles W. 1920. *A Family Matter*. New York: Scribner's.

Grant, Madison. 1916. *The Passing of the Great Race or The Racial Basis of European History*. New York: Scribner's.

Greenough, Sarah, and Juan Hamilton. 1983. *Alfred Stieglitz: Photographs and Writings*. New York: Callaway Editions.

Gribayedoff, Valerian. 1897. "Incendiarism." *Frank Leslie's Illustrated Weekly* 84 (Feb. 18): 102.

Gropper, William. 1927. Letter to Kalman Marmor, n.d. Box 11, Folder 117, W. G. 205. YIVO Archives, New York.

Groseclose, Barbara. 1978. "Painting, Politics, and George Caleb Bingham." *American Art Journal* 10 (Nov.): 5–19.

Gross, Charles. 1891. "Causes of Russia's Persecution of the Jews." *Frank Leslie's Illustrated Newspaper*, Aug. 29, 50.

Gurock, Jeffrey. 1981. "Jacob Riis: Christian Friend or Foe? Two Jewish Views." *American Jewish History* 71 (Sept.): 29–47.

Hales, Peter. 1984. *Silver Cities: The Photography of American Urbanization*. Philadelphia: Temple Univ. Press.

Halpern, Ben. 1979. "The Americanization of Zionism, 1880–1910." *American Jewish History* 69 (Sept): 15–33.

Handlin, Oscar. 1951a. "American Views of the Jew at the Opening of the 20th Century." *Publications of the American Jewish Historical Society* 40 (June): 323–44.

———. 1951b. "How U.S. Anti-Semitism Really Began." *Commentary* 12 (Jan.): 541–48.

Hapgood, Hutchins. [1902] 1965. *The Spirit of the Ghetto*. New York: Funk and Wagnalls.

Harap, Louis. 1974. *The Image of the Jew in American Literature from the Early Republic to Mass Immigration*. Philadelphia: Jewish Publication Society of America.

———. 1987. *Creative Awakening: The Jewish Presence in Twentieth-Century American Literature*. New York: Greenwood Press.

Hart, Mitchell B. 2011. *Jews and Race: Writings on Identity and Difference, 1880–1940*. Waltham, MA: Brandeis Univ. Press.

Hartman, Geoffrey H. 1992. "The Book of Destruction." In *Probing the Limits of Representation: Nazism and the Final Solution*, edited by Saul Friedlander, 318–34. Cambridge, MA: Harvard Univ. Press.

Harvey, William. 1894. *Coin's Financial School*. Chicago: Coin.

Hays, Samuel P. 1957. *The Response to Industrialism, 1885–1914*. Chicago: Univ. of Chicago Press.

Hegman, Susan. 1999. *Patterns for America: Modernism and the Concept of Culture*. Princeton, NJ: Princeton Univ. Press.

Hendrick, Burton J. 1907. "The Great Jewish Invasion." *McClure's Magazine* 28 (Jan.): 307–20.

———. 1913. "The Great Jewish Invasion." *McClure's Magazine* 40 (Mar.): 127–65.

Higham, John. 1984. *Send These to Me: Immigrants in Urban America*. Rev. ed. Baltimore: John Hopkins Univ. Press.

———. [1955] 1992. *Strangers in the Land: Patterns of American Nativism, 1860–1925*. New Brunswick, NJ: Rutgers Univ. Press.

Hills, Patricia. 1977. *Turn-of-the-Century America*. New York: Whitney Museum of American Art.

Hindus, Milton. 1947. "F. Scot Fitzgerald's Literary Anti-Semitism: A Footnote on the Mind of the 20s." *Commentary* 4: 508–16.

Hobbes, Thomas. [1651] 1958. *Leviathan, Parts I and II*. Indianapolis, IN: Bobbs-Merrill.

Hoffman, Katherine. 2011. *Alfred Stieglitz: A Legacy of Light*. New Haven, CT: Yale Univ. Press.

Huneker, James. 1915. *The New Cosmopolis*. New York: Scribner's.

Hyman, Paula. 1980. "Immigrant Women and Consumer Protest: The New York City Kosher Meat Boycott." *American Jewish History* 70 (Sept. 1): 91–105.

"Israel on the Crank." 1881. *Puck*, Dec. 14, 227.

James, Henry. 1907. *The American Scene*. London: Chapman-Hill.

"Jew Cartoons." 2009. *Journal for the Study of Anti-Semitism* 1 (June): 85–87.

Jewish Messenger. 1881. Editorial, Dec. 9, 4.

"Jews in Congress." 1883. *The Judge*, Jan. 20, 2.

"Joseph Seligman." n.d. *Wikipedia*. At https://en.wikipedia.org/wiki /Joseph_Seligman.

"*Judge* Magazine Illustration Collection." Delaware Art Museum. Finding aid to the collection in the Helen Farr Sloan Library & Archives at http://www.delart.org/wordpress/wp-content/uploads/2015/02/Judge -Magazine.pdf.

Kaufman, Yehezkiel. 1949. "Anti-Semitic Stereotypes in Zionism: The Nationalistic Rejection of Diaspora Jewry." *Commentary* 8 (1949): 239–45.

Keppler, Joseph. 1891. *A Selection of Cartoons from* Puck. New York: Keppler and Schwartzmann.

Kibler, M. Alison. 2015. *Censoring Racial Ridicule: Irish, Jewish, and African America Struggles over Race and Representation, 1890–1930*. Chapel Hill: Univ. of North Carolina Press.

Kirke, Edmund. 1889. "Wit and Humor—Old and New." *North American Review* 148 (Jan.): 33–46.

Klehr, Harvey. 1984. *The Heyday of American Communism: The Depression Decade*. New York: Basic Books.

Kotek, Joël. 2009. *Cartoons and Extremism: Israel and the Jews in Arab and Western Media*. Translated by Alison Jaffa. Edgeware Middlesex, UK: Valentine Mitchell.

Kounstamm, Lorenzo T. 1881. "The Russian Arrivals." *Jewish Messenger*, Dec. 2, 1.

Kraut, Alan M. 1982. *The Huddled Masses: The Immigrant in American Society, 1880–1921*. Arlington Heights, IL: Harland Davidson.

Kroiz, Lauren. 2012. *Creative Composites: Modernism, Race, and the Stieglitz Circle*. Berkeley: Univ. of California Press.

Krugman, Paul. 2016a. "Hillary and the Horizontals." *New York Times*, June 10, A27.

———. 2016b. "The Pastrami Principle." *New York Times*, Apr. 15, A27.

Lang, Berel. [1999] 2004. "Self-Description and the Anti-Semite: Denying Privileged Access." In *Those Who Forget the Past: The Question of Anti-Semitism*, edited by Ron Rosenbaum, 91–95. New York: Random House.

Leavitt, Julian. 1919. "American Jews in the World War." In *American Jewish Year Book 1919*, 141–50. Philadelphia: Jewish Publication Society of America.

Lennon, John B. 1901. *Reports of the Industrial Commission on Immigration*. Washington, DC: US Government Printing Office.

Levinger, Rabbi Lee J. [1925] 1972. *Anti-Semitism in the United States: Its History and Causes*. Westport, CT: Greenwood Press.

"Levy's Out!" 1881. *Puck*, Aug. 3, 367.

Lewin, Kurt. 1941. "Self-Hatred among Jews." *Contemporary Jewish Record* 4 (June 1): 219–32.

Life. 1897. Dec. 7, 30.

———. 1903. June 4, 510.

———. 1905a. Apr. 27, 480.

———. 1905b. Apr. 27, 488.

"*Life's* Confidential Guide to the Theatres." 1903. *Life*, Apr. 23, 372.

Lipton, Sara. 1999. *Images of Intolerance: The Representation of Jews and Judaism in the Bible Moralisée*. Berkeley: Univ. of California Press.

———. 2014. *Dark Mirror: The Medieval Origins of Anti-Jewish Iconography*. New York: Metropolitan Books.

Lodge, Henry Cabot. 1891. "The Restriction of Immigration." *North American Review* 152 (Jan.): 27–36.

Lozowick, Louis. 1983. *William Gropper*. Philadelphia: Philadelphia Art Alliance.

Marcus, Kenneth L. 2015. *The Definition of Anti-Semitism*. New York: Oxford Univ. Press.

Marling, Karal Ann. 1982. *Wall-to-Wall America: A Cultural History of Post-Office Murals in the Great Depression*. Minneapolis: Univ. of Minnesota Press.

Marx, Karl. 1972. "On the Jewish Question." In *The Marx–Engels Reader*, edited by Richard C. Tucker, 24–51. New York: Norton.

Masserman, Paul, and Max Baker. 1932. *The Jews Come to America*. New York: Bloch.

Mayo, Louise A. 1988. *The Ambivalent Image: Nineteenth-Century America's Perception of the Jew*. Rutherford, NJ: Fairleigh-Dickinson Univ. Press.

Mazow, Leo G. 2012. *Thomas Hart Benton and the American Sound*. University Park: Pennsylvania State Univ. Press.

McCall, Walter. 1924. *Patriotism and the American Jew*. New York: Plymouth.

McCausland, Elizabeth. 1934. "Stieglitz and the American Tradition." In *America and Alfred Stieglitz: A Collective Portrait*, edited by Waldo Frank, 227–32. Garden City, NY: Doubleday Doran.

McCracken, Harold. 1947. *Remington, Artist of the Old West*. Philadelphia: Lippincott.

Medoff, Raphael, and Craig Yoe. 2015. *Cartoonists against the Holocaust*. Middletown, DE: Clizia.

Mendes, Pereira. 1887. "Why Am I a Jew?" *North American Review* 144 (June): 596–608.

Michael, Robert. 2005. *A Concise History of American Anti-Semitism*. Lanham, MD: Rowman and Littlefield.

Michaels, Walter Benn. 1995. *Our America: Nativism, Modernism, and Pluralism*. Durham, NC: Duke Univ. Press.

Millhiser, Ian. 2015. *Injustices: The Supreme Court's History of Comforting the Comforted and Afflicting the Afflicted*. New York: Nation Books.

Milosz, Czeslaw. 1981. *Native Realm: A Search for Self-Definition*. Berkeley: Univ. of California Press.

"The Mission of the Jews." 1893. *Harper's New Monthly Magazine*, Dec., 259–66.

Mitchell, J. A. 1889. "Contemporary American Caricatures." *Scribner's Magazine* 6 (Dec.): 728–45.

Moore, Debra Dash. 1981. *At Home in America: Second Generation New York Jews*. New York: Columbia Univ. Press.

Morais, Nina. 1881. "Jewish Ostracism in America." *North American Review* 133 (Sept.): 265–75.

Morgan, James Morris. 1899. "An American Forerunner of Dreyfuss." *The Century* 58 (Sept.): 796–800.

Morley, Christopher. 1933. Foreword to William Murrell, *A History of American Graphic Humor*, vol. 1, ix–xi. New York: Whitney Museum of American Art.

Mosse, George L. 1993. *Confronting the Nation: Jewish and Western Nationalism*. Hanover, NH: Brandeis Univ. Press.

Mott, Frank Luther. 1938. *A History of American Magazines, 1865–1885*. Cambridge, MA: Harvard Univ. Press.

Murphy, Paul. 1964. "Sources and Nature of Intolerance in the 1920s." *Journal of American History* 51 (June): 60–76.

Murrell, William. 1933. *A History of American Graphic Humor*. Vol. 1. New York: Whitney Museum of American Art.

Nemerov, Alexander. 1995. *Frederic Remington and Turn-of-the-Century America*. New Haven, CT: Yale Univ. Press.

Nemes, Hody. 2014. "How a Jewish Infant Came to Be the Aryan Poster Child for the Third Reich." *Forward*, July 28, 3.

Newman, Sasha M. 1981. *Arthur Dove and Duncan Phillips, Artist and Patron*. New York: Braziller.

Nirenberg, David. 2013. *Anti-Judaism: The Western Tradition*. New York: Norton.

Norman, Dorothy. 1973. *Alfred Stieglitz: An American Seer*. New York: Random House.

"Objectionable Immigrants." 1891. *Frank Leslie's Illustrated Newspaper*, June 13, 322.

"On the Immediate Tasks of the CUSA." 1935. *The Communist* 14 (Feb.): 120–26.

Packer, George. 2015. "Dark Hours: Violence in the Age of War on Terror." *New Yorker*, July 20, 72–75.

Parsons, Talcott. 1942. "The Sociology of Modern Anti-Semitism." In *Jews in a Gentile World: The Problem of Anti-Semitism*, edited by Isacque Graeber and Stuart Henderson Britt, 101–22. New York: MacMillan.

Pells, Richard H. 1973. *Radical Visions and American Dreams: Culture and Social Thought in the Depression Years*. New York: Harper & Row.

Pennell, Joseph. 1892. *The Jew at Home: Impressions of a Summer and Autumn with Him*. New York: Appleton.

———. 1925. *The Adventures of an Illustrator Mostly in Following His Author in America and Europe*. Boston: Little, Brown.

Peters, Madison C. 1910. *Justice for the Jew: The Story of What He Has Done for the World*. New York: Trow.

Phagan, Patricia. 2000. "William Gropper and 'Freiheit': A Study of His Political Cartoons." Ph.D. diss., City University of New York.

Pizer, Donald. 2008. *American Naturalism and the Jews: Garland, Norris, Dreiser, Wharton, and Cather*. Urbana: Univ. of Illinois Press.

Press, Charles. 1981. *The Political Cartoon*. Rutherford, NJ: Fairleigh Dickenson Univ. Press.

Puck. 1877. Editorial, June 27, 2.

———. 1884. Dec. 17, 248.

"*Puck* Illustration Collection." n.d. Delaware Art Museum. Finding aid to the collection in the Helen Farr Sloan Library & Archives at http://www .delart.org/wordpress/wp-content/uploads/2015/02/Puck-Illustration -Collection.pdf.

Rebak, Gil. 2012. *Gentile New York: The Images of Non-Jews among Jewish Immigrants*. New Brunswick, NJ: Rutgers Univ. Press.

Reid, Sydney. 1908. "Because You're a Jew." *Independent* 65 (Nov. 16): 1212–17.

Reiter, Paul. 2012. *On the Origins of Jewish Self Hatred*. Princeton, NJ: Princeton Univ. Press.

Remington, Frederic. 1894a. "Chicago under the Law." *Harper's Weekly*, July 28, 703.

———. 1894b. "Chicago under the Mob." *Harper's Weekly*, July 21, 680–81.

———. [1979] 1986. *The Collected Writings of Frederic Remington*. Edited by Peggy Samuels and Harold Samuels. N.p.: Castle.

Rendell, Kenneth W., and Samantha Heywood. 2016. *Power of Anti-Semitism: The March to the Holocaust 1919–1939*. Boston: Museum of the Second World War.

Rhine, Alice Hyneman. 1887. "Race Prejudice at Summer Resorts." *Forum* 36 (July): 523–31.

Ribuffo, Leo. 1983. *The Old Christian Right: The Protestant Far Right from the Great Depression to the Cold War*. Philadelphia: Temple Univ. Press.

Riis, Jacob. 1890. *How the Other Half Lives: Studies among the Tenements of New York*. New York: Scribner's.

———. [1890] 2010a. "Jew Town." In *How the Other Half Lives: Studies among the Tenements of New York*, edited by Sam Bass Warner Jr., 101–14. Cambridge, MA: Harvard Univ. Press.

———. [1890] 2010b. "The Sweaters of Jewtown." In *How the Other Half Lives: Studies among the Tenements of New York*, edited by Sam Bass Warner Jr., 115–28. Cambridge, MA: Harvard Univ. Press.

Roche, John. 1963. *The Quest for the Dream: The Development of Civil Rights and Human Relations in Modern America*. New York: MacMillan.

Rosen, Armin. 2016. "The First Post–Nuclear Deal Holocaust Cartoon Contest Is Coming to Tehran." *Tablet*, May 13. At http://www.tablet mag.com/scroll/202427/the-first-post-nuclear-deal-holocaust-cartoon -contest-is-coming-to-tehran.

Rosenblatt, W. M. 1872. "The Jews: What Are They Coming To?" *Galaxy* 13 (Jan.): 47–60.

Ross, Edward Alsworth. 1904. "The Value Rank of the American People." *Independent* 57 (Nov. 10): 1061–63.

Rush, Nancy. 1991. *The Paintings and Politics of George Caleb Bingham*. New Haven, CT: Yale Univ. Press.

"Russian Jews and Gentiles: From a Russian Point of view." 1882. *Century Illustrated Magazine* 23 (Apr.): 903–21.

Sacher, Harry. 1940. "Revenge of the Prophets: A Psychoanalysis of Anti-Semitism." *Menorah Journal* 28 (Oct.–Dec.): 243–53.

Salpeter, Harry. [1937] 1973. "William Gropper, Proletarian." *Esquire*, Sept. Reprinted in *Social Realism: Art as a Weapon*, edited by David Shapiro, 191–202. New York: Frederick Ungar.

Samuel, Maurice. [1940] 1988. *The Great Hatred*. Lanham, MD: Univ. Press of America.

Sanford, M. Bourchier. 1891. "In Favor of the Jew." *North American Review* 152 (Jan.): 126–28.

Sarna, Jonathan. 1981. "Anti-Semitism in American History." *Commentary* 71 (Mar.): 42–47.

———. 2012. *When General Grant Expelled the Jews*. New York: Nextbook.

Sarolea, Charles. 1936. "The Religion of Race." *Menorah Journal* 24 (Jan.–Mar.): 1–7.

Sartre, Jean-Paul. 1948. *Anti-Semite and Jew*. Translated by George Becker. New York: Schocken Books.

Schoener, Alan, ed. 1967. *Portal to America: The Lower East Side, 1870–1925*. New York: Rinehart and Winston.

Seligmann, Herbert, ed. 1966. *Alfred Stieglitz Talking*. New Haven, CT: Yale Univ. Press.

Sifton, John. 2015. *Violence All Around*. Cambridge, MA: Harvard Univ. Press.

Slezkine, Yuri. 2004. *The Jewish Century*. Princeton, NJ: Princeton Univ. Press.

Slowcus. 1880. "No Yankee Need Apply." *Puck*, Dec. 8, 225.

Smith, Goldwin. 1891. "New Light on the Jewish Question." *North American Review* 153 (Aug.): 129–43.

Sokolsky, George. 1935. "We Jews." *New Masses* 14 (Feb. 12): 27.

Sorin, Gerald. 1992. *A Time for Building: The Third Immigration, 1880–1920*. Baltimore: Johns Hopkins Univ. Press.

Splete, Allen, and Marilyn D. Splete, eds. 1988. *Frederic Remington—Selected Letters*. New York: Abbeville.

Stav, Arieh. 1999. *Peace: The Arabian Caricature of Anti-Semitic Imagery*. Jerusalem: Gefen.

Steinberg, Milton. 1945. *A Partisan Guide to the Jewish Problem*. Indianapolis, IN: Bobbs-Merril.

Steinberg, Stephen. 1989. *The Ethnic Myth: Race, Ethnicity, and Class in America*. Boston: Beacon.

Stephens-Davidowitz, Seth. 2014. "The Data of Hate." *New York Times Sunday Review*, July 13, 4.

Stieglitz, Alfred. 1940–41. "Ten Stories." *Twice a Year* 5–6: 135–63.

———. 1978. *Georgia O'Keeffe, a Portrait*. New York: Viking.

———. [1921] 2000. "A Statement." Anderson Galleries, New York. Reproduced in *Stieglitz on Photography: His Selected Essays and Notes*, edited by Richard Whelan, 226. New York: Aperture.

Stoddard, Lothrop. 1920. *The Rising Tide of Color against White World-Supremacy*. New York: Scribner's.

———. 1927. *Re-forging America: The Story of Our Nationhood*. New York: Scribner's.

Strauss, Loren B. 2004. "Painting the Town Red: Jewish Visual Artists, Yiddish Culture, and Progressive Politics in New York, 1917–1938." Ph.D diss., Jewish Theological Seminary of America.

Strong, Donald S. 1941. *Organized Anti-Semitism in America: The Rise of Group Prejudice during the Decade 1930–40*. Washington, DC: American Council on Public Affairs.

"Studies in American Immigration." 1901. *Chicago Record Herald*, Sept. 25, no page number.

Sypher, Wylie. 1956. "The Meaning of Comedy." Appendix in *Comedy*, 193–258. New York: Random House.

Thaoor, Ishaan. 2016. "Iran Revs Up for Its Latest Holocaust Cartoon Contest." *Washington Post*, May 12, no page number.

Thomas, Samuel J. 2004. "Mugwump Cartoonists, the Papacy, and Tammany Hall in America's Gilded Age." *Religion and American Culture: A Journal of Interpretation* 14 (Summer): 213–50.

Todd, A. L. 1964. *Justice on Trial: The Case of Louis D. Brandeis*. New York: McGraw-Hill.

Trachtenberg, Alan. 2010. Introduction to Jacob Riis, *How the Other Half Lives: Studies among the Tenements of New York*, edited by Sam Bass Warner Jr., xiii–xxxii. Cambridge, MA: Harvard Univ. Press.

Trumbul, Alfred. 1877. "The Jews in America." *Frank Leslie's Popular Monthly*, Aug., 129–44.

Twain, Mark. 1899. "Concerning the Jews." *Harper's Magazine* 99 (Sept.): 527–35.

"UNESCO Condemns Iran's Holocaust Cartoon Contest." 2016. Jewish Telegraph Agency, May 16. At http://www.jta.org/2016/05/15/news -opinion/israel-middle-east/unesco-condemns-irans-holocaust-cartoon -contest.

Urofsky, Melvin. 1975. *American Zionism from Herzl to the Holocaust*. New York: Doubleday.

Van Rensselaer, Mrs. Schuyler. 1892. "Picturesque New York." *The Century* 45 (Dec.): 164–77.

Vorpahl, Ben Merchant, ed. 1972. *The Fredric Remington–Owen Wister Letters*. Palo Alto, CA: American West.

Waldman, Morris D. 1932. "The International Scene in Jewish Life." *Jewish Social Science Quarterly* 9 (Dec.): 9.

Walkowitz, Abraham. 1946a. *Faces from the Ghetto*. New York: Machmadin Art Editions.

———. 1946b. *Ghetto Motifs*. New York: Machmadin Art Editions.

Ware, Louise. 1938. *Jacob Riis: Police Reporter, Reformer, Useful Citizen*. New York: Appleton-Century.

Watson, Forbes. 1930. "The All American Nineteen." *The Arts* 16 (Jan.): 303.

Weinberg, Louis. 1917. "Jewish Artists in America: Abram Walkowitz." *American Hebrew and Jewish Messenger*, Aug. 31, 410, 426.

Weingarten, Irving. 1979. "The Image of the Jew in the American Periodical Press, 1881–1920." PhD diss., New York Univ.

Wenger, Beth. 1996. *New York Jews and the Great Depression: Uncertain Promise*. New Haven, CT: Yale Univ. Press.

West, Richard Samuel. 1968. *Satire on Stone: The Political Cartoons of Joseph Keppler*. Urbana: Univ. of Illinois Press.

Wheatley, Richard. 1892a. "The Jews of New York." *The Century* 43 (Jan.): 323–42.

———. 1892b. "The Jews of New York." *The Century* 43 (Feb.): 512–33.

White, G. Edward. 1968. *The Eastern Establishment and the Western Experience: The World of Frederick Remington, Theodore Roosevelt, and Owen Wister*. New Haven, CT: Yale Univ. Press.

Winter, William. 1918. *The Life of David Belasco*. Vol. 2. New York: Moffat and Yard.

Wolff, Justin. 2012. *Thomas Hart Benton: A Life*. New York: Farrar, Straus and Giroux.

Young-Bruehl, Elisabeth. 1996. *The Anatomy of Prejudice*. Cambridge, MA: Harvard Univ. Press.

Zagat, Ida, ed. 1972. *Samuel Zagat: Jewish Life on New York's Lower East Side, 1912–1962*. New York: Rogers Book Service.

Zuckerman, William. 1944. "Currents in American Jewish Life." *Contemporary Jewish Record* 7 (Apr. 1): 160–63.

Zurier, Rebecca, Robert W. Snyder, and Virginia M. Mecklenberg. 1995. *Metropolitan Lives: The Ashcan Artists and Their New York*. Washington, DC: National Museum of American Art.

Index

Italic page numbers denote illustrations.

Matthew Baigell is emeritus professor of art history at Rutgers University. He has authored, coauthored, edited, and coedited twenty books and has written widely on nineteenth- and twentieth-century American art. His most recent books include *Jewish American Artists and the Holocaust* (1997), *Jewish Artists in New York: The Holocaust Years* (2002), *American Artists, Jewish Images* (Syracuse University Press, 2006), *Jewish Art in America: An Introduction* (2007), and *Social Concern and Left Politics in Jewish American Art, 1880–1940* (Syracuse University Press, 2015).